A happy birthday B in £4.50 Tra 32/23

J.H.

Roy:

اقرأ بتمعن

THE LAKERS
The First Tourists

HONISTER CRAG AND PASS

THE LAKERS

The First Tourists

by

NORMAN NICHOLSON

ROBERT HALE & COMPANY
LONDON

First published in Great Britain 1955

Reprinted October 1972

ISBN 0 7091 3490 8

Robert Hale & Company
63 Old Brompton Road
London S.W.7

Printed in Great Britain by
Redwood Press Limited
Trowbridge, Wiltshire

"The Lakers are those persons who visit the beautiful scenes in Cumberland and Westmorland by distinction styled the Lakes."

(EUROPEAN MAGAZINE, Vol 34, 1798. Review of THE LAKERS, *a Comic Opera in Three Acts*. Clarke, 2s.)

ACKNOWLEDGMENTS

MY grateful acknowledgments are due to the many people who have helped me during my work on this book. In particular, I must name Mr Frank Warriner, who first interested me in the Picturesque, and who has advised and guided me throughout my studies in the subject. With him I would associate Mr J. L. Hobbs and Mr F. Barnes (Borough Librarian at Barrow-in-Furness), both of whom have taken much trouble to search for special information and to verify particular points. In addition I am obliged to Mr Barnes for help with my bibliography, and, together with the Barrow Library Committee, for permission to consult the unpublished manuscript of a tour of the Lakes by Sir William Gill and Sir Busick Harwood, made in 1796. Similarly, I am indebted to Miss Kathleen Coburn and the Governors of Toronto University for the loan of a transcription of passages dealing with the Lakes in the unpublished Notebooks of Samuel Taylor Coleridge. I am also indebted to notes on the early Lake visitors written in 1916 by the late Mr W. B. Kendall, to which I was granted access by kind permission of Mr Harold Kendall of Machynlleth.

For research into certain other points. I must thank Mr K. Smith of Carlisle City Library and Mr D. Hay of Whitehaven Borough Library. To these two librarians, together with Mr Barnes, Mr A. Davis of Millom Public Library, and to the Cumberland County Library I am grateful for the great pains they have taken to obtain the books I needed—some of them very scarce. The staff of the Millom Library, indeed, have written many letters and climbed many ladders for the sake of this book. Finally, I would like to mention that nearly all the local books referred to in these pages can be seen in the Jackson Library, Tullie House, Carlisle—a magnificent collection of the literature of Cumberland, Westmorland, and North Lancashire, without which any study such as this could scarcely have been possible.

1955   N.N.

CONTENTS

ILLUSTRATIONS

ACKNOWLEDGMENTS TO ILLUSTRATIONS

The following drawings and prints are reproduced by permission of the Carlisle Public Library and Museum Committee :

A view of Derwentwater from Crow Park, by Thomas Smith (known as Thomas Smith of Derby), 1761.

Keswick Lake from Barrow Common, by William Westall. From *Views of the Lakes and of the Vale of Keswick*, published by Hurst, Robinson & Co., 1820.

Honister Crag, by T. Allom. From *Westmorland, Cumberland, Durham and Northumberland Illustrated*, by T. Rose and T. Allom, 1832.

The following are reproduced by permission of the Trustees of the British Museum :

A View of Windermere, by William Burgess, 1794.

Castle Crag and Bowderstone, by J. Farrington. From *The Lakes of Lancashire, Westmorland and Cumberland Delineated*, 1816.

Blea Tarn, and Stockgill Force, by T. H. Fielding. From *Cumberland, Westmorland and Lancashire Illustrated*, 1822.

Rocky Scenery, by William Gilpin. From *Observation Relative Chiefly to Picturesque Beauty in the Mountains and Lakes of Cumberland and Westmorland*, 1786.

The nine illustrations of present-day scenes in the Lakes are reproduced from photographs taken by Mr. J. Allan Cash, London.

CHAPTER ONE

THE HEART OF THE PICTURE

THIS IS not going to be a book about the Lakes, but about the way people look at the Lakes; not about the fells, but about a view of the fells. It is a view which has changed a good deal, which has often been inaccurate, fantastic and misleading, yet which contained at all times something of the shape of truth. Through all the varying misconceptions and distortions, the land itself remained constant, or as nearly constant as a living thing can be. Now in this book we will be concerned more with those very misconceptions and distortions than with the objective truth, but because we can only measure change in relation to that which does not change, it will help us to understand how people looked at the Lakes if, first of all, we look for ourselves, though we must remember that our vision may be just as subjective in its own way as was theirs.

To begin with, we must define the limits of our area. The Lake System spreads a long way beyond the lakes themselves. To the north it extends over the Cumberland Plain nearly as far as Carlisle; to the south along the shores of Morecambe Bay to Lancaster. West it reaches the coast, and includes the coal-mines of Workington and Whitehaven, the iron-ore districts of Egremont, Millom, and Furness, and the manufacturing towns of Kendal and Barrow. East it is blocked from Northumberland, Durham and Yorkshire by the Pennines. All these, however diverse they may seem, are part of one geographical system and their people have roots in a shared history and tradition. It is a system built around a central mountain dome, gouged out with radiating valleys, down which not only the rivers but the very life and communications flow outwards to the perimeter, while round the edge of the mountain dome there is a surrounding basin of lowland, which stretches a great

I

way to the north and south, but in the west is planed off by
the sea, and in the east is walled in by the Pennines.

The northern lowlands are of sandstone, a rich stone, which
wears and weathers into the fat farming soil around Wigton
and Wetheral, and gives the building material of churches and
castles, farms and walls—a clean plant-pot pink when new,
and when old, a dark blackberry purple, mildewed as damp
leather, and greened and furred with moss and weed. In a
broken ring round the central dome, between the sandstone
and the mountains, the rock is limestone—soft and silvery
around Morecambe Bay, severe and grey in the Pennines, and
fussy and speckled with shell-pink in the iron-ore districts.

The travellers of the late eighteenth century visited only a
part of the area, and those of the nineteenth century still less.
Indeed, the fashion has been largely to concentrate on more
and more intensive exploration of a continually shrinking area.
For as the roads have improved and brought coaches and
hotels to the lower dales, the mountain-snob[1] has moved upwards and inwards. Long ago he deserted the pastoral lakes,
Windermere and Esthwaite, leaving them first to the pony-cart
and then to the limousine. Already he is snooty about the larger
villages, and soon he will retreat, like a melting glacier, to the
daleheads, or become one of those who deny the true name of
Cumberland to anything below two thousand feet.

The earlier travellers were less selective. Young included the
Lakes in a six months' tour of the north; Pennant called on his
way to and from Scotland; Gilpin extended his journey to
Carlisle and the Border. Yet by the end of the eighteenth
century the tourist boundaries had been laid down; in modern
terms of reference they may be described as the old
Workington–Penrith railway in the north; the Penrith–Shap–
Carnforth railway on the east; the coast on the west and the
shore of Morecambe Bay on the south. To this area should be
added the mountain block of Skiddaw and Saddleback to the
north of the Penrith line, while the industrial west coast may
mostly be ignored. The tourist area, therefore, consists of the
central mountain dome with its radiating valleys, and the inner
ring of the lowland country into which these valleys open.

[1] "The mountain-snob is a Wordsworthian fruit."—W. H Auden.

Within this area the travellers find three main types of scenery. In the north there is the Skiddaw range, and the block of fells round the lakes of Bassenthwaite, Buttermere, Crummock and Loweswater, together with the country as far west as the borders of the Egremont iron-ore district. These are all of Skiddaw slate, which appears also in several outlying patches, notably that of Black Combe, above Whicham Valley, in the extreme south of the county. Now these fells, which were the last to be seen by the traveller who approached from the south, probably impressed him more immediately than the rest, for they are bolder, more obtrusive, more self-assertive. They tend to be rather isolated, standing apart as individuals, unlike the fells of the central dales, which lap and fold over and around one another like the sheaths of a house-leek. No doubt Skiddaw has its secrets, but, on first meeting, it is frank and open, hands on the table—not particularly friendly, but with nothing to conceal. Even Charles Lamb, who was far from being a mountain lover, could not ignore it. "Oh, its fine black head,' he wrote in 1802, "and the bleak air atop of it, with a prospect of mountains all about and about, making you giddy." The average traveller rarely got himself into the right position to see the more tucked-away and secluded fells, such as Langdale Pikes, but he could not help getting a clear view of Skiddaw.

Now the rock of these northern mountains is a dark mud rock, which does not easily disintegrate into scree or splinter into crag. Its typical form is a solid, smooth-sided block, rounded like Dent above Egremont, or pyramidal like Melbreak. From the bottom its slopes seem to slide so evenly upwards that they look neither steep nor high until some object catches your eyes—perhaps a stone wall which runs up and up till it is no more than a pencil-mark on the flank of the fell. At Grassmoor, beside Crummock, the broom grows alongside the road, lemon tags and curlings of bloom with the stamens cocked like little fingers, and the eye follows them up a slope no steeper, apparently, and not much longer than the high street of a country town. Then, all at once, you realize that where the broom gives way to bracken, the yellow bushes seem the size of pollen grains, and immediately the fellside comes into perspective and you feel the whole height and weight and mass of it hulking above you like a boot above a beetle.

Because this rock is uniformly more durable than the rocks of the central dales, it has worn into simpler, more regular shapes, and has less variety of texture than, say, the fells of Eskdale or Langdale; instead of a continual contrast of crag and turf, we find an even surface of grass and bracken or sometimes heather. It is smooth, even sleek, yet it is tough and alive like the hide of an animal. In those places (as on Skiddaw Dodd) where the Forestry Commission have planted rectangles of fir trees crossed by geometrical rides, the effect is that of a green tartan pulled round its haunches.

The early traveller, looking north or west from Friar's Crag at the foot of Derwentwater, had a view of Skiddaw and the Newlands that was so deliberate, so self-explanatory, that it might be called a demonstration. It was magnificent and, as he would say, "awful", yet it seemed to be within his powers of understanding. But if he turned and gazed to the fells round the head of the lake, he was face to face with a different sort of country altogether, a country which seemed to him to have all the mystery and secretiveness which were what he asked from romantic scenery. It might not impress itself on his mind as clearly as Skiddaw and Saddleback, but nevertheless it blew across his imagination like the wind across the strings of an Æolian harp.

This was the country of the dales, the hub of the lakes; the land of the passes, and tight, crooked valleys, where the fells queued up one behind the other, so packed, close and anonymous, that you scarcely realized that from many of them you could look down on Grassmoor and Saddleback, and even, from one or two, on Skiddaw. This central area is of the volcanic rocks which Professor Sedgwick called "green slates and porphyries". The rock here, being formed of different sorts of volcanic matter—lava, ashes, breccias and conglomerates—varies very greatly in hardness, and therefore weathers in many different ways even in the same fellside. At times it is as hard as steel, thrusting a great plated hulk into the rough seas of cloud, letting the waters run away down spouts and grooves of rock. Such is the rock-face of Pavey Ark about Great Langdale, or the knob of Castle Head near Derwentwater which may perhaps have been the central neck of lava in one of the former lake volcanoes. In other places the rock wears no better than plaster, rotting and crumbling in the rain, slithering into scratches and slaverings of scree. Such are the screes of Wastwater, where a whole fellside has disintegrated, turning back into its own element, and seeping down to the water which once shaped and raised it from mud to mountain.

Yet it is not these vast exhibitions of crag or scree which are typical of the dales, but rather the continual juxtaposition of each to each, so that even the lower hills are both bony and scurfy, are knobbed and scabbed, gnarled and scraped, whiskered and downy, almost at one and the same time. The turf climbs among the crags, carrying sedges and the mountain flowers, and larches heave in great heaped tidal waves up the narrowing channels of ghylls and clefts. Gorse swarms like bees, and rowans and thorn trees grow high up in hollows and clearings scythed out of the bracken by a beck. From lakeshore to the tops the land is populous with flower and seed and bird and living water.

Moreover, it is not just the substance of the rock which has given the dales their character, but the forces which have been at work on it, and, in particular, that of glaciation. In the Ice Ages, the Lake valleys manufactured each its own glacier which squirmed to the lowlands along the track taken now and before by the rivers. But this ice-flood left the shape of the dales greatly changed. It sliced away the sides, giving a U-shape to a cross-section of the valleys instead of the former V-shape. Today, a flat matting of meadowland is laid along the beckside right up to the dale-heads, while the fells, cut clean to the bone, look on with water dribbling down their chins. Where the streams were of any size they were often left "hanging" in the air, so that now they may drop all at one go in a waterfall, or bob and bubble and bounce their way down a ghyll carved out of the rock like a slice cut from a cake. When the drop is steep, even a beck so small that it would not drown a hedgehog can dig a trough deep enough to hide a house.

It was the glaciers, too, which gave the dales their lakes, either by damming the exit with a moraine, or by scooping beneath the old river-bed and then leaving the water to flood the hole. For this reason the lakes of the dales are very like rivers. Bassenthwaite and lower Derwentwater spread out beneath a wide sky, with plenty of room for the sun to shine on them and for the traveller to view them whole. They seem detached, separate from the fells, pretending to be under no obligation, and the fells, for their part, seem aloof. Buttermere and Crummock are more hemmed in, lying as in the bottom of a cup, but they too are curiously independent, not accepting High Style or Robinson or Melbreak as being of their order or genus. But the lakes of the central dales are the brides and bed-mates of the rocks. Ullswater links arms with the crags, crook-ing elbow and ankle around them, turning back to see itself, bending at the knees and again at the hips, slapping the mascu-line thighs of the fells and wriggling like an adolescent. Elter-water, which drains both of the Langdales, never quite makes up its mind when to cease to be a lake and begin to be the Brathay. Just below the entrance of the stream from Colwith, the lake is narrowed by a long promontory, but it opens out again into another reach almost as large as the higher one. Then it contracts itself to a river, shallow enough for a dog to wade through, flows a hundred yards or so between widening meadows and woods, and, without any excuse, opens out into a pool nearly as deep as the lake. But from that moment there is no more shilly-shallying, for Skelwith Force has got its pull on the water which now flows straight and fast till it makes that full-bodied dive into the rock-pools above Skelwith Bridge.

It is futile to assess such country in terms of views. The view flattens the scene to a man-made dimension; it measures the landscape from the borders of an imaginary picture-frame; it reduces life to a postcard. It imposes a rigid and unnatural rule of proportion on our eyes, and makes us reject so much of what our other senses tell us. Even in our own memories, Coniston Old Man is not just a design in shape and colour seen from this or that angle—a double-propped marquee from the Duddon Estuary; a single-ridged peak, like a shoe-nut, from Torver; a great kangaroo-bellied amphibian, seen from the opposite side of Coniston Lake. It is also the man-made screes beside the quarries; the whitewash on the old miners' cottages, a stone playing ducks-and-drakes on Levers Water, making the black tarn throw up waves like a magician's steel rings; a small dog nosing its way alone up the track from Low Water to the summit; a scrap of silver paper curled round a stone like lichen; dirty snow in a culvert of rock; rowan berries, the red-green of mouldy raspberry jam, making the end twigs bend under their weight; wheatears; the split and spit of thin ice; a pulled muscle in the thighs; a wind making a spread map roll and ripple like the sea; herdwicks; the smell of cut bracken; clouds; handkerchiefs. And yet all these impressions, and a thousand more, add up only to a one-sided, personal and entirely superficial memory, which ignores all that the mountain may mean to those who have lived for years beside it. It ignores still more what the mountain may mean to itself—not as a thing to be seen or climbed or thought about, but merely as a thing that is.

Looking east from Coniston Old Man, towards Kendal and the Yorkshire border, you see the third main division of the Lake scenery: the Windermere country. It includes no fells of any great height, no crags, no screes, no major waterfalls. Instead, it consists of easy-going hills, undulating as gently as an eiderdown, with wood, park-land, gardens, garages, and country houses. Much of it is now turned into a mountain watering-place, an upper-outer-suburb, yet in its less publicized spots it is still as homely and wholesome as new-made bread. There are gulleys and ghylls in the hills behind Brantwood which are far less visited than the top of Scafell Pike.

The glaciers, in widening and sometimes deepening the valleys, emphasized still more the main structure of the Lake System, which falls roughly into the shape of a wheel, the hub at Esk Hause, and ranges of fells running outward like spokes with the dales in between. This comparison to the wheel was first made popular by Wordsworth, who took it from William Green, though John Briggs, writing in *The Lonsdale Magazine* about 1821, said that he had heard the same analogy made by a farmer in Little Langdale:

"This", observed my uncle, "is very like the account given by Mr. Wordsworth, in his late publication. Have you ever seen this book?" "No," replied the old man, "I see no books. But if we were on Bowfell, I could let you see down all these vallies in a two hours' walk; though I am so plagued with rheumatism now, I don't think I could get up so high." "Are we to suppose", said my uncle, "that Mr. Wordsworth has borrowed this idea from an old dalelander, and then published it as his own?" "Oh, no," said my father, "Mr. Wordsworth will call it a coincidence of ideas!"[1]

Briggs is probably inventing this episode since, like many others, he was rather suspicious of Wordsworth, but at least his comments seem to show that the image of the wheel was fairly well known by this time.

Such was the general appearance of the country, but it will be necessary also to know something of the sort of people who lived there before the tourists came.

We need not say much about the very early people—the barrow-building folk; the early Celtic tribes whose villages were set on the cold moors above the level of swamp and forest; the megalith-builders, who left us the great stone circles at Little Salkeld (Long Meg and her daughters), Castlerigg near Keswick, and Swinside near Broughton-in-Furness. The Romans, too, left their memorials for the antiquaries, though they left little else. Cumberland was Celtic before they came and Celtic after they left. Yet though Welsh remained the language almost till the Norman Conquest, and though the Welsh gave their name to the county of Cumberland, there is little that is Celtic in the main tradition of the dales. The shepherds of the nineteenth century still counted their sheep in Celtic numerals, yet otherwise their dialect was largely Norse and English. Carlisle and Penrith retain their Celtic names, and so do a few rivers like the Derwent and a few mountains like Helvellyn. One small hill near the foot of Dunnerdale, a conical pimple rough as a Harris tweed with bracken and scree, still calls itself, as in a dead language, The Pen, but elsewhere Norsemen have plastered their names like posters across the hoardings of the fells.

For it was the Norseman, above all others, who bred the dalesman, and gave him his bone, his language, and his way of

[1] John Briggs: *Letters From The Lakes* (Kirkby Lonsdale, 1825).

life. How they came, nobody quite knows. Probably it was not by invasion but by a gradual infiltration from Ireland, from the West of Scotland, and especially from the Isle of Man. For Man stands almost equidistant between England, Galloway and Northern Ireland, with North Wales not too far away to the south. From almost any point on the coast between St Bees Head and Walney Island, you look across the sea, some thirty or forty miles to Man. In summer weather, with a haze over the water, it is often unseen for days at a time. Then suddenly a wind frisks up from the south-west and the air is clear for an hour or two before the rain reaches the land, and the island shines out, shadowed with dark blue, with the sun behind it. Or in November, when every hill is lathered with cloud and the trees make spouts for the vapour to run down without even condensing to rain, a wind will tear off a strip of cloud along the horizon, and the island will float out into a green sun which we in England have not seen throughout the day.

Looking across from Man, the Cumbrian hills must have seemed just as near as Snaefell does to us, but bigger, stretching north and south till they were lost in the curve of the sea. It must have seemed, at this distance, a country very like Norway and, indeed, wherever the settlers may have landed— on the south coast of Cumberland, between Ravenglass and the Duddon, or perhaps on the convenient peninsula of Furness— they would find, when they moved inwards, a country well suited to the sort of life they were used to—long, narrow, private dales, with fertile land beside the becks, and a great wall of crag for defence, so that the colonists could set up a system of land-ownership very similar to that of Norway. In every dale there developed a number of small family farms, each owning its couple of hundred acres or perhaps much less. They were in communication with one another, but they were independent, and with certain modifications many of them remained independent until as late as the eighteenth and nineteenth centuries. The men who farmed them were the statesmen (or "estates men") whom Wordsworth admired, who cultivated their own fields, passing them on from father to son, and grazing their sheep in the fells. Even the sheep, the Herdwicks, may have come in with the Vikings, though his-

torians now think that they may be a native Cumbrian breed,
older in local genealogy than the men who herd them.

In many ways, the dalesman remained a Viking for centuries. He kept much of the grit of his old tongue in his dialect,
for long a seeming-barbarous language, quite unintelligible to
the Southerner. Even today he speaks with a grating, clattering
grutch, which is as indigenous as the sound of the wind in
bare sticks or a stone slithering down a scree. His vocabulary is
as Scandinavian as a lemming, and he has stamped it on the
landscape till you cannot think of it in Anglo-Saxon. Tarn,
beck, ghyll, fell, dale—these are all Scandinavian words, as are
the typical suffixes of the place names: -thwaite, -wick, -biggin,
-keld, and -knott, and to use such words is not only to name
and describe a place, but to acknowledge its ownership. Even
an Englishman must learn the language of the native when he
visits Cumberland.

The independence of the statesman was maintained only
with a struggle during the years which followed the Black
Death. He still kept his old love of individualist sports—
wrestling and the fell race—but he found it hard to make a
living. By the time of Wordsworth, many of the dale farmers
must have been very poor, and the sons were not looking forward to the family inheritance. In truth, Wordsworth's account
of the dale community was idealized, telling partly of what
was no longer true and partly of what never had been. Yet, if
his words are read with understanding there is truth in them,
and they describe a state which, if never quite fulfilled, has
always been aimed at, or, at least, hoped for:

Towards the head of these Dales was found a perfect
Republic of Shepherds and Agriculturists, among whom the
plough of each man was confined to the maintenance of his
own family, or to the occasional accommodation of his neighbour. Two or three cows furnished each family with milk
and cheese. The chapel was the only edifice that presided over
these dwellings, the supreme head of this pure Common-
wealth; the members of which existed in the midst of a
powerful empire like an ideal society or an organised community, whose constitution had been imposed and regulated
by the mountains which protected it. Neither high-born

nobleman, knight, nor esquire was here; but many of these humble sons of the hills had a consciousness that the land, which they walked over and tilled, had for more than five hundred years been possessed by men of their name and blood; and venerable was the transition, when a curious traveller, descending from the heart of the mountains, had come to some ancient manorial residence in the more open parts of the Vales, which, through the rights attached to its proprietor, connected the almost visionary mountain republic he had been contemplating with the substantial frame of society as existing in the laws and constitution of a mighty empire.[1]

Travelling is a reciprocal activity. Or, to put it in terms of grammar, "visit" is a transitive verb: it needs the visitor and the visited. In the case of the Lakes, the visited was not just a place but a people, and the rise of the tourist trade was due as much to the wish of the inhabitants as that of the tourists themselves, as much to conditions inside the Lakes as to fashions outside.

The old statesman would have had nothing to do with the travellers: there was a fierce independence about the Norse farmers which had little use for foreigners. But the statesman had been in decline for centuries and, indeed, by the end of the Middle Ages he had already begun to look outside his farm for extra livelihood. The boom in the cloth trade, which transformed so much of the English countryside in the fourteenth century, made its mark even on the Lakes. Kendal and, to a larger extent, Keswick both became centres for collecting wool and manufacturing cloth. By Tudor times Kendal was famous for its coarse woollen products (known as "Kendal Cottons") and for its dyes—especially the Kendal Green of Falstaff's "misbegotten knaves". In this district there was not only wool from the fells but water-power for the fulling-mills, so that soon trade became so prosperous that it spread from Kendal into the lower valley and over the hills to Windermere, Ambleside, Grasmere and Langdale. Here, in the villages, the fullers and dyers set up their mills, but the early stages of manufacture,

[1] William Wordsworth: *Description of the Scenery of the Lakes* (1822 and later editions).

the spinning of the thread and weaving of the cloth, were still
carried on in the cottages by the housewife and her husband.
The statesman, home from his few fields or his heaf on the fell,
would turn to his loom in the evening, while mother and
daughters worked at the spinning-wheel. Many cottagers who
had no land at all took on full-time piece-work from the village
mills, and soon the valleys held a population much greater than
that which could have been maintained by agriculture alone.
Langdale, in particular, had far more people than it has today.

Then, in the reign of Elizabeth, the trade began to decline.
Kendal was able to keep going by supplying cloth for the negro
slaves in the American colonies, but the trade largely disappeared from the smaller villages. And on top of this, plague
came to the district. Tradition says that it was particularly
severe in Langdale, while it is recorded that 2,260 died in the
parish of Penrith and 2,500 in the parish of Kendal. The
valleys were now left half-derelict. Desperate attempts seem
to have been made to plough a few extra acres at the dale-
heads or on the flanks of the fells, trying to wring a bucketful
of oats from the grudging rock. In Cumberland, Fuller could
commend black-lead, copper, and pearls:

> . . . mussels (and also oysters and other shell-fish) gaping
> for the dew, are in a manner impregnated therewith; so
> that some conceive that as dew is a liquid pearl, so a pearl
> is dew consolidated in these fishes.

But for Westmorland, he could see no hope at all from natural
resources:

> Here is cold comfort from nature, but somewhat of
> warmth from industry. That the land is barren, is God's
> pleasure; the people painful, their praise.[1]

Sir David Fleming of Rydal, writing rather later than Fuller,
in 1671, could say of the county:

> . . . Because it lyeth among moors and high hills, and was
> antiently for the most part unmanured, [it] came by this
> name in our language, for such barren places which cannot
> easily, by the painful labour of the husbandman be brought
> to fruitfulness, the northern English men call *moores*, and

[1] Thomas Fuller: *Worthies of England* (1662).

Westmoreland is nothing else but a western moorish country.[1]

Real poverty came to the dales in the seventeenth and eighteenth centuries. The statesman had been ready to do spare-time work for the factories, but he was too proud to hire himself out to work on another's land, so that, in spite of unemployment, we find that wages, especially wages for casual labour, remained as high as (or higher than) those in South Lancashire and the Midlands.[2] But without supplementary work, the farms were too small and too primitive to yield a reasonable living, so that the younger people began to drift away. The little farms became empty and rotted into piles of grass-covered stones, while Wordsworth's story of the Ruined Cottage, in the first book of *The Excursion*, is typical of what was happening to those who depended entirely on casual jobs. In *Michael*, too, the poet gives a picture of one of the old statesmen, struggling with an inheritance which was already mortgaged before it came to him. By a lifetime of hard work he has paid off the debt, running the place entirely on his own—tilling the fields, herding the sheep, building walls and byres, repairing implements, and, in the evening, carding wool for his wife to spin. But his son Luke, who was to follow him, has no liking

---

[1] Daniel Fleming: *A Description of Westmoreland*. Printed as a tract in 1882 for the Cumberland and Westmorland Archæological Society. The name probably means "district of those living west of the moors"—i.e. the Pennines.

[2] Here are the rates of labour in the Penrith district in 1768, as reported by Arthur Young:

In harvest, 1s. 6d. and beer.
In hay-time, 1s. 3d. and ditto.
In Winter, 10d. and ditto.
Reaping corn, 3s. to 5s.
Mowing grass, 1s. to 2s. 6d.
Ditching, 8d. a rood.
Threshing wheat, 2d. to $2\frac{1}{2}$d.
     ,,   barley, $1\frac{1}{2}$d.
     ,,   oats, $1\frac{1}{2}$d.
Head man's wages, £12 to £14.
Next ditto, £9.
Boy of ten or twelve years, £3.
Dairy maid, to £6.
Other maids, £3 to £4.
Women, per day, in harvest, 10d. and beer.
In hay-time, 8d. and ditto.
In winter, 6d. and ditto.

Arthur Young: *A Six Months Tour through The North of England* (1770).

for the dale life and takes the first chance that comes to get
away from the district. The old man waits, year after year,
carrying on the duties of the farm as well as he can, but without the heart to continue with the plan of improvement and
modernization symbolized by the projected sheep-fold. There is
a splendid bareness about the lines as well as considerable
social significance:

> His bodily frame had been from youth to age
> Of an unusual strength. Among the rocks
> He went, and still looked up to sun and cloud,
> And listened to the wind; and, as before,
> Performed all kinds of labour for his sheep,
> And for the land, his small inheritance.
> And to that hollow dell from time to time
> Did he repair, to build the Fold of which
> His flock had need. 'Tis not forgotten yet
> The pity which was then in every heart
> For the old Man—and 'tis believed by all
> That many and many a day he thither went,
> And never lifted up a single stone.

The position of the statesman can be gauged from the surveys made at the instigation of the Board of Agriculture and
published in 1794—that of Westmorland by Andrew Pringle,
and that of Cumberland by John Bailey and George Culley.
Arthur Young, too, visited the two counties, but seems to have
been interested mostly in the larger and better-equipped farms
of the lowlands and the more accessible valleys. From these
surveys it becomes obvious that the statesmen, with their small
resources, could not keep pace with the revolution which was
then taking place in farming. Many of them sold out, and John
Fisher of Townend told his neighbour, Miss Wordsworth, that
soon there would only be two ranks of people in the dales, the
very rich and very poor—"for those who have small estates are
forced to sell, and all the land goes into one hand."[1] Dorothy,
daughter of the Lowthers' agent, could not help but know
whose. Other men hung on grimly to their few fields, saving
all they could to pay the "fines" which were often a term of
their ownership. They had no means of raising the capital

[1] Dorothy Wordsworth: *Grasmere Journal.*

needed to make their land really productive, but they still worked desperately in the fields, women and girls as well as men. Pringle reports with some feeling that "... it is not uncommon to see sweating at the dung-cart, a girl, whose elegant features and delicate nicely-proportioned limbs seemingly but ill accord with such rough employment." Mawman, in 1804, tells how he saw girls helping with the hay-making in the meadows between Buttermere and Crummock, and how, "without the least consciousness of indelicacy", they would lie flat on their faces to drink from the beck.

There were prejudices to overcome also. The dale farmer had obsolete ideas about crop-rotation. He believed that natural grass was more profitable to him than corn, and grew the latter largely to free the ground of moss and prepare it for more hay. He was suspicious of clover, seed-grass and turnips. Even the standard of his sheep had deteriorated through lack of cross-breeding between herds. We are told of a shepherd at Penruddock who, when asked about "some singularly rough-legged, ill-formed sheep", replied: "Lord Sir, they are sik as God set upon the land, we never change any."[1] One of his customs, however, was eventually adopted by others, for the dale farmers (most of whom could only afford one horse) had taken to the single-horse cart at a time when the rest of England still used the cumbersome three- or four-horse wagon or wain.

In the large estates of the lower land, methods of agriculture were being brought up to date. At Lowther, near Penrith, and at Muncaster, at the foot of Eskdale, many experiments were carried out, together with extensive plantings. Lord Muncaster was a pioneer in scientific agriculture, making a careful study of crop-rotation, and availing himself of the Ravenglass Estuary to try out every possible kind of manure: not only the customary seaweed, but also "slake or mud, left by the tide", and most intriguingly, mussels "at the rate of five or six cartloads per acre"—a dressing which, according to Pennant, was used some twenty-five years earlier at Walney Island, off the end of the Furness peninsula.

The enterprise and capital of these lowland farmers were

[1] Andrew Pringle: *General View of the Agriculture of the County of Westmorland* (1794).

much needed in the dales. Bailey, Culley, and Pringle report everywhere the need for drainage of the fellside mosses, for reclamation of peat-bogs, and enclosure of much waste land, especially the fairly low-lying commons of parts of Westmorland. They also anticipated the Forestry Commission by recommending the plantation of larches. They were impatient with old systems and customs, unsympathetic towards those whose lives could not easily be adjusted to the new plans, intolerant of anything which hindered their vision of the factory-farm. They showed much the same romantic enthusiasm as did John Dyer in *The Fleece*, with that mixture of adventure, energy and greed which was already beginning to build the new world of Victorian capitalism.

It is impossible to look forward without emotion to that day when these neglected wastes shall have received that degree of improvement of which they are susceptible; when they shall wave with valuable crops of corn, bleat with profitable flocks, or be clothed with stately timber; and when there may be seen in every corner the industrious husbandman at once enriching himself and advantaging the community in a manner the most substantial.[1]

All of this, of course, needed money, and some of it needed legal enclosure. The statesman, who could afford neither to improve his own land nor to enclose more, was an economic anachronism. Unless he could find some source of extra income to take the place of the clothing trade, he was bound to disappear like the eagles and the mountain cats.

The wool trade was not the only important supplementary industry in the Lakes—there was also mining. This was of great antiquity, for the Romans knew of the presence of iron, copper, lead and silver, while the Celtic tribes before them dug for copper; indeed, copper-mines on Coniston Old Man have been worked, on and off, for about two thousand years. In the time of Elizabeth, when a colony of German miners settled in the district, Keswick was an important centre, dealing with ore not only from Newlands but also from as far off as Caldbeck and Coniston. Near Keswick, too, in Borrowdale was the

[1] Andrew Pringle, *op. cit.*

famous "black lead" mine, which was much visited by the early tourists. At the same time the valleys around Coniston and Hawkshead became a small Black Country with charcoal-burners living in huts in the woods, and little bloomeries or furnaces set up nearly everywhere to smelt iron from Furness.

This trade did not really decline, but in the seventeenth and eighteenth centuries it moved from the dales to the surrounding lowlands. There were still small mines in the fells, but by now geologists and mining engineers were beginning to get some idea of the huge deposits of ore that were waiting to be found in Low Furness and in West Cumberland, and of the enormous wealth of the Whitehaven-Workington coalfields. With the development of the cold blast furnace in the early eighteenth century, the small bloomeries were shut down, and large furnaces were built both in Furness and West Cumberland. The first to be opened in the district (and one of the first in Great Britain) was at Backbarrow, near Greenodd, while there was another at Duddon Bridge, just at the foot of Wordsworth's Dunnerdale. The latter can still be seen, some hundred yards from the road, hidden in a clearing among overhanging woods, its great slate walls and shafts dribbling with fern and weed.

On the opposite side of the district, at the foot of the Ennerdale Fells, the industry was already well established, for by 1700 the Lowther pits at Whitehaven were producing 27,000 tons of coal a year, and in the middle of the century the town was one of the three or four leading ports in England. And now the whole of this coastal strip, from St Bees to Maryport, began to expand, and Sir James Lowther, who managed the Whitehaven estate, "had the satisfaction" (in William Gilpin's amusing phrase) "to die the richest commoner in England". Everywhere people felt the thrust of ambition, the lift of self-confidence:

> Before my view an ample bason pours
> Her waves swift-rolling on the western shores,
> While num'rous masts beneath delight the eye,
> The growth, WHITEHAVEN, of thy industry,
> There infant Parton's neighb'ring village hails
> Her mother town, and spreeds her lesser sails.[1]

[1] James Eyre Weeks: *A Poetical Prospect of Whitehaven* (1752). A rare pamphlet.

Parton, now, is a half-wrecked village jammed between the sea and the collier cliffs, with the ruins of works standing all round it, and the tide blowing black froth over seaweed and sand. It is hard to remember that the whole of this coast, from Whitehaven to Maryport, which is now re-emerging after the desperate days of the 1920s, was once a place of high industrial adventure. Whitehaven then shipped great quantities of coal to Ireland and at one time seemed likely to win much of the new trade with America. Its broad, square streets were planned by one of the Wren circle, and its eighteenth-century houses and warehouses have the bold, open, hand-above-the-counter look of a confident trader. It was proud of its rapid growth, proud of its sudden enterprise.[1] One of its main residences (now the Waverley Hotel, a fine, late-seventeenth-century building) was given the name of Tangier House, a sign that here, on this isolated coast, walled round by mountains and blocked for centuries from all main centres of commerce and culture, the people were beginning to look across wider skies. They remembered that the Solway was part of the Atlantic.

Moreover, there was an excitement about those times, a new stirring of the imagination, a new credulity, a sense of Cumberland as part of the greater world, a queer hope, too, that it might be a leader in that world. Whitehaven was the Plymouth of the Lakes, the port of departure not only for America but for the future. Here, on a barren strand which for so many centuries had limped behind the rest of England, there was now a new romantic vision, a "scientific" mirage:

> From Hundy, Scoofe, and Seaton, there you see
> The Carriage plying from the Colliery;
> The Land-banks there with jetty Treasures teem,
> Fertile, and ripened by the Solar beam;
> Wher'e'er you look, on ev'ry side around,
> The Coal-mines num'rous in the hills abound.

[1] "About a hundred years ago there was not one house here, except Sir John Lowther's, and two others, and only three small vessels; and for the next forty years, the number of houses encreased to about twenty. At this time [1772] the town may boast of being one of the handsomest in the north of England, built of stone, and the streets pointing straight to the harbour, with others crossing them at right angles. It is populous as it is elegant, containing twelve thousand inhabitants, and has a hundred

There down the Pits descend the *human moles*,
And pick their passage thro' the Veiny Coals,
Maintain thro' ev'ry obstacle their Way,
And force their entrance ev'n beneath the Sea.
Still as their dang'rous Conquests they extend,
The Works with mighty Pillars they defend,
To prop the pond'rous Roof that hangs above,
Which threatens Ravage to their deep Alcove;
Tremendous crush! how dreadfully they die,
When ill-supported, tumbling from on high
Upon their heads the heavy Ruins lye.[1]

Weeks, a Workington man, could not help but be aware of the
great danger of coal-mining, for time after time men, boys,
horses, and even women and girls were killed from explosions,
falls of rock, and inrushes of water. But he sees the danger not
as a deterrent, but as an extra excitement, while experiments in
mining engineering have for him the interest of exploration:

Near are the coalworks, Lowther's treasur'd mines,
Whence the foul-air, thro' artful tube refines,
Like a Volcano the perennial Flame
Sulphureous burns in nature much the same,
Yet so by art contriv'd that thro' the fire
The pestilential vapour may transpire,
The air expung'd above, and free to breathe,
Th' adventurous collier works insur'd beneath.

The prosperity of Whitehaven undoubtedly helped the
farmer by providing a ready market, but it drew the young
people away from the dales, and, at the same time, it made the
dalesman aware of the rising standards of middle-class comfort,
so that the living he made from his fields seemed meaner than
ever. Prospects were not good. The fell mines and the quarries
employed quite a number of men, but it could not then be perceived that quarrying would greatly increase in the nineteenth
century to supply roofing-slates for the new industrial towns of
northern England. Many small-holders sold out, or sometimes

and ninety great ships belonging to it, mostly employed in the coal trade."
Thomas Pennant: *A Tour in Scotland and Voyage to the Hebrides in
1772* (1774–6).
    [1] Weeks: *A Poetical Prospect of the Coast, Town and Harbour of
Workington* (1752).

even deserted their homes, and Lancaster, as John Briggs reports, was full of beggars. Briggs, though he wrote his *Letters from the Lakes* in the character of a young tourist from Preston, was in fact a local man, the son of a swill-maker, born near Cartmel on Christmas Day 1788. His *Letters* are written in the form of the usual itinerary, but he showed a much greater knowledge of social conditions than was usually acquired by the visitor. His account of the distressed young woman from "Wyersdale", who threw herself into the River Lune just in time for the Preston party to fish her out, seems rather highly coloured, but most of his stories have an authentic ring and his details are as convincing as Crabbe's. He tells, for instance, of a father, a joiner, out of work through ill-health, and of the wife boiling "a pint of grey peas in water" to serve as a meal for herself and her eight children. "Unsound flour, being cheaper, was their only bread, and clean water their only beverage. I have more than once seen Thomas make a dinner of two potatoes and a small onion."[1]

Such was an exceptional case, and one, unfortunately, not peculiar to the dales, but Briggs's account of a Lake District inn is of particular interest. He is writing, about 1821 or 1822, of Kentmere, but the inn he describes is a survival of the mid-eighteenth century, so that the conditions he sees—though they had surely disappeared from the more prosperous houses by 1820—are those which must have been met by earlier travellers in the 1770s and 80s.

"The floor", he says,

> was bespread with tubs, pans, chairs, tables, piggins, dishes, tins, and other equipage of the farmer's kitchen. In the dusk of the evening, and the darkness of the house, the things were only just visible; and we felt some hesitation in approaching the fire, lest some accident might befal us in working our way through the innumerable obstacles that intervened between us and the *cozey hearth*. A robust girl, in a short petticoat of *Kendal bump*, however, with more agility than might have been expected from her very unpromising appearance, presently pushed the tubs and pots aside, and by that means formed a tolerable avenue to the fire. . . .

[1] Briggs: *Letters From The Lakes* (Kirkby Lonsdale, 1825).

My uncle now requested that something might be added to the fire, as we were thoroughly wet and very cold. "Put some mear peats tet fire," said the landlord, "thur folks are verra ill drabbled." While the maid was reconstructing the fire, we had time to reconnoitre our quarters.

There was no fire-place; but a paved area of aböut 2 square yards, raised 6 inches from the floor, and attached to the end wall, formed the hearth where the fire burned. Parallel to the end wall, a beam, belonging to the room floor above us, crossed the house about 2 yards from the end wall. The space above this beam was shaped like a pyramid; gradually tapering to the top, where it could not be above a yard square. Up this funnel or chimney the smoke ascended in fine convolving wreaths, very amusing to us, as it gave a dingy hue to the small speck of sky which appeared like the lid of a chimney. . . .

As we began to warm, we began to feel faint, and my uncle requested the maid to bring my sister a glass of warm shrub, as he supposed they would keep no wine, and each of us a glass of his favourite rum and new milk. The girl stood and looked "unutterable things". But the landlord replied, "We hae nae rum." "A little gin and water then," said my uncle. "We niver keep nae spirits," replied Boniface. "Let us have something at any rate," replied my father. "We hae capital ale," observed the landlord; "bring 'em ivery yan a pint." "And a pint for your master," added my uncle. The landlord's face brightened up at this; and all was very pleasant till we tasted the nauseating beverage. However, it was all we could procure; and it was our duty to submit to necessity. Besides, whatever our comforts might be, we might rank them among the curiosities of our lake tour.[1]

This passage should not be taken too credulously. The boorishness of the landlord is obviously exaggerated, and one suspects, in spite of Briggs's scoffing, that the serving-girl was not altogether unattractive. Briggs was a poor man. The two excursions on which his letters were based were made on foot, and he avoided the inns, because of their charges, and slept at farm-houses and cottages, feeding on "a little oat-cake and a pennyworth of milk", and starting off usually at five o'clock each morning. It may be that he resented the difference be-

[1] John Briggs, *op. cit.*

tween his way of travelling and the comfort of the tourists (the very last sentence in the passage quoted may be a concealed sarcasm). Or it may be that when he called at one of the inns he was treated casually because of his poverty. Certainly he seems determined here to get his own back, and to enjoy, vicariously, the pleasure of patronizing the landlord (" 'And a pint for your master,' added my uncle.") Yet his description of the place itself seems true enough—he was writing largely for a local audience and knew he could not get away with gross inaccuracies. The picture—though it may not be typical— certainly suggests a country where money is very scarce, and where wealthy tourists would be as welcome as Father Christmas.

By the time that Briggs was writing the tourist trade had already brought something like prosperity to the more populous centres, but well into the nineteenth century the living conditions of the poorer classes in the dales remained very bad. Harriet Martineau, a shrewd if somewhat town-minded observer, reports that sanitation is often deplorable. She tells also, probably from hearsay, that mothers in Wasdale would not wash the hands and arms of their children till they were six months old, as otherwise they would grow up to be thieves. But the small farmers were becoming aware of the higher material standards of living in the rest of England. Up to the mid-eighteenth century they rarely ate butchers' meat, but lived on bread, porridge, cheese and milk. The statesman, understandably, was dissatisfied with this traditional and rather primitive way of life. He wanted to better himself, but so long as he was dependent on the produce of his few poor fields he could not do so. He welcomed the tourist, therefore, both with a canny eye on his pocket and, one fancies, with a genuine curiosity about the world which he represented, the world beyond the mountains. Caged monkeys are interested not just in the nuts but in the men on the other side of the bars.

CHAPTER TWO

THE EXPLORERS

IN THE Middle Ages nature was mysterious and menacing. There were dangers from wild beasts, storms, avalanches, shipwrecks. Everywhere, outside the small enclosures of man, was famine, desolation, barrenness, evil. In the mountains and the forests the old pagan gods still lived changed to evil spirits—gnomes, trolls, banshees and boggarts. With the Renaissance the spiritual dangers of the woods evaporated like mist in the morning sun, and by the end of the seventeenth century the physical dangers had disappeared too. In England, if not in the rest of Europe, people began to think themselves free from the risk of war, though it was not till the subjection of the Highlands that they felt really safe. The country was now secure and confident. Society was settled. Travellers of earlier days, Leland and Camden, had looked to the past, but the new travellers looked to the future. They felt a lively curiosity about the physical world in which they lived. Science was revealing the conjuring tricks of matter; natural history was bringing the wonders of traveller's tales into their own lanes and back gardens. They became aware of the potentialities, the resources, the variety of their own country. The Middle Ages had seen the village as a tiny clearing of order among the illimitable wildness of nature; the seventeenth century saw the mountains as the last defiance of disorder among the colonies of civilization. These dark woods and mountains were to them as was the first chaos to God; England had her Newton, so let her now have light. At this very time travel, instead of being discouragingly dangerous and laborious, began to look almost as if it might become a pleasure. Highway robbery was decreasing, roads were improving; turnpikes were opened. The time was right for the exploration of England and the discovery of the Lakes.

*　　*　　*

Among the first to take part in that discovery was Daniel Defoe—if, indeed, he ever reached Cumberland at all. For Defoe was such an accomplished liar, his imagination was so vivid, his news sense so sure, that there is no need whatever to doubt the authenticity of his account merely because it may be fiction. Even if Defoe himself never saw Windermere we may be certain that what he says about it would be precisely what a middle-class man of his like would have said if he had been there. And what he did say was chiefly confined to the potted char. His remarks on the mountains are more interesting and more famous:

> Here we entered Westmoreland, a country eminent only for being the wildest, most barren and frightful of any that I have passed over in England, or even in Wales itself; the west side, which borders on Cumberland, is indeed bounded by a chain of almost unpassable mountains, which, in the language of the country, are called Fells.

Now these lines have often been quoted to show how false and absurd was the eighteenth-century attitude to mountain scenery. In fact, they show only that Defoe was a good journalist. He was not struck dumb with horror as many have tried to make out; he was merely determined to see that his readers got their money's worth. His steady use of superlatives, instead of seeming to exaggerate, has quite the opposite effect of sober realism. In fact, it was no great exaggeration to say that Westmorland was the most barren and frightful country *"of any that I have passed over in England"*. He was making comparison not with the Alps, but with the Midlands and the South Downs. Moreover, the word "barren" had not, for him, the emotional force it has for us. It did not call up vast landscapes of desolation; it meant merely country on which nothing profitable would grow, and what, for an eighteenth-century business man, could be more frightful than that? He does not seek to exploit the credulity of his readers—legends like that of St Bega and the founding of St Bees he leaves where he finds them: "(viz.) among the rubbish of the old women and Romish priests". A few archæological details are required, but these could be copied from Camden.

Yet though his material might be gathered in the most casual way, it was assembled and presented with the cunning of a confidence trickster. Of the stables at Lowther Castle, he says "... having not taken an exact view of them myself, I am loth to say, at secondhand, what fame has said"—and immediately you believe every word. His account is short, slick, completely unreliable, and aimed at the reader as deliberately as a bullet.

Celia Fiennes, on the other hand, aimed her story at no one. It is purely personal, entirely without purpose—the overheard mumblings of a talkative old maid. She took her "Great Journey to Newcastle and to Cornwall" in 1698, about twenty-five years before Defoe, but in many ways she anticipated the later travellers more than he does. It is not that she is more interested in landscape, but she is more interested in herself. Defoe travelled, in the first case, to collect information for a Minister of State; Miss Fiennes travelled only for her own entertainment. The scene around her mattered less for its own sake than because it could divert and amuse her. She is an extraordinarily interesting character: prudish, strict, exacting, and possibly sharp-tongued, and at the same time hardy, determined, and adventurous. To travel all over England in the reign of William and Mary demanded not only courage, but great physical toughness, yet Celia Fiennes was something of a hypochondriac, and became an expert visitor of "Spaws", where she went, not for cards and dancing, but for almost brutal treatment in icy-cold water. The Lakes, unfortunately, had little of this sort to offer, which may be one of the reasons for delay in their discovery by people of quality; for the visiting of watering-places was not just a fashion in medicine, it was a relic—though far removed—of the old pilgrimages to holy wells and miracle-working fountains.

Miss Fiennes's account of her visit to the Lakes is specially valuable because she was unprepared by the writings of others. She comes with no preconceived ideas; she did not feel that any particular reaction was expected of her. Her mind was entirely free from the suggestions of guide-book stars; she had neither to notice them nor to avoid them. Moreover, she knew of no prescribed grading of subjects. To her the purchase of curios made of "canal coal" at Wigan was quite as worthy of comment as the crossing of Kirkstone Pass. She had little of the later preoccupation with scenery, and would ride for miles without noticing anything which stuck in her mind, yet when her interest is really roused she can be a most perceptive reporter, especially (and here she may be compared with later women travellers) in matters of inns, cooking, and housewifery. Thus she enjoys the potted char from Windermere ("big as a small trout rather slenderer and the skinn full of spotts some redish, and part of the whole skinn and the finn and taile is red like to finns of a perch, and the inside flesh looks as red as any salmon"[1]); and, since rye bread makes her sick, she is relieved to find that she can digest the Westmorland Clapbread, which played an important part in the diet of the Lake counties.

Her route, unlike her prose, was straightforward enough. From Lancaster (where her horse stumbled in the street) she went through Kendal to Windermere, over Kirkstone into Patterdale, and thence to Penrith and on to Carlisle. In all her descriptions of the fells it is noticeable that she is quite uninfluenced either by Italian painting or by English poetry. Probably, being a Puritan, she had not read even such a poet as Spenser; certainly she arrived in the district quite unrehearsed in vocabulary. Such stock terms as "cataract" and "precipice" do not come easily to her mind, and this conditions her actual vision, for, instead of being able to fit the scenery into accepted categories, she is forced to stare hard and try to take each object to pieces and put it together again, like a savage trying to understand a watch. The extraordinary circumlocutions caused by this effort, together with the natural garrulity of a seventeenth-century Gertrude Stein, make her style as hard to follow as the course of a straw in a rocky stream, but they do tell us what she really saw and not just what she expected to see. In the whole history of Lake travel, there are few people who have described their first impressions with such honesty and such charm:

> ... at last I attained to the side of one of these hills or fells of rocks which I passed on the side much about the middle;

[1] *The Journeys of Celia Fiennes,* edited by Christopher Morris. (The Cresset Library, 1949).

for looking down to the bottom it was at least a mile all full
of those lesser hills and inclosures, so looking upward I was
as farre from the top which was all rocks and something more
barren tho' there was some trees and woods growing in the
rocks and hanging over all down the brow of some of the hills;
from these great fells there are severall springs out of the
rock that trickle down their sides, and as they meete with
stones and rocks in the way when something obstructs their
passage and so they come with more violence that gives a
pleaseing sound and murmuring noise.

The attraction of Celia Fiennes's account of the Lakes lies
in its spontaneity. She had little idea of what she was going to
see and none at all of what she ought to feel about it. She had
no thought of publication, and her work was not in any sense
an advertisement, so that we can see in her journal perhaps the
last truly unconditioned reflex to Cumberland landscape.

Soon after wild scenery first began to be popular, attention
was directed north by two publications: Dr John Brown's
Description of the Lake and Vale at Keswick, and Dr J. D.
Dalton's *Descriptive Poem* addressed to two young ladies (the
Misses Lowther) after their return from viewing the mines near
Whitehaven. Neither of these is very accomplished in itself, but
together they played a most important part in the discovery
of the Lakes, being the direct cause of the visits of Gray and
Young. From this time onwards, it was almost impossible for
the educated man to see the Lakes through his own eyes alone,
to see them clear and fresh, without having to compare the
visual image with the mental image, without having to compare what he really saw with what he had been led to expect.
From this time onwards he could not look into the bottle without having to stare at the label.

Brown starts by calling Keswick "a vast amphitheatre in
circumference about twenty miles" and this image makes clear
where he found his criteria. His picture of Keswick is, in fact,
an Italian picture. The hills are exaggerated to the heights of
the Apennines; the "furniture" of the scene—groves, cliffs,
clouds, waterfalls, eagles—is that of a classic landscape seen
through romantic eyes; the very colour is the full-fruited,

golden-brown of hills cooked in a hotter sun than that of Cumberland:

> ... at Keswick, you will on one side of the lake, see a rich and beautiful landskip of cultivated fields, rising to the eye in fine inequalities, with noble groves of oak, happily dispersed, and climbing the adjacent hills, shade above shade, in the most various and picturesque forms. On the opposite shore, you will find rocks and cliffs of stupendous height, hanging broken over the lake in horrible grandeur, some of them a thousand feet high, the woods climbing up their steep and shaggy sides, where mortal foot never yet approached. On these dreadful heights the eagles build their nests; a variety of water-falls are seen pouring from their summits, and tumbling in vast sheets from rock to rock in rude and terrible magnificence.

Dr Brown's prose is not without merit. He does not lash himself into a frenzy of enthusiasm; he does not exaggerate beyond an agreed degree. Moreover, he was one of the very first among the Lake writers to get above lake level. Not that he got very high—only to the top of Walla and Falcon Crags beside Derwentwater—but he does catch something of the excitement of height, the slight breathlessness, even dizziness, which is rather surprisingly absent from the writings of many of his contemporaries. It is not absent, however, from the verse of Dr Dalton,[1] who tips on to the page a whole cartload of picturesque bric-à-brac, image rolling after image like stones down the slope of a scree:

> Horrors like these at first alarm,
> But soon with savage grandeur charm,
> And raise to noblest thoughts the mind:
> Thus by thy fall, Lowdore reclin'd,
> The craggy cliff, impending wood,
> Whose shadows mix o'er half the flood,
> The gloomy clouds, which solemn sail,
> Scarce lifted by the languid gale,
> O'er the capp'd hill, the dark'ned vale;
> The rav'ning kite, and bird of Jove,

---

[1] John Dalton, D.D., who was born at Dean, between Cockermouth and Arlecdon, should not be confused with John Dalton, the pioneer of the atomic theory, who was born only a couple of miles away at Eaglesfield. Dr Dalton became a prebendary of Worcester, where he died in 1763.

Which round the aerial ocean rove,
And, floating on the billowy sky,
With full expanded pinions fly,
Their flutt'ring or their bleating prey
Thence with death-dooming eye survey;
Channels by rocky torrents torn,
Rocks to the lake in thunders borne,
Or such as o'er our heads appear
Suspended in their mid-career,
To start again at his command
Who rules fire, water, air and land,
I view with wonder and delight.

Brown and Dalton, however, were ahead of the main fashion by a decade or two. In the 1760s and early 1770s, æsthetic enjoyment of scenery had not yet replaced the inquiring curiosity about the physical world which excited so many eighteenth-century travellers. And chief among such was Thomas Pennant, who today is remembered as the man to whom Gilbert White addressed some of the Selborne letters. At the bottom, he was a humanist, interested more in men than in mountains. He had all the typical eighteenth-century pride in England's expanding trade, and he was supremely confident in the greatness of his age and in the soundness of the English social structure. But though he was a humanist he was no humanitarian. He had common sense but little imagination, and he had some of the hardness which is often to be found below the elegance of his time. At Whitehaven workhouse he could "look with pleasure" on the sight of old people, idiots, and "even infants of three years of age, contributing to their own support, by the pulling of oakum", and at Carlisle he received a similar pleasure from "twelve little industrious girls spinning at once at a horizontal wheel, which set twelve bobbins in motion". He had a strong distrust of all extravagances in thought, word and emotion, and in this was curiously unlike most of those who were to follow him to the Lakes. He had learned the jargon, of course. He knew when to call a scene "horrid" or "stupendous", but the words had no emotional content for him—they were merely the accepted terms for describing that sort of scenery.

For all this, he was a true romantic, and his romanticism expressed itself in science. Science, in the mid-eighteenth century, was revealing enormous new vistas and potentialities; it was making man more aware of his physical environment; it was making the discovery of that environment into an adventure—and it was to this adventure that Pennant's life was dedicated. To him the mere collection of facts was the most exhilarating thing in life, for every fact added to the sum of knowledge, and through knowledge the whole world was opening out to man. To Pennant, no fantasies of poetry, no prophecies of religion, offered such scope to the human imagination as did the phenomena of the natural world. No myth could move him to such wonder as did theories and speculations about the geography of the world or the physical structure of vertebrates.

He felt to the full that sense of adventure, of discovery, and even of mystery which lay behind the catechism distributed about this time by the Society of Antiquaries among "the Gentlemen and Clergy of North Britain":

QUERIES

Relating to the Natural History of the Parish

1. What is the appearance of the country in the parish; is it flat or hilly, rocky or mountainous?
2. Do the lands consist of woods, arable, pasture, meadow, heath, or what?
3. Are they fenny or moorish, boggy or firm?
4. Is there sand, clay, chalk, stone, gravel, loam, or what is the nature of the soil?
5. Are there any lakes, meers, or waters, what are they, their depth, where do they rise, and whither do they run?
6. Are there any subterraneous rivers, which appear in one place, then sink into the earth and rise again?[1]

The questions approach subject after subject—antiquities, agriculture, soil, stock, customs, storms; the words are flat and

[1] Printed as an appendix to Pennant's *Tour in Scotland in 1769* (1771). For a further extract from his questionnaire see Appendix A in the present volume.

precise, yet almost liturgical in the repetitions, with something of the tone of a prosaic *Hymn to David*, a humanist *Benedicite*.

Except as an ornithologist, Pennant was merely an amateur in the sciences—unlike Arthur Young who on his Northern Tour of 1768 brought the trained eye of a specialist in farming. But what he lacked in knowledge he made up in curiosity. There was no scraping of information that failed to interest him, no rumour or hint that did not catch his fancy. Horace Walpole called him a smatterer in history, who "picks up knowledge as he rides", but Johnson, defending him against Bishop Percy, said: "He's a Whig, sir; a sad dog. But he's the best traveller I have ever read; he observes more things than anyone else does". Yet his journals are rather cold-bloodedly impersonal—almost entirely devoid of anecdote, of reference to friends or even to the weather. He could take an artist with him as a modern traveller might take a camera, never thinking of the man as a friend, scarcely, even, as a human being.

On his first tour of Scotland, in 1769, Pennant passed through the Lakes only on the way back, by which time he was obviously tired by his long journey. He had had enough of marvels, and hurried through Carlisle and Penrith, anxious to get home to his children, "after an absence" (as he naïvely and not very convincingly says) "equally regretted by all parties".

On his second visit, in 1772, his mind was set once again on Scotland and the Hebrides, but this time he called in at the Lakes on the way up. He travelled as before through Lancashire as far as the county town, but planned the rest of his journey so that his new route did not coincide with his former one till he reached Carlisle.

After crossing Morecambe Bay he came to Furness and thence to Coniston. This was the first English lake he had seen at close hand and he seems rather puzzled at what to say, not knowing whether to use his superlatives or to reserve them for places more celebrated. "The scenery", he says, choosing a word which is not really one of the more conventional ones, ". . . is extremely noble", but he seems glad to direct his attention to the slate quarries and the price of fish. Neither Esthwaite nor Windermere impressed him greatly, though he inquired again

about the fish and tells us that there are wild cats in the woods
—but at Derwentwater he was faced with what was already
accepted as the scenic climax to the Lakes, the "Elysium of
the North". Here he is clearly much more enthusiastic and his
prose begins to warm up into passages which were to be quoted
over and over again in the years which followed. But, though
he is quite sincere (which is more than could be said of many
of his readers), he could not keep up that strain for long, for
he was exhausting both his sense of rapture and his rather
small vocabulary. Luckily, there was more to interest him. He
turns from the lake and mentions, with his usual delight at any
piece of stray information, that it is not long since the stipend
of the vicar of Crosthwaite (the parish church of Keswick) "was
five pounds per annum, a goose-grass, or the right of common-
ing his goose; a whittle-gait, or the valuable privilege of using
his knife for a week at a time at any table in the parish; and
lastly, a hardened sark, i.e. a shirt of coarse linnen."

He now had the good fortune to meet Dr Brownrigg, a man
after his own stamp, who was then retired and living at Orma-
thwaite near Keswick. Brownrigg, next to John Dalton the
most distinguished chemist Cumberland has yet produced,
had been in practice as a surgeon at Whitehaven where he
invented an instrument "for the more immediate extraction
of drowning bodies from the water",[1] and began important
experiments with fire-damp and other poisonous or explosive
gases which caused so many accidents in the mines. Nor was
Pennant his only visitor that year, for Benjamin Franklin
stayed there, preoccupied, quite literally, with the problem
of pouring oil on troubled waters. He, Brownrigg and the Rev.
Charles Farish of Carlisle carried out experiments on Derwentwater, and one wonders if anyone protested when the three of
them rowed out from Friar's Crag and tipped barrels of oil
on to the choppy surface of the lake. Perhaps there were oil-
casualties among the water-fowl even as early as the eighteenth
century.

Pennant stayed for two days with Dr Brownrigg and then
set off for Whitehaven, of which, no doubt, he had heard much
from his host, and the town interested him more than anything

[1] William Hutchinson: *History of Cumberland* (Carlisle, 1794).

BUTTERMERE WITH FLEETWITH PIKE

ROCKY SCENERY by William Gilpin

he had yet seen. And, indeed, as he approached over the moors, the streets and harbour below him were a sight to take the breath away. In those days the low hills round the port would be barren of cultivation and bare of buildings, crouching over the roofs like Rugby players in a scrimmage. Yet, in the hollow, the streets were laid out in clean lines and right-angles, deliberate as heroic couplets. Moreover, this outpost of civilization among the barbarous hills had set itself to tame and subdue the still more barbarous sea, and stone piers stretched into the water, making "a fine and expensive" harbour, "where the ships may lie in great security". From the hill above Brackenthwaite these piers would seem to cross each other and overlap, as if hugging the water, holding the docks in a huge mother-of-navies, mother-of-empires embrace.

It was a sight which every liberal Englishman would have admired, but for Pennant the town had a still greater fascination. Mines brought out all that was romantic in his nature. As a scientist he was interested both in the engineering problems of the work and in the coal itself. Again, the dark caves, strangely lit by the miners' lamps, the awareness of danger, of remoteness from the normal world, of a hidden and hazardous way of living—all these appealed deeply to his sense of the mysterious. They aroused wonder and perhaps awe, stirring the damped-down dreams of the subconscious yet presenting them in a solid, measurable, demonstrable form which he could not put aside as he might put aside the mysteries of metaphysics:

Visit the collieries, entering at the foot of a hill, not distant from the town, attended by the agent: the entrance was a narrow passage, bricked and vaulted, sloping down with an easy descent. Reach the first beds of coal which had been worked about a century ago: the roofs are small and spacious, the pillars of a sufficient strength to support the great superstructure, being fifteen yards square or sixty in circumference; not above a third of the coal having been worked in this place; so that to me the very columns seemed left as resource for fuel in future times. The immense caverns that lay between the pillars, exhibited a most gloomy appearance: I could not help enquiring here after that imaginary inhabitant, the creation of the labourer's fancy,

The swart Fairy of the mine,

and was seriously answered by a black fellow at my elbow, that he really had never met with any; but that his grand-father had found the little implements and tools belonging to this diminutive race of subterranean spirits.[1]

He went on next to inspect the result of Dr Brownrigg's research:

At about 80 fathoms depth began to see the workings of the rods of the fire-engine, and the present operations of the colliers, who now work in security, for the fire-damps, formerly so dangerous, are almost overcome; at present they are prevented by boarded partitions, placed a foot distant from the sides, which cause a free circulation of air through-out: but as still there are some places not capable of such conveniences, the colliers, who dare not venture with a candle in spots where fire-damps are supposed to lurk, have invented a curious machine to serve the purpose of lights: it is what they call a steel-mill, consisting of a small wheel and a handle; this they turn with vast rapidity against a flint, and the great quantity of sparks emitted, not only serves for a candle, but has been found of such a nature as not to set fire to the horrid vapour.

Formerly the damp or fiery vapour was conveyed through pipes to the open air, and formed a terrible illumination during the night like the eruptions of a volcano; and by its heat water could be boiled; the men who worked in it in-haled inflammable air, and, if they breathed against a candle, puffed out a fiery stream.

It is as near to poetry as Pennant can ever get. He had not seen this last phenomenon; it was only hearsay to him. Yet he turns over the idea in his mind, enjoying the mental image more thoroughly than he had enjoyed any actual view of lake or fell. In his own limited way, he is warming his wits at the sort of scientific fantasy which, over a hundred years later, was to burst into the full flame of the Wellsian romance.

After this, the rest of Cumberland was an anticlimax. He made for Carlisle and Scotland, with the Border Ballads blow-

[1] Thomas Pennant: *Tour in Scotland and Voyage to the Hebrides in 1772* (1774-6).

ing their horns, and so passes out of the county. For a long time, however, his name and his words were repeated by the Lake travellers to whom he seemed a pioneer. And, indeed, so he was, though his interests were more serious, more enduring, than the fashion which he helped to create. As a writer he is neither lively nor original. Defoe could make the eighteenth-century scene come alive in a few sentences, and Miss Fiennes, with her trails and tangles of words, could always make at least herself come alive. Pennant had not this gift. Too often he descends into a sort of gentlemanly journalism. Yet of all the early travellers in the Lakes, he is the one for whom I feel the most sympathy. His interests were confined almost entirely to the natural and material world around him, but they were the beginnings of a great new awakening to the physical and spiritual predicament of man. His view was limited, but it was a real view; he saw only in part, but what he did see was really there. He did not invent his own landscape, and his very lack of imagination, his literal and materialist way of thought, represents the basic, objective view of the Lakes to which every now and then we must return to renew our sense of perspective. Pennant's mountains may not point to heaven, but at least you can stand on them.

CHAPTER THREE

WILLIAM GILPIN

WILLIAM GILPIN was born in 1724 at Scaleby Castle,[1] near Carlisle. His family was notable both in Cumberland and Westmorland, and could claim Bernard Gilpin, the "Apostle of the North", among its members. William's great-grandfather, Dr Richard Gilpin, bought Scaleby Castle during the mid-seventeenth century, leaving it to his son, William Gilpin, who spent most of his life as a lawyer at Whitehaven. Of this William's several sons, John Bernard, the fourth, became the father of the picturesque traveller, and, as he was in the army, his wife and their son, William, were allowed to live at Scaleby, till the castle had to be sold, after which the boy went to Carlisle where his father was put in charge of the garrison. (It was not Captain Gilpin, however, who surrendered to Bonnie Prince Charlie, but the

---

[1] Here is part of Gilpin's description of his birthplace, taken from *Observations on the Lakes* (1786):

"The castle is more perfect than such buildings commonly are.... It preserved its perfect form, till the civil wars of the last century; when the castle, in too much confidence of its strength, shut its gates against Cromwell, then marching into Scotland; who made it a monument of his vengeance.

"What share of picturesque genius Cromwell might have, I know not. Certain however it is, that no man, since Henry the eighth, has contributed more to adorn this country with picturesque ruins. The difference between these two masters lay chiefly in the style of ruins, in which they composed. Henry adorned his landscapes with the ruins of abbeys; Cromwell, with those of castles. I have seen many pieces by this master, executed in a very grand style; but seldom a finer monument of his masterly hand than this. He has rent the tower, and demolished two of its sides; the edges of the other two he has shattered into broken lines....

"The area within the mote, which consists of several acres, was originally intended to support cattle, which should be driven thither in times of alarm. When the house was inhabited ... this area was the garden; and all around, on the outside of the mote stood noble trees, irregularly planted, the growth of a century. Beneath the trees ran a walk round the castle; to which the situation naturally gave that pleasing curve, which in modern days hath been so much the object of art. This walk might admit of great embellishment."

officer who succeeded him on the orders of the Duke of Cumberland.)

William was educated first at St Bees, and then at Oxford, where he was studying at the time of the Rebellion of '45. He took a degree, married his cousin, held several curacies, and finally was put in charge of the Rev Daniel Sanxay's school at Cheam in Surrey, running it on the new evangelical principles which were just beginning to be felt in education. The school was so successful that by 1777 Gilpin had amassed £10,000, and was able to resign his headship, handing it over to his son, and to begin to look for a quiet living in which to spend his old age. He wanted a rest from schoolmastering, and, above all, he wanted the leisure to make a study of picturesque landscape from material which he had gathered during his tours of the Wye, the Lakes, Wales and Scotland, carried out chiefly during the school holidays.

When, in the introduction to the *Lakes Tour*, Gilpin expressed the hope that his work may not be thought "inconsistent with the profession of a clergyman", the reader is likely to think that this is merely a conventional concession to propriety. For Gilpin seems to be typical of the easy-going yet cultured eighteenth-century country parson, a good conversationalist, something of a scholar, an amateur of the arts and the sciences, but not a zealot for the duties of his calling. In fact, he was by no means a man of this sort. Boldre, in the New Forest, was not a wealthy parish, and when Gilpin accepted the living he found his parishioners in social and moral squalor, picking up a livelihood mostly by poaching on the game of the forest. Immediately he made it his duty to reform this state of things, visiting every house in the parish, giving away a considerable amount of his income (he managed nevertheless to keep four servants), and preaching and teaching with admirable directness and force.

Soon he realized that if the children of the foresters were to be raised much above the level of savages, he would have to build and endow a school. But this needed money, and though he now had a considerable fortune, he hesitated to spend it on such a project, for he feared that this would be unfair to his own family. On the other hand, he felt that the proceeds of his "amusements" (as distinct from his capital and his stipend) were his own to do with as he liked, and he decided, therefore, to devote the entire earnings of his books and drawings to the upkeep of the school. Pastorate and Picturesque were thus most conveniently combined.

The cult of the Picturesque[1] was primarily an attempt to educate the eye to a new way of looking at the natural world. In its simplest and purest sense the word had none of the implications of rusticity and quaintness which it has today. It just meant the art of seeing the world aesthetically. People had got into the habit of using the eye mainly for information, mainly in order to know. The Picturesque trained them to use it for sensation.

Burke, in his *Inquiry into the Origin of Our Ideas of the Sublime and Beautiful* (first published in 1756), had ascribed æsthetic taste to two fundamental instincts, that of self-propagation and that of self-preservation. All objects, because they were perceived by the senses, appealed in some degree to one or other of these two instincts: those which were pleasing and gentle, suggesting ease and safety, appealed to the instinct of self-propagation; those that were great and vast, suggesting fear and wonder, appealed to, or aroused, the instinct of self-preservation. The first category was that of the Beautiful, the second, that of the Sublime.

William Gilpin was among the first to realize that what was beautiful or sublime in nature did not always come off in art, to explain which he invented a third category which he called Picturesque Beauty, meaning, quite simply, that form of beauty "which would be effective in a picture". Gilpin became the travelling salesman of the Picturesque, yet when he used the term he did not, at first, envisage beauty of a different *kind* from that of the Sublime or the Beautiful. It was not till the publication in 1794 of Uvedale Price's *Essay on the Picturesque* that this type of beauty was recognized as one to which neither of Burke's generalizations could be applied. The characteristics of the Picturesque, said Price, were diametrically

---

[1] Those who wish to study this movement in detail should consult Mr Christopher Hussey's invaluable book, *The Picturesque* (Putnam, 1927).

opposite to those of the Beautiful. Where the Beautiful was smooth, gentle, with easy gradations of colour and texture, the Picturesque was rough, asymmetrical, irregular, with abrupt and surprising variations.

Gilpin, anticipating Price by some years, applied the theory more specifically. The proportions of a Palladian mansion, he says make it into a *beautiful* object, but a broken ruin is more *picturesque*. Similarly, a wilderness is more picturesque than an ordered garden, dishevelled hair than a powdered wig, an old, wrinkled face than a young, pretty one. Smoothness, the conventional idea of beauty, may actually have a part in a picturesque composition because it provides a contrast to the rougher parts. Thus, the smoothness of lakes enhances the ruggedness of the rocks above them, and "an old head is greatly improved by the smoothness of the bald pate".

This last ridiculous example shows one of the many dangers of Gilpin's point of view. The object loses all significance in itself, it becomes nothing but its own shape, and may even be admired solely for its decrepitude. "We admire the horse, as a *real object*; the elegance of his form; the stateliness of his tread; the spirit of all his motions; and the glossiness of his coat. But as an object of picturesque beauty, we admire more the worn-out cart-horse." Or, in Sidney Smith's words: "The vicar's horse is beautiful, the curate's picturesque."

Once the connoisseur has learned to recognize the Picturesque he naturally sets off in search of it. Picturesque travel, in fact, is a sort of collecting. "The pleasures of the chase are universal", says Gilpin, ". . . And shall we suppose it a greater pleasure to the sportsman to pursue a trivial animal, than it is for the man of taste to pursue the beauties of nature?"[1] Yet the sort of beauties which are really satisfactory are not easy to find. Nature, indeed, rarely seems to pass the test. Among all her splendours she so often lacks composition, or spoils a fine distance by an indifferent foreground. Too often all that can be said of the most celebrated prospect is that it is "amusing". Indeed, Catherine in *Northanger Abbey*, who learned to reject the whole of the city of Bath as unworthy to make part of a landscape, was no more severe a critic than William Gilpin.

[1] William Gilpin. *Three Essays on Picturesque Beauty*, etc. (1792).

In all his tours he never departed from the purity of his æsthetic principles. He was concerned solely with the *visual* aspect of the scene, and would not allow any other considerations to affect his judgment. The true character of the districts he visited, the real life of the people—these interested him not at all. If men were included in his landscape it was purely as picturesque objects, or because they suggested the proportions of the scene. There was a certain inhumanity in all this, of course, and Gilpin, though he was not callous by nature, tended at times to see poverty as picturesque.

Again, he refused to admit the relevance of all those romantic associations which were beginning to rise like a mist around medieval ruins and ancient abbeys. It was not legitimate to include a ruin in a landscape merely as a stimulus to the imagination; to justify its inclusion it must be interesting in *shape*. Gilpin preceded Wordsworth not only in the Lakes but at Tintern, and it is most entertaining to compare his comments with Wordsworth's poem. For Gilpin, the abbey "... does not make that appearance as a *distant* object which we expected. Though the parts are beautiful, the whole is ill-shaped."[1] There are a number of unbroken gable-ends which "hurt the eye with their regularity, and disgust it by the vulgarity of their shape", and he suggests that this might be improved by breaking them up with a mallet. But while he obviously preferred a ruin to a living building, he had too much common sense to copy the late-eighteenth-century affectation for the sham Gothic. Like Cowper, he was contemptuous of artificial ruins. Time and nature alone could produce a convincing ruin—without their aid "you may as well write over the gate: Built in the year 1772. Deception there can be none."[2]

His drawings may not rank very high as works of art, but they have much charm, and admirably reveal what he saw in landscape. He aims, as he repeatedly tells us, not at portraits, but at the general character of the scene, and for accurate and detailed representation he has nothing but scorn—it is merely "a painted survey, a mere map". On the other hand, the artist "... who works from imagination—that is, he who culls from

[1] *Observations on the River Wye* (1782).
[2] William Gilpin. *Observations on the Lakes* (1786).

nature the most beautiful parts of her productions—a distance here; and there a fore-ground—combines them artificially; and removing everything offensive, admits only such parts, as are *congruous* and *beautiful*; will in all probability, make a much better landscape, than he who takes all as it comes."[1]

The anonymous author of Dr Syntax's *Tour* has his own characteristic comment. Syntax, lost on a moor with his horse, Grizzle, finds only an old guide-post with all its lettering defaced:

> ... But, as my time shall not be lost,
> I'll make a drawing of the Post;
> And, tho' a flimsy taste may flout it,
> There's something *picturesque* about it;
> 'Tis rude and rough, without a gloss,
> And is well cover'd o'er with moss;
> And I've a right—(who dares deny it?)
> To place yon group of asses by it.
> Aye! this will do: and now I'm thinking,
> That self-same pond where Grizzle's drinking,
> If hither brought 'twould better seem,
> And faith I'll turn it to a stream:
> I'll make this flat a shaggy ridge,
> And o'er the water throw a bridge:
> I'll do as other sketchers do—
> Put any thing into the view;
> And any object recollect,
> To add a grace, and give effect.
> Thus, though from truth I haply err,
> *The scene preserves its character.*
> What man of taste my right will doubt,
> To put things in or leave them out?
> 'Tis more than right, it is a duty,
> If we consider landscape beauty:—
> He ne'er will, as an artist shine,
> Who copies Nature line by line:
> Whoe'er from Nature takes a view,
> Must copy and improve it too.
> To heighten ev'ry work of art,
> Fancy should take an active part:

[1] Gilpin, *op. cit.*

Thus I (which few I think can boast)
Have made a landscape of a Post.[1]

Now if Gilpin were merely laying down the rules of land-scape-painting there would be no need for us to bother about him; but, in fact, he is dictating the way in which to look at nature. He is advocating that the connoisseur should mentally falsify (or, as he would say, correct) the scene before his eyes, setting to right Nature's deformities, and adding extra accessories where desirable. That this is so is shown by the way he limits this practice by the rules of propriety. The artist should introduce nothing alien to the scene, and the alterations he makes must be in character with the country. He may plant trees if he wants to, or remove them; he may change a "spreading oak" into a withered stump if this improves his composition. Yet he has no right to add "a magnificent castle, and impending rock, or a river, to adorn his fore-ground". Such are new features, and Gilpin clearly feels that to add them is not quite playing fair. But he may certainly break an ill-formed hillock; and shovel the earth about him, as he pleases, without offence. He may pull up a piece of awkward paling—he may throw down a cottage—he may even turn the course of a road, or a river, a few yards on this side, or that.

It is impossible not to feel that there is a note of condescension in a passage like this. Gilpin did not fall into the typical trick of the romantics, did not glorify his own ego by equating it with wild nature and especially with mountains. Yet in his very objectivity there is a sort of pride; in his very detachment there is an assumption of superiority. As he went on his tours, "corpulent but not unwieldy", giving Helvellyn and Loch Lomond so many out of ten, we feel that he enjoyed the actual scenes less than the fantasies he could build from memory when he was safe in his inn at the end of the day. Then, in the large sketchbook of his mind, he could touch up the untrained designs of Nature, and persuade himself that he was a perceptive observer of the countryside, when, in fact, he was little more than a collector of lantern-slides.

*　　*　　*

[1] *The Tour of Dr Syntax in Search of the Picturesque.* (Published anonymously, 1812).

Gilpin set off in May 1772 from Cheam and passed through the Midlands, visiting and criticizing several of Capability Brown's "embellished" estates, and passing through Manchester and Preston to Lancaster. He approached the Lakes by Kendal and Ambleside, and sailed up and down Windermere, noting the changes in distance and prospect as he moved along the surface of the water. He had no eye for detail, but he did have a lively interest in what might be called the series of dissolving views which is revealed as a bay slides out from behind a promontory, as the shores approach each other or open apart, or as hills emerge above hills or sink and recede in the distance. The landscape, if it is only a picture, is at least a moving picture. From Windermere he passed over Dunmail Raise, along Thirlmere, then still treeless and bridged about the middle, and on to Keswick, whence he made excursions to Lower Borrowdale, to Buttermere and Crummock, and to Bassenthwaite. He views Derwentwater appreciatively but critically, and does not fall into the raptures of many of the other visitors. He quotes the famous saying of Charles Avison, organist and composer, of Newcastle-upon-Tyne: "Here is beauty indeed—Beauty lying in the lap of Horrour!" He tells also the rather odd story of an artist who painted a series of views of the lake from St Herbert's Island, and then hung them around the walls of a circular room, "whence, as from a centre, he might see it in rotation".

Borrowdale, however, made rather more of an impression on him. Here, he went first as far as Rosthwaite, and thence by the track that curves behind Grange Fell, into the small Watendlath valley, and his story of this journey was so often quoted and repeated that the phrase "Which way to Watendlath?" has become almost a local proverb. And it is, indeed, a curiously intriguing phrase and one which, if spoken in the presence of Wordsworth, might have led to a poem, another "What, are you stepping westward?"

"Which way to Watenlath?" said one of our company to a peasant, as we left the vale of Borrodale. "That way," said he, pointing up a lofty mountain, steeper than the tiling of a house.

To those, who are accustomed to mountains, these perpendicular motions may be amusing; but to us, whose ideas were less elevated, they seemed rather peculiar. . . . To move upwards, keeping a steady eye on the objects before us, was no great exercise to the brain : but it rather gave it a rotation to look back on what was past—and to see our companions below *clinging*, as it appeared, to the mountain's side; and the rising breasts and bellies of their horses, straining up a path so steep, that it seemed, as if the least false step would have carried them rolling many hundred yards to the bottom.

The last lake he visited was Ullswater, where he was entertained with the french horns which will be heard echoing through later chapters of this book. He got a glimpse of the King of Patterdale, fishing on the lake, collected a few stories about thrifty curates and great storms and then passed along to Carlisle and the Border. He had been only five days in the Lakes and his impressions were bound to be superficial, yet for two or three generations people would look at those scenes through his eyes. He had made, in fact, the first picturesque survey of the district.

Gilpin's limitations are obvious, yet he avoided most of the absurdities of his contemporaries. He has little of the traveller's usual wish to astonish those who stayed at home, and seems deliberately to keep his enthusiasm in check (if, indeed, he was capable of much enthusiasm), and to remind the reader that not every scene in Cumberland and Westmorland is "correctly picturesque". This cold, analytical approach may suggest that he was incapable of accurate observation, but this is not quite true. Whenever a scene has a picturesque effect which particularly interested him, he takes careful notice of the physical details which produce that effect. He notices, for instance, the variations of light on the side of a mountain, and how the surface which seems flat and dull at one time of day, can take on an exciting texture of gleam and shadow as the sun shifts to another angle. He notices too, how great tides of shadow wash round the bases of the mountains and in the clefts between them, ebbing and flowing with the sun. Like James Thomson, he was much concerned with light, and his comments on the surface of the lakes have an accuracy and understanding quite astonishing for one who spent so little time among them:

In clear windy weather, the breezy ruffled lake ... is a shattered mirror: it reflects the serenity; but reflects it partially. The hollow of each wave is commonly in shadow, the summit is tipped with light. The light or shadow therefore prevails, according to the position of the waves to the eye.

There is another appearance on the surfaces of lakes, which we cannot account for on any principle either of optics, or of perspective. When there is no apparent cause in the sky, the water will sometimes appear dappled with large spots of shade. ... The people will often say, "It will be no hay-day, today, the lake is full of shades".

It is in his love of certain effects of light—particularly of mist, vapours, shadows and twilight—that Gilpin approaches closest to one aspect of romanticism. He was the forerunner of those who look to art to escape from the world of physical necessity into a blurred, hazy, intangible world of the imagination. He was, in fact, one to whom distance lends enchantment to the view,[1] because distance moves out of fact into fancy.

But what does his doctrine imply in its purest form? It implies first of all a disastrous break between man and the external world. The method of generalization has completely betrayed its main aim. The generalization of the eighteenth-century artists like Reynolds aimed at penetrating through the particular to the ideal. The conventional diction of some eighteenth-century poetry had a similar effect: a "verdant grove" may not apply very aptly to this spinney or that copse, but it does suggest a memory of woodlands. The worst that could be said

[1] Why to yon mountain turns the musing eye,
Whose sunbright summit mingles with the sky?
Why do those cliffs of shadowy tint appear
More sweet than all the landscape smiling near?
'Tis distance lends enchantment to the view,
And robes the mountain in its azure hue.
            Thomas Campbell—*The Pleasure of Hope* (1799).
Compare this with a typical Elizabethan sentiment:—
Kind sir, near-dwelling amity indeed
Offers the heart's inquiry better view
Than love that's seated in a farther soil:
As prospectives, the nearer that they be,
Yield better judgement to the judging eye;
Things seen far off are lessened in the eye,
When their true shape is seen being hard by.
            Henry Porter—*The Two Angry Women of*
                        Abingdon (1599)

of these artists and poets is that they could not see the trees for the wood. But the connoisseurs of the Picturesque could not see even the wood—all they saw were perspectives, backgrounds and foregrounds, diagonals and parallels and correspondences, depositions of mass and gradations of tone.

They set up an entirely false relation between themselves and nature. For the Picturesque is a complete distortion of perception. It has not even the swagger of those romantics who inflated their own egos till they fill the universe, for it reverses that procedure and reduces the universe to the size of a man's eyeball. There were idealists like Blake who were at times doubtful of the reality of the external nature which they saw around them; but if they felt that nature might be an hallucination, a vision, they believed also that it was a glorious vision, an act of creation by God through the human imagination. In the Picturesque, the only creative act is that of man himself, a small, mean, self-satisfied manipulation of an abstract landscape. The Picturesque reduces the world to a mere scribbling-pad for man; it makes a convenience of nature. It denies all dimensions to nature except one—and that a false one. It denies the intricate reality of the world, the biological, geological, organic, physical complexity of which rock, water, air, grass, tree, bird, beast, and man himself are all part. It is, in fact, not even a half-truth, or a quarter-truth, but a lie.

CHAPTER FOUR

THOMAS GRAY

IN THE popular literature of the Lakes, Gray has been made the butt of all those who think themselves better men because they can climb Scafell or walk across Striding Edge. As early as 1787 James Clarke, in his *Survey of the Lakes*, was spreading the story that Gray was so terrified by the precipices of Skiddaw that he drew the blinds of his chaise. Others told how he had been equally terrified when crossing Windermere by boat. Both stories appear to be false, and in any case we shall never understand the effect of the Lake scenes on his complex personality unless we try to understand something of the man himself.

Gray was born in 1716 in London of what we would now call bourgeois parents. His father was a scrivener, while his mother and her sister ran a shop or warehouse on the profits of which the boy was sent to Eton. Here he made friends with Horace Walpole, Richard West and Thomas Ashton—a quartet of adolescent æsthetes, precocious, highly intelligent, elegant, detached, sophisticated.

In these days at school Gray's temperament seemed to take shape. He was nervous, delicate, and physically unsure of himself, shrinking from contact with the world and with women. From men he could accept a friendship which seemed safer because it made less physical demands, but which, in the end, probably caused much nervous strain. About the close of his life—a few months after his visit to the Lakes—he formed a violent attachment to a young Swiss, called Bonstetten, from which he was only just able to recover without a mental breakdown. Moreover, the years of loneliness and frustration acting on the tenderness of his nature must have heightened the sensibility with which he turned to landscape, art and antiquities, so that to Gray the Picturesque was, in a way, a substitute for sex.

After Eton he went to Cambridge which at first he did not like, but where, after a time, he was able to settle down to his intense and systematic, but essentially private, studies. When he left in 1738, however, he had next to no plans for making a living for himself. His health was not good; he was shy and painfully self-conscious, and altogether unfitted for the harsh professional world of the eighteenth century, so it was a merciful escape from immediate problems when he was invited by Walpole to come as his guest on a continental tour. They left in March 1739, travelling by Paris, Dijon, Lyons, and on to Florence.

The first part of the tour was a success, for Gray was tremendously excited by the Alps, and could have spent all his life wandering among the rivers of Rome, but in the end the arrangement between the two of them did not quite work. Walpole, as the son of one of the most powerful statesmen in Europe, was welcomed into the brilliant society of Italy; Gray sat in a corner and sulked. He became moody, touchy, ready to take offence and very conscious of the fact that it was Walpole who paid the bills. A break was inevitable, and, though we do not know all the details of the quarrel, Gray returned to England on his own in the autumn of 1741.

The loss of Walpole's friendship affected him very deeply. The young aristocrat had brought into his life a whiff of the great world of Whig politics which had always fascinated him. Now he seemed to be shut out from that world for ever, and at the same time to have lost his greatest friend. Let it be said, quite fairly, that this second loss affected him the more. To Gray, the Arcadian friendship of Eton had been more real than to the others, less of a game, less of a pretence, so that when, in 1742, the estrangement with Walpole was followed by the death of West, he felt wounded and alone. The thin shell of his defence was cracked like that of a trodden-on snail, and he was left exposed and raw to the world. Ill-health was beginning to take up its lifelong lodging with him, and he was unprepared for the future and scared of it.

In October 1742, he acknowledged that he was beaten. He

GREAT GABLE FROM CASTLE CRAG IN BORROWDALE

A View of Derwentwater &c. from Crow Park.

DERWENTWATER
FROM
CROW PARK
by Thomas Smith

would try to face the world no longer; he would find another shell and crawl into it. He returned, therefore, to Peterhouse, Cambridge, where he could live free of charge, and settled down to a life of retirement and order—a life as punctual, as solitary, and almost as frugal as that of a monk.

But was this really a defeat? If Gray had tried to square up to life he might perhaps have written more passionate poetry, but he would certainly have been dead within a few years or mad within less. As it was, he lived to work the *Elegy* into perhaps the most popular poem in English, to make himself one of the most learned men in Europe, and in his own odd, ingrown, secretive way, to get a great deal of satisfaction out of life. He was never very lively, of course, and he suffered much from depression and inertia of the spirit, yet at most times his was not despair but rather what he himself called a "white melancholy". Like Cowper, he had that touch of spiritual toughness which sometimes helps a physically broken man to last longer than the heroes. If Gray had been Shelley he might never have written the *Ode to the West Wind,* but he would have taken good care not to be drowned.

For our own purpose we may look on the next thirty years of Gray's life as a preparation for his visit to the Lakes. As a scholar he carefully equipped himself to appreciate every aspect of the Picturesque. From the Classics he passed on to Provençal, Anglo-Saxon, Old and Middle English, Old Norse, and the Icelandic Sagas. His love of ruins led him to Gothic architecture, heraldry, archæology and medieval history; his love of landscape led him to botany and zoology. Though he was always living on the edge of a physical crisis, so that a puff of wind or a slammed door might have knocked him over, and though he went for many days at a time in lassitude, weakness, and depression, he succeeded in putting the stamp of order upon his private world, a world which with most men would have collapsed into helplessness and chaos. He became precise, finicky, exacting, systematizing the most trivial everyday matters, until he was able to bring perpetual interest, significance, and even excitement into a life which from the outside seems deadeningly dull.

This comparative security, however, this near equilibrium,

was gained only at a great price. The seclusion and monotony in which he lived so guarded him from outside stimulus that his creative gifts could rarely break through the apathy which, followed. Again, his continual (and, admittedly, necessary) care of himself resulted in the most painful neurosis. He watched his health, Lord David Cecil says[1], as a scientist watches an experiment. Like most nervous patients he became passionately attached to the place where he lived. The familiar rooms and furniture, the measured stairs and streets, and, above all, the known and regular routine gave him a sense of stability without which he could scarcely have kept his mental balance. Any break or disturbance in this routine could put his whole system into a wobble—a practical joke played on him by students drove him for ever from Peterhouse to take shelter at Pembroke.

In the same way, any temporary absence from home was a great nervous strain. A holiday was always an adventure, because he had removed himself from the place of safety. He planned his journeys for days, even months, beforehand, constantly revising his arrangements and trying to foresee every eventuality or possible accident. From the moment he left to the moment when he returned he was in a state of prolonged agitation; indeed, it is probable that he did not really enjoy his holidays till he had got back.

But though Gray was something of an oddity he was not in any way naïve. Before we are tempted to try to debunk him, we must remember that we are dealing with a brilliant intellect, with a man of subtle and unending humour, the close associate of some of the wittiest men of his time. The mere fact that Walpole chose him as his companion shows that he was capable of extreme sophistication, of diagnosing and satirizing all the fashionable foibles and pretences. He had, in fact, an ear, an eye and a nose for every over-emphasis, every exaggeration, every strained pose. It is dangerous to ridicule one with so acute a sense of the ridiculous.

Gray's response to landscape was bound up very closely with his sense of history. He first began to enjoy the natural scene at Eton and Windsor, where the meadows took half their beauty

[1] In *Two Quiet Lives* (Constable).

in his eyes from the Tudor mists that hung about the old walls. At Cambridge he could not look at the "brown o'er-arching grove" of the "willowy Camus" without seeing

> High potentates, and dames of royal birth,
> And mitred fathers in long order go.[1]

It was not just that he peopled his landscape with a pageant of the past, but that the fields took their colouring from other eyes, that they existed at one and the same time in his own sight and in someone else's memory. It is not the "light that never was on sea or land", but a light that once was and, to all except Gray, is now no more. Things seen, things remembered, and things imagined are blended together into a delicate landscape which is half reality and half dream, but in which the dream helps to clarify rather than to obscure that which is really there.

It may be that Gray's antiquarian enthusiasm faded to some extent as he grew older; perhaps the shimmering, ambiguous vision was a strain on the nerves and he needed to rest his thoughts on more solid things. Anyway, in his visit to the Lakes he did not go out of his way to satisfy historical curiosity. Indeed, in the last years of his life he studied botany and the natural sciences rather than history and archæology, though again his passion for tidiness showed itself—he was trying to set in order his experience of nature. Classification, therefore, became one of his chief interests, and, as well as this scientific order, he sought to impose a personal order. In his letters to Dr Wharton he is continually constructing lists and calendars: the date when he sees plants in bloom, the date when he sees them in fruit, together with notes on the wind and the weather. He watched flowers, fruit, the air and the sky, even in a Cambridge garden, even in a London yard, as carefully as he watched his own health—his calendars are temperature charts of nature in which he himself is the thermometer. A note on the weather could fill the horizon of his thoughts as completely as the affairs of nations:

> This is a very critical time, an action [the Battle of Quiberon Bay—N. N.] being hourly expected between the

[1] Thomas Gray: Ode for Music.

two great fleets, but no news yet. I don't know where my thermometer left off, but I do not find any observations till after 8th September.

Often, too, his lists of flowers have a simple direct poetry which may attract us more than his elaborate odes, and the keenness of his interest in botany can be seen from the marginal notes in the Flora[1] which he used—appropriately enough the *Flora Anglica* of William Hudson, himself a native of the Lake District, born at the White Lion Inn, Kendal. These include many small drawings of leaves and seeds as well as corrections of the classification. Hudson, for instance, includes in the genus Geranium both the flowers which we call Cranesbill (e.g. Herb-Robert) and those we call Storksbill, but Gray rightly classifies the latter as Erodium. There are one or two supplementary notes written in the blank leaves at the front of the book, such as a recipe for curing hams ("Sal. petri 1 oz. Treacle, coarsest(?) sugar and salt, each ½ a pound. 3 cloves of Garlick").[2] We are reminded that, like many men who are deprived of normal sexual experience, Gray occasionally found a compensatory pleasure in good food and good cooking—he took a cold tongue with him on his trip to Grange in Borrowdale, and sent Wharton an enthusiastic account of the butter, the milk, oatcakes and ale. Trout was out of season, but, like all the travellers of his time, he shows great interest in the pike and the perch—indeed, sometimes one feels that the eighteenth century looked even on Derwentwater primarily as a gigantic fish-pond.

Gray's tour was made only at a second attempt. The first had been in August 1767, and was abandoned when his companion, Dr Wharton, was taken ill at Keswick. Two years later he tried again, and once more Wharton was ill, but this time Gray continued on his own from Brough, writing his *Journal* and posting it piece by piece, so that his friend could share the experience he had just missed. This journal remained unpublished till after Gray's death, but was included in William Mason's memoir of the poet (1775) and five years later was

---

[1] This copy is now in the Jackson Library, Tullie House, Carlisle.
[2] I cannot be certain that I have deciphered correctly every word in the script.

printed as an appendix to the second edition of West's *Guide to the Lakes*.[1]

Gray's ten days in the Lakes were well planned for one who did not want to exert himself overmuch. He arrived at Penrith on September the 30th, climbed the Beacon Hill, and the next day visited Ullswater, returning to Penrith for the night. On the 2nd of October he went on to Keswick and stayed there several days, visiting Bassenthwaite, Borrowdale, the Wad Mine, and the Druid Circle at Castlerigg, and spending the rest of the time sauntering through the meadows and beside the lake. On the 8th he left by Dunmail Raise and Grasmere for Ambleside, but continued as far as Kendal because the best bedroom at the Ambleside inn was "dark and damp as a cellar". At Kendal he spent two nights, taking a trip to Sizergh before going on to Lancaster, and thence by Ingleborough and Settle, through Yorkshire to join Mason in Derbyshire.

Throughout this tour he carried with him a Claude-glass, described by Mason as "a plano-convex mirror, of about four inches in diameter, on a black foil, and bound up like a pocket-book". On clear days a dark glass was used; in dull weather, one laid on silver foil, or tinted to give the classical golden glow of Claude. "The mirror", says West,[2] "is of the greatest use in sunshine; and the person using it ought always to turn his back on the object that he views. It should be suspended by the upper part of the case, holding it a little to the right or left (as the position of the parts to be viewed requires) and the face screened from the sun."

The primary effect of the glass was to reduce the landscape to the size of a postcard, so that the shape, balance, and perspective could be seen at a glance. The advantage to artists is obvious (indeed, some of them still use a similar device) and it is possible that the drawings of Gilpin, both in their oval shape and the carroty colours of the aquatints, were in part an imitation of the image in the mirror. Moreover, it deflated and simplified the scene. Detail was lost; movement, except on the scale of a large storm, was scarcely perceptible; and the whole

[1] See Chapter V. My quotations are taken from this version since that was the form in which the work was known to the majority of the Lake travellers.
[2] *Guide to the Lakes*, by the author of *The Antiquities of Furness* (1778).

smell and taste and feel of a place were bled away till it became merely a design under glass, a dead world, indeed a world that had never lived.

Gray certainly enjoyed this toy, which, he says, "played its part divinely" in lower Borrowdale, and the view from the Parsonage at Crossthwaite is specifically described as "a picture in the glass". But he was not restricted to this view. He could put down the glass and look about him, often with a clarity of vision for which he has not often been credited. It is true that he rarely focuses his eye or his interest on a small object, or on one that was near at hand. He notices that at Grange in Borrowdale the Derwent shows under its bridge "every trout that passes", but, to our loss, he gives us none of the botanical notes and comments which so often fill his letters from Cambridge or London. Even as late as October there must have been many flowers of the dales and mountain pastures which were still to be seen and recognized—goldenrod, lady's mantle, betony, white deadnettle (Gray would probably have called it the white "archangel"), lousewort, and grass of Parnassus, together with the peculiar bitter-orange seeds of bog asphodel, the berries of rowan, tutsan and bird-cherry, and all the brown rag-mat of dying leaf and fern. Of this he mentions only a few lichens and the gale or wild myrtle, yet we have many glimpses that are clearer, cleaner, truer, with more line and edge to them than anything which had been written before. There is Ullswater, "smooth as a blue mirror", with "white farm houses looking out among the trees, and cattle feeding"; there is, at seven in the morning, the hoarfrost "which soon melted and exaled in a thin bluish smoke"; there · is Saddleback, "whose furrowed sides were gilt by the noonday sun, whilst its brow appeared of a sad purple from the shadow of the clouds as they sailed slowly by it". Nor does he restrict his notice entirely to the countryside, for outside Kendal he is intrigued with the Tenter Grounds, where the bleached cloth was stretched to dry, and, in a delightful phrase, says of the houses of this town that they ". . . seem as if they had been dancing a country-dance, and were out: there they stand back to back, corner to corner, some up-hill, some down, without intent or meaning".

Whenever he settles himself to sketch a complete landscape he does so with a real sense of composition, giving us foreground, and middle distance, with side-screens and backscreen, arranged formally yet not artificially. In his picture of Ullswater, for instance, the eye is led from the lake up through lake meadows to the lower hills and then checked, encircled and enclosed by the fells so that it cannot overrun its subject. Yet, unlike Gilpin, he does not sacrifice everything else to the art of formal composition. The landscape is simplified, but it is not distorted; it retains much of its true character and colouring. Indeed, if Gilpin's descriptions often resemble his own vague and misty aquatints, Gray's are more like the type of colour print with which we have become familiar in the better type of railway poster—stylized, romanticized, yet with a certain, almost photographic literalness. At the same time, they are drawn with true feeling, with genuine and not prefabricated excitement, and with delicate shading of poetry. Gray had not Worsdworth's gift of seeing in the forms of nature a tremendous and transcendental significance, but he could look at them straight and could delight that they were what they were. As Mason says in a footnote: "When Mr. Gray described places he aimed only to be exact, clear, and intelligible; to convey peculiar, not general ideas, and to paint by the eye not the fancy." From Mason this was an apology rather than a compliment, for he obviously preferred Gilpin's tour (which he had read in manuscript), but today we can see in Gray not only more precision but also more poetry:

Next I passed by the little chapel of Wythburn, out of which the Sunday congregation were then issuing; soon after a beck near Dunmail-Raise, where I entered Westmorland a second time;[1] and now began to see Helm-Crag, distinguished from its rugged neighbours, not so much by its height as by the strange broken outlines of its top, like some gigantic building demolished, and the stones that composed it flung across each other in wild confusion. Just beyond it, opens one of the sweetest landscapes that art ever attempted to imitate. The bosom of the mountains spreading here into a broad bason discovers in the midst Grasmere-water; its

[1] He had been to Appleby in the earlier part of his tour.

margin is hollowed into small bays, with bold eminences; some of rock, some of turf, that half conceal and vary the figure of the little lake they command; from the shore a low promontory pushes itself far into the water, and on it stands a white village, with the parish church rising in the midst of it; hanging inclosures, corn-fields, and meadows, green as an emerald, with their trees, and hedges, and cattle, fill up the whole space from the edge of the water; and just opposite to you is a large farm-house at the bottom of a steep smooth lawn, embosomed in old woods, which climb half-way up the mountain's side, and discover above them a broken line of crags that crown the scene. Not a single red tile, no gentleman's flaring house,[1] or garden walls, break in upon the repose of this little unsuspected paradise; but all is peace, rusticity, and happy poverty, in its neatest, most becoming attire.

So far we have dealt only with what Gray *saw*, with the sense of sight. But he was by no means limited to this one sense in his appreciation of nature. For him a landscape was not merely a scene, but an environment. He could not feel, as Wordsworth could, that he himself was part of that environment, absorbed into it, sharing its life, yet he did feel that it was all round him, encircling him and bending over him. It was the element in which he moved, as a bird moves in air or a fish in water.

It is perhaps significant that he came to the district in October, which may seem a strange choice for a man of delicate health, until we remember that October, in its brown autumnal varnish, is pre-eminently the month of the Picturesque. It is also the month when a view is almost tangible. In the turnip-purple mist that rises from the stubble the senses are inter-mingled. You *smell* the brownness, you *feel* the manure-smells, the harvest- and orchard- and dead-bracken-smells, and the yellow light drifts round your head like mist.

Gray was "no lover of dirt", nor of damp. We often catch his fastidious and hypochondriac shudder at the soft humidity of the Lake air, and he obviously approved of the local description of Derwentwater as "the Devil's chamber-

[1] Thus Mason's transcription. Gray had actually written: "No flaming gentleman's house."—Gray: *Works* (Edm. Gosse), Vol I, 1902.

pot". As he walked, well muffled up, stepping cautiously, even his feet collected sensations which contributed to his experience, noticing, for instance, at Dunmallet, that the meadow is "spongey" to stand on. It is, however, his sense of the height and steepness of the scene, rather than of its texture or mass, that makes his *Journal* memorable—his sense of the lift, the jaggedness, the Gothic upsurge of the central dales. The mountains seemed to him to have an inexplicable malice which made itself visible in the shape of overhangs of rock, filling his mind with fear of falling stones. His awareness of the landscape was intensely physical, but, unlike that of John Wilson and of modern hikers and rock-climbers, it was entirely passive. He did not try to impose his own personality on it, he did not try to break it to his will. Instead, he endured it, suffered it, felt it directing itself against him, impinging on him, leaning over and overshadowing him.

All this can be seen in his account of lower Borrowdale— probably the most quoted and most ridiculed passage in the writings of the early Lake travellers. As description it is obviously preposterous: Mason's claim that Gray painted "with the eye not the fancy" is not valid here. But though he did not describe what he saw, he did describe what he felt. The landscape is an image of his own nervous agitation, and about this, at least, he did not exaggerate. Here we must remember what sort of man he was—his temperament, his state of health, his susceptibility to nervous fears, his extreme anxiety when travelling, his sense of insecurity when among unfamiliar surroundings, all of which helped to make his journey almost into a nightmare. The landscape became a fantastic dream, not just in memory, but before his very eyes, and he could not differentiate between dream and reality:

> ... a little farther, passing a brook called Barrow-beck, we entered Borrowdale; the crags named Lowdore-banks begin now to impend terribly over the way, and more terribly when you learn that three years since an immense mass of rock tumbled at once from the brow, barred all access to the dale (for this is the only road) till they could work their way through it. Luckily no one was passing by at the time of this fall; but down the side of the mountain, and far into

the lake, lie dispersed the huge fragments of this ruin, in all shapes and in all directions. . . . Soon after we came under Gowdar-crag—the rocks at the top deep-cloven perpendicularly by the rains, hanging loose and nodding forwards, seem just starting from their base in shivers. The whole way down, and the road on both sides is strewed with piles of the fragments, strangely thrown across each other, and of dreadful bulk; the place reminds me of those passes in the Alps, where the guides tell you to move with speed, and say nothing, lest the agitation of the air should loosen the snows above, and bring down a mass that would overwhelm a caravan. I took thus counsel here, and hastened on in silence.

"Non ragionam di lor, ma guarda, e passa."[1]

The man who wrote that is very different from him who wrote to Walpole, thirty years earlier, that a district was "exceeding fruitful in ravens and such black cattle"; but he is not, in any way, less intelligent nor less critical. On the contrary, his mind has become stored with literary, historical, and scientific studies, and every scene evolves rich and complex associations. The quotation from Dante gives an instance. It comes from the third canto of *The Inferno* where Dante and Virgil, having just entered Hell, see the souls of the Trimmers, those who were never really alive because they never committed themselves to the reality of good or of evil. We should not examine the reference too closely—it was probably intended facetiously. Nevertheless, it shows the thoughts which were in his mind—thoughts which to him were part of the pleasure of the scene. For in his tentative, tremulous way he was a seeker for sensation. He delighted in the idea of danger so long as it remained only an idea, and he delighted, too, in a sense of obscurity and strangeness. It pleased him to think of secret passes among the mountains, and he would even assume for a moment a primitivism which was not quite in his nature in order to say that "the mountains know well that these innocent people [the dalesmen] will not reveal the mysteries of their ancient kingdom, 'the reign of *Chaos* and *Old Night*' ". He anticipated more than one aspect of the later Picturesque. By

[1] "Let us not discuss them, but take a look and pass by."

his more exact observations, by his greater sensitivity to the personality of place, by his more sensual response to landscape, he advanced far beyond the visual æstheticism of Gilpin and foreshadowed the splendid understanding of Wordsworth. But by his substitution, here and there, of imaginative fantasy for objective observation, by his cult of the nerves, by his desire for an irrational and to some extent self-manufactured excitement, he pointed the way to the most ludicrous affectations and self-deceptions, and gave them, or seemed to give them, the authority of his approval and example.

CHAPTER FIVE

ECHOES OF ANTIQUITY

THE HISTORICAL sense, one of the main ingredients of the Picturesque, was left out of Gray's *Journal*, but the omission was made good by two other travellers, each of whom was both an historian and a connoisseur, though otherwise they had little in common.

William Hutchinson (1732–1814) was a solicitor at Barnard Castle, with ambitions both as an imaginative writer and as an antiquary. He made a good many tours through the Border counties, and published valuable histories of Durham County (1785) and of Cumberland (1794), the latter of which is, in fact, a picturesque work.

Hutchinson was in many ways typical of his time—robust, quick-witted, impressionable, now and then naïve, with all the varied interests, the restless, shifting curiosity of his class and culture. He was like a child, always wanting to be on the roundabouts whenever he was on the swings. He seems to jump from one theme to another, changing his style to suit his purpose. Thus he will describe the local antiquities in an account as plain and factual as an auctioneer's catalogue, and then, suddenly, will put away his notes and break into "a train of melancholy sentiments", for when "rebellion adds its horrid dye to darken the retrospection, the soul recoils at the sad unnatural scene; and tears start from the eye, to weep the sins of fell ambition, and the pride of man".

Hutchinson, we feel, is fond of adding the horrid dye. His writing is often highly coloured in the most literal sense, yet it conveys such enthusiasm, such genuine enjoyment, that we scarcely feel the strain of exaggeration or over-emphasis. He may be like a child, so eager to cheer that he cheers before the runners are off, but at least there is nothing half-hearted about his cheer; he is not just striking an attitude, not just waving his cap to call attention to the feather in it.

He made two visits to the Lakes for his *Excursion*, the first in 1772, when he was accompanied by his brother, a frail, melancholy-looking young man, who died the same year. They travelled by Bowes and Brough to Penrith, visited Ullswater, on to Keswick, where they climbed Skiddaw, and thence to Ambleside, Kendal, and home by Kirkby Stephen. The ascent of Skiddaw was enlivened by a thunderstorm, in which Hutchinson revels like a Wagnerian at *Tristan*, giving us a rather incredible picture of the guide, lying on the earth, "terrified and amazed . . . accusing us of presumption and impiety". On the second visit, in the following year, taking the same route as far as Keswick, and climbing Skiddaw this time on horseback (a procedure he does not recommend), he passed through Cockermouth to the coast, then north to Carlisle, and back by the Roman Wall. As he went through Cockermouth it is possible that Wordsworth, then three years old, may have been playing in the garden behind the house in the main street.

The new complexity of response which Hutchinson brought to the Lakes, his virtuosity on the five-manual organ of the senses, can be seen in the account of his favourite, Ullswater. The party of which he was a member started from Askham, beside the River Lowther, so that they first saw the lake from the hills which lie between Lowther and Pooley Bridge. Then, having reached the shore, they left their horses at an inn, and went aboard one of the pleasure barges placed there by the Duke of Portland. Rowed by four men, they ascended as far as Watermillock where they landed to picnic. The lake, which before had been ruffled by the wind, now "became a shining mirror", with the water so transparent that they could "perceive the fish and pebbles at the depth of six or eight fathom". They set off again, passing "Gobery Park" (the Gowbarrow Park of Wordsworth's daffodils), and Hutchinson, who all the time has been looking about him with excited interest, now begins to feel the full evocative power of the scene, to move, as it were, from the swell to the great. As they sail along, one peak is disclosed behind the other, the prospect continually unpacking itself like a parcel. The clouds hang about the mountain, jutting out from its sides, or descending up and down, in the strange way clouds behave above the lakes. I myself, very early one summer morning at Cockley Moor, above Airey Beck, have seen a new lake of mist, identical with Ullswater in size and shape, lying some fifty or a hundred feet above it, as if it had grown a second storey.

Then, leaving the gentlemen on shore, the barge put out into the lake to rouse the echoes, for which purpose it was fitted with six brass cannon, mounted on swivels, while some of the men had French horns to add to the harmony. The passage in which Hutchinson describes these echoes is one of the most famous in all Lake writing, and will go on repeating itself in guide-book after guide-book, reverberating like the sounds it describes. It is the climax of what we might call the sensational approach to the Lakes—the moment before the wave breaks, before the bubble bursts, before the swing swings back:

The report was echoed from the opposite rocks, where by reverberation it seemed to roll from cliff to cliff, and return through every cave and valley; till the decreasing tumult gradually died away upon the ear.

—The instant it had ceased, the sound of every distant water-fall was heard, but for an instant only; for the momentary stillness was interrupted by the returning echo on the hills behind; where the report was repeated like a peal of thunder bursting over our heads, continuing for several seconds, flying from haunt to haunt, till once more the sound gradually declined;—again the voice of water-falls possessed the interval,—till to the right, the more distant thunder arose upon some .other mountain, and seemed to take its way up every winding dell and creek, sometimes behind, on this side, or on that, in wondrous speed, running its dreadful course;—when the echo reached the mountains within the line and channel of the breeze, it was heard at once on the right and left, at the extremities of the lake.—In this manner was the report of every discharge re-echoed seven times distinctly.

It is impossible not to like Hutchinson. There is a boyish eagerness about him, an almost adolescent acceptance of a new world of the senses. His intellect was not profound, but it was lively. If he was not one of those who opened new vistas of experience for humanity, he was still, within his limitations, adventurous, enterprising, never disappointed, never bored. Moreover, his echoes give us an apt analogy for the Picturesque at this stage. To him, to his contemporaries, the landscape was chiefly a sounding-board. They sailed into the middle of the lake, fired off the guns of their own ego, and waited, patiently yet excitedly, to hear the echoes return to them. The world itself did not matter—what concerned them was the sound of their own voices. They looked on mountain, lake, and sky to prove that their eyes were open; they kicked at a stone to feel their own feet. They opened all the doors and windows of their senses so that they might feel their own selves blowing gently back to them. It was not just that they saw the mountains reflected in a mirror or in a Claude-glass—they saw their own souls reflected in the mountains.

Father Thomas West,[1] author of the *Antiquities of Furness*, was much more of a true historian, but he had nothing of the charming eagerness of Hutchinson. By his time the Picturesque was already becoming a planned pleasure, a Butlin Camp of the sensibilities, with all its possibilities tasted, tested, tried, recorded, and mapped out. The Lakes soon were to become less of a discovery than a fashion, and West himself did much to bring about this change through his *Guide to the Lakes*, published in 1778. He died in 1779, but the guide was reissued the following year, revised and enlarged by William Cockin of Burton-in-Kendal, who also added an appendix which is a most important anthology of pre-Wordsworthian writing on the Lakes, and it was here, rather than in the original editions, that the majority of the tourists first met Gray's *Journal*, Brown's *Description of Keswick*, and Dalton's *Descriptive Poem*.

[1] According to the registers of St Mary of Furness, Ulverston, published by the Catholic Record Society, West was born in 1717 (*D.N.B.* gives 1720, and Close, editor of the second edition of the *Antiquities*, 1703). He was educated at Edinburgh and became a commercial traveller for a time, and later went to the Continent and entered the Society of Jesus, under the name of Daniel, in 1751. After various appointments in England he came to Dalton-in-Furness sometime in the 1760s, living at Titeup Hall near Lindal, where he wrote the *Antiquities*. Later he moved to Ulverston, where he published his *Guide to the Lakes* in 1778. He died the following year when on a visit to Sizergh Castle, in Westmorland, and is buried in Kendal Parish Church. (See *Lancashire Registers*, Vol III. Published by the Catholic Record Society, London, 1916.)

West has the merit of knowing the district he describes, but he catches little of the adventure and excitement which we feel with Gray or Hutchinson. His *Guide* helps the traveller to find his way, tells him what to look for, but it never makes the scene appear before his eyes. He wrote at a time when the vocabulary of picturesque travel had already hardened into a convention, and, while this spared him the effort of searching for the right word, it meant that his language is too blunted to have much effect. His rivers invariably "serpentize", his mountains are "most horrid and romantic". Moreover, he was not really happy among rocks and crags. A dale without a lake meant nothing at all to him. The centre of his interest was always water, and he would jump from one lake to the next with scarcely a glance at the intervening country. With Gilpin as guide, he directed the traveller to a progression of "Stations", or, as we would call them, viewpoints—each lake being divided into Station One, Station Two, and so on—comparing one view with another, judging them like exhibits at a flower show.

We can illustrate West's method by quoting from his account of Coniston which he approached from Ulverston, reaching the lake at the southern tip. He gives his directions with characteristic detail:

STATION I. . . . From the rock, on the left of the road, you have a general prospect of the lake upwards. This station is found by observing where you have a hanging rock over the road, on the east, and an ash-tree on the west side of the road. On the opposite shore, to the left, and close by the water's edge, are some stripes of meadow and green ground, cut into small enclosures, with some dark coloured houses under aged yew trees. Two promontories project a great way into the lake; the broadest is finely terminated by steep rocks, and crowned with wood; and both are insulated when the lake is high. Upwards, over a fine sheet of water, the lake is again intersected by a far-projecting promontory, that swells into two eminences, and betwixt them the lake is again caught, with some white houses at the feet of the mountains.

There is nothing slipshod or haphazard about that. West is obviously determined that no one shall miss any detail of the view, yet he never catches the imagination, and succeeds in giving only what Gilpin would have called a catalogue and not a landscape. For all this, his stations are chosen with knowledge and care and the next one, from the "far-projecting promontory" just mentioned, has already been canonized by the National Trust. It is that small headland, about a mile and a quarter from the foot of the lake, where a fist of reddish rock thrusts out of the cuff of the shore to make a miniature Hebridean island of tiny cliffs, screes and ledges, with bracken and elder, heather and wild thyme, a picnic-sized back-of-beyond. "From thence," says West, "the coast is beautifully diversified by a number of green eminences, crowned with wood; and sequestered cottages, interspersed amongst them, half concealed by yew trees, and, above them, a wave of rocky spiral mountains dressed in brown vegetation, form the most romantic scenes."

"The spiral mountains", dressed in inevitable brown, are left as vague as the hints of landscape in a Raeburn portrait, and indeed, they are probably nothing more spectacular than the gentle mounds of Beacon Hill and the Blawith Fells. But, as we look north, the land rises to the ridge of Coniston Old Man, and the groove in which the lake lies begins to look like what it never quite is—a dale. From here, and still more from points nearer Brantwood, the lake gains a grandeur from the backing of the Coniston fells and the Yewdale crags which is never seen by those who view it from Coniston village. West knew this very well, and he knew, too, the right time of day to make his approach, choosing the morning when the sun is behind the traveller and the shadows of the shore woods lie on the shillet by the lake, while the Torver and Coniston fells are broadside to the light. In the evening, from the same spot, the light skids on the water as on black enamel, and the fells are only a vague flat shape, over which great Niagaras of sun-dazzle seem to pour and splash, blurring every line and contour. Then, if you want to see the lake, you must go out in a boat and look back to the eastern shore, and watch all the tide-mark of oaks and alders held in a yellow level light that catches the under-side of the leaves as well as the top-side, and throws shadows above as well as below.

It is just such knowledge which distinguishes his book from

those of the other travellers. Had he restricted himself to the things which really interested him—the history of the district, its monuments, abbeys, castles and churches, and the plain plan and geography of the Lakes—he might have produced a local classic.

As it is, he tried to dress to a fashion he did not really understand, so that his work lacks the vitality which we find in writers much less informed. Already, by 1778, he was demonstrating the deadening results of the conventional response.

CHAPTER SIX

THE NEW RAMBLER

B Y NOW we have heard practically all the themes which go to make the full chorus of the early Picturesque. There is the scientific curiosity of Pennant, the pure æsthetics of Gilpin, the romantic æsthetics of Gray, and the æsthetic sensation of Hutchinson. There is also Gray's imaginative response to history, together with the antiquarianism of Hutchinson and West, and their interest in local customs and the like. This pattern of interests, this counterpoint of curiosity with connoisseurship and of imagination with the senses, remained for many years the aim and object of tourists in the Lakes. But as visitors became more frequent and the district better known, as the tour became less of an exploration and more of a routine, we find that these main themes diminish in scope and in pitch. The curiosity of the scientist becomes a mere itch for oddities; the artist's careful assessment of the landscape in terms of visual beauty and design becomes a mere taste for prettiness; the painstaking (if rather amateur) research of the historians becomes a mere eye for a monument and an ear for a legend; and the genuine virtuosity of sensual response cultivated by such men as Hutchinson becomes a mere search for thrills. After 1790, the tourists were no longer pioneers or explorers; they were holiday-makers. Their main aim was just to enjoy themselves, and for this purpose they could, if they liked, change direction as often as the wind—one moment praising the primitive life of the dales and the next grumbling at the lack of town comforts in the inns. Yet in all their freaks and foibles they were looking at nature, for the main part, in the same way as the pioneers—they were regarding it subjectively, making a picture of it, making a convenience of it, using it as a stimulus to their own egos. The Claude-glass had been replaced by the silver buckle of a vanity-case or the stopper of a brandy-bottle,

but it still reflected the same view and for the same purpose.
The Dark Ages of the Lakes were over for ever—

> And now, when bright thy day of honour dawns,
>   Which quells the darksome shades of many a year,
> What wond'ring crowds, to trace thy fairy lawns,
>   At summer's call, in gayest trim appear!
>   Sure this is praise sincere!
>   See o'er thy rocks, along thy glades,
>   They rove with raptured eye;
>   Now mark thy rills, and bold cascades,
>   Or scale some mountain high;
> Inspired by TASTE, to Nature's interest true,
> They deem all labour light, which brings thy charms
>   to view.[1]

About this time, Captain Joseph Budworth strode into the
literature of the Lakes like Long John Silver into *Treasure
Island*. Like Silver he was purposeful, independent, cheerfully
arrogant and superbly alive. Like Silver, too, he was something
of a cripple, though it was an arm that he had lost and not a
leg. While he is before your eyes you can look at no one else.
The people he meets are acted off the stage or are remembered
because of what he said of them. Even his occasional affectations,
his delights and shudderings, seem to be merely freakish dis-
guises of his own true personality.

Budworth's reactions to the Lakes are perhaps the freshest
and most spontaneous since those of Celia Fiennes. In spite of
his one arm (he had lost the other at the Siege of Gibraltar), he
was essentially a whole man, having the energy which was lacking in Gray, and the balance and animal spirits which were
lacking in most of the rest. He could at times invent his own
little pretences, but he was never one of those who cried, as
he himself tells: "Good God! how delightful!—how charming!
—I could live here for ever!—Row on." Such sham ecstasies
provoked him to nothing but scorn. He would like to paint
Kendal, he says, but the roads were so ill-paved that he could
mind nothing but his feet. In the same way his descriptions
often have a little hard knob of reality, which tells us more

---

[1] William Cockin: *Ode to the Genius of the Lakes*. First printed 1780,
Reprinted in *The Rural Sabbath* 1785.

than a hundred stock epithets. Grasmere, for instance, has a
"green rump-shaped island"; Ullswater, seen from a spot on
Helvellyn where Place Fell interrupts the view, has the shape
of a pair of breeches; while Red Tarn is like a Bury pear.

Moreover, unlike West, he did not go from view to view
without noticing what happened in between. For quite a lot
happened, especially food. The route from Ambleside to Keswick did not just include Dunmail Raise, it included a mid-
morning breakfast of mutton-ham, eggs, buttermilk, whey, tea,
bread and butter, and cheese—and all for sevenpence. Many
of the early travellers had enjoyed the trout and the potted
char, but none, we feel, brought such an eager appetite as
Budworth. His pleasure still hangs to the pages like the smell
of a savoury, while he licks his lips over a meal such as that at
Robert Newton's in Grasmere:

> Roast pike, stuffed
> A boiled fowl
> Veal-cutlets and ham
> Beans and bacon
> Cabbage
> Pease and potatoes
> Anchovy sauce
> Parsley and butter
> Plain butter
> Butter and cheese
> Wheat bread and oat cake

Three cups of preserved gooseberries, with a bowl of rich
cream in the centre:
For two people, at ten-pence a head.[1]

After this he set out to climb Helm Crag, and it is not surprising that the hill looked formidable, and "not less so, to speak
in plain English, from having a complete bellyful".

For he was not content to stay at lake level. As well as the
usual Skiddaw, he climbed Helvellyn, Coniston Old Man,
and Langdale Pikes, and he was the first of all the travellers
to begin to see the fells as a physical challenge. He did not face
that challenge as boldly as "Christopher North", but he was

---

[1] *A Fortnight's Ramble to the Lakes* (1792, 1795), by "A Rambler".
By Joseph Budworth (1810). All quotations here are from the third edition.

able to accept physical effort, if not with enjoyment, yet with a cheerful toughness. When he tells of his struggle to climb a frozen grass slope near Scale Force, you are conscious not only of pride in his endurance, but of a certain heightened physical awareness, a translation of the hill from terms of visual scenery to the tactile impression of feet and legs and muscles :

> I made many efforts to overcome the glassy hill; and although I had sharp nails in the balls of my shoes, and large stubbs to the heels, with a pike to my hazel stick, my efforts were useless; I tumbled twice, and slid bodily down the hill again. . . . Although the surface was ice, the rough grass and water oozing through had made it both hollow and rotten. It soon got over my shoe-tops, and up to one knee, and then I felt myself conquered, gave up the pursuit, and determined to bear a great disappointment with due meekness.

Here at last is a landscape you can really touch, can really get hold of. Budworth is exaggerating—the average Youth Hostel schoolgirl of today would be up that slope with a sandwich in one hand and an ordnance map in the other. But he is exaggerating in a new way. Unlike Young, Gilpin and Hutchinson, he is not making the view conform to a preconceived image. Instead, he is exaggerating as a sportsman exaggerates. His descriptions are like fishing stories—lies told within a certain convention, certain accepted limits, which are understood by the listener as well as the teller. He is not so much deceiving as spinning a yarn.

This comes out very clearly in the account of his climb of Langdale Pikes on the 7th of November 1797. He tells us little of the actual ascent, but on the way down he followed a sheep-track which traversed "a large bulging part of the mountain, across a sward nearly perpendicular, and of immoderate height". His guide, Paul Postlethwaite, a lad of fifteen, said he had passed that way hundreds of times, but Budworth was scared and wanted to return to the summit. Days are short in November, however, and there was no time for this, so at last he agreed to descend. First of all he tied up his right eye, in order not to see the drop beneath him, then, keeping his left eye focused on the trod, he held out his staff to the boy and was thus led across the slope. Ridiculous as it sounds, it was a feat of which he could well be proud, for, one-eyed, one-armed, hunched and groping as he was, the crossing must have been nearly as dangerous as walking a tight-rope.

Budworth is distinguished from all others of his time not only by his physique but by his quick interest in people. He made friends with the landlords of all the inns, and gathered the local gossip from them. He wished, he said, to "give free scope to everyone he spoke to", so that an old grandmother at Dunmail Raise proved that she had "the clack of her sex", and told him that she had been too often on Skiddaw in her youth to be ill in her old age. Even his guides, Paul Postlethwaite and Robin Partridge, obviously liked him, though they may have laughed at him many a time behind his back.

Yet inevitably he was a man of his time, and his view was not free from the distortion of the Picturesque. Just as he had exaggerated about the mountains, so now he struck an attitude about the people. Against the evidences of his own sense, he had to feel that the Cumbrians were a strange, primitive, pastoral race, far away from everyday problems, far away from the vices and corruptions of civilized society, shut off from the rest of the world (as John Housman said) "by those natural barriers infinitely stronger than the great wall of China".[1]

The Primitive was the picturesque view of man: Rousseau's dream of a Noble Savage realized in a people who were not quite savages. Because of this, when Budworth watched a village wedding, somewhere between Leeds and Kendal, and when he attended a dancing-class at Heversham, he reported both of them in the tone of a lady traveller describing racial customs of the Balkans. Because of this, again, when he saw a young girl serving at an inn in Buttermere, he indulged in a sentimental daydream which was to distort the shape and course of her life and to make her name known throughout the country.

Mary Robinson, daughter of the landlord of the Fish Inn, Buttermere, was first seen by Budworth in 1792. She was then about fifteen, shy enough to keep out of his way at first, and

[1] John Housman: *Topographical Description of Cumberland, Westmorland and Lancashire* (Carlisle, 1800).

for a man like Budworth, in early middle-age, she had all the sentimental, might-have-been, poignantly-sensual charm of adolescence. It is possible that he scarcely spoke to her, for he gets her name wrong in the first two editions of his book. Yet he wrote of her in self-indulgent and unguarded praise.

Her hair was thick and long, [he says] of a dark brown, and, though unadorned with ringlets, did not seem to want them; her face was a fine oval, with full eyes, and lips as red as vermillion; her cheeks had more of the lily than the rose; and, although she had never been out of the village (and I hope will have no ambition to wish it), she had a manner about her which seemed better calculated to set off dress, than dress *her*. She was a very Lavinia,
"Seeming, when unadorn'd, adorn'd the most."
When we first saw her at her distaff, after she had got the better of her first fears, she looked an angel; and I doubt not but she is the reigning Lily of the Valley."[1]

Now, without casting doubt on Mary Robinson's good looks, we can easily see that those lines are almost pure fantasy. The wish that the girl should never leave her own valley gives Budworth away. He wanted her to live out for him the myth of the Primitive; he wanted her to act his own dreams. Unfortunately, his very words destroyed his hopes, for when *The Ramble* was published, it drew everybody's attention to the girl, and sent all the Keswick tourists to Buttermere on the chance of seeing her. Many of them paid attentions that were not wanted. J. Grant, who went in 1797, tells of a friend who left some

---

[1] This account should be compared with De Quincey's description of her as she appeared a few years later: "Her figure was, in my eyes, good— but I doubt whether most of my readers would have thought it such. She was none of your evanescent, wasp-waisted beauties; on the contrary, she was rather large in every way; tallish, and proportionably broad. Her face was fair, and her features feminine; and, unquestionably, she was what all the world would have agreed to call 'good-looking'. But, except in her arms, which had something of a statuesque beauty, and in her carriage, which expressed a womanly grace, together with some degree of dignity and self-possession, I confess that I looked in vain for any *positive* qualities of any sort or degree. *Beautiful*, in any emphatic sense, she was not. Everything about her face and bust was negative; simply without offence."— There is a faint hint, however, that this negative effect may have been due to the fact that the girl was more friendly with Wordsworth and with Southey than with De Quincey—he is always inclined to be a bit jealous of those to whom Wordsworth showed any favour.

black stockings in her empty shoes, and when he returned the next year found that she had not dared to wear them, fearing that someone might come back to claim them. Budworth, who could be thoughtless but never mean or callous, realized that he had been rather a fool, and in January 1798, on his second visit to the Lakes, he called again at the Fish Inn. Here, "taking the opportunity of our being alone", he revealed his identity, and gave Mary a little homily on the dangers of vanity. Strangers would come, he said, some of them with "very bad intentions", and he hoped that she would never suffer from them. She was, he added rather naïvely, not really so handsome as he had thought she was, and was glad to have had the chance to undo any harm caused by his former flattering report.

He returned home, published an account of his visit in *The Gentleman's Magazine*, and sat back with an easy conscience, congratulating himself on having carried out a moral duty which ("taking the opportunity of our being alone") he had rather enjoyed.[1] But his complacency was not justified. In July 1802 there arrived at the Queen's Head, Keswick, one calling himself the Hon. Alexander Augustus Hope. This man, a rather flashy but evidently well-to-do tourist, soon wormed his way into the local society, making friends among others with Mr Crump, the Liverpool business man who built Allan Bank and rented it to Wordsworth. Before very long he found his way to Buttermere, then famous for its char-fishing, and immediately included Mary in the sport. They were married at Lorton on the 2nd of October, and, as the girl was something of a celebrity, the wedding was reported in the newspapers, where it came to the notice of people who knew that the real Colonel Hope had been abroad all the summer and was then in Vienna. Inquiries were made and a warrant was issued, and "Hope" was formally arrested, but was allowed to fish on the lake in the charge of a constable, from whom he managed to escape, crossing over Stye Head Pass to Wasdale and Raven-

---

[1] In the Jackson Collection, Tullie House Library, Carlisle, there is a copy of the second edition of *The Ramble*, interleaved with written corrections and additions for the third edition. In one of these notes, in what is presumably Budworth's own handwriting, there is his final apology for having brought so much public attention to Mary Robinson.

glass, where he hid for some days on board a small ship. Eventually he was captured in South Wales and taken to Carlisle for trial, by which time it had been discovered that his real name was John Hatfield, and that he was a bigamist with several children by his first wife. The case aroused enormous interest, and when he was found guilty and condemned to be hanged on the 3rd of September 1803, the county rustled with rumours of a pardon or of the postponement of the execution. Large crowds gathered around the gaol. Wordsworth and Coleridge, who were passing through Carlisle at the beginning of their Scottish tour, tried to obtain an interview with the prisoner, who would agree to meet only the former, though Coleridge seems to have caught a glimpse of him as he walked in the yard, with chains on his legs, taking exercise and air. One of the bystanders told them that Hatfield's fate was a warning against meddling with pen and ink.[1]

At the execution, which took place on the banks of the River Eden, Hatfield behaved with all the courage and bravura of a French aristocrat or an English highwayman. He dressed carefully, showed great politeness to the chaplain who attended him, gave his last half-crown to his executioner, and asked that his body should be buried at Burgh-by-Sands. Mary, who had had a child about this time, later married a local man and settled down to what seems to have been quite a happy marriage.

There would be no need to retail this rather squalid little story were it not for the immense excitement which it caused throughout England. It was repeated in dozens of letters and magazine articles and journals. It was written up on a broadsheet and acted in London as a melodrama. Nor was it just a seven-days' wonder, for as late as 1841 it was the subject of a novel, *James Hatfield and the Beauty of Buttermere,* set in the over-manured ripeness of the high Victorian landscape. Now when a story appeals even to the less discriminating readers of two ages so different as that of the Prince Regent and that of the Prince Consort, we can be sure that it must have some inner

---

[1]See Dorothy Wordsworth: *Recollections of a Tour made in Scotland*; and also James Denholm: *A Tour to the Principal Scotch and English Lakes* (1805).

vitality or significance. There can be no doubt, I think, that
the people of the Industrial Revolution saw in the tale of
Buttermere, consciously or unconsciously, a kind of allegory.
To them Mary represented the sweet natural innocence of
man living in an almost classical landscape, a modern Golden
Age of shepherds and mountains. Hatfield, on the other hand,
stood for the corruption of that new society, which was destroy-
ing the peasantry and the rural way of life, and imposing a new
economic compulsion on all classes of men. He stood, also, for
the evil in human nature, an evil which men were to believe in
less and be aware of more. The Buttermere story, in fact, was
popular because it was both a social allegory and a moral allegory. It was a story of the Fall, in which modern man could
identify himself both with Mary and with Hatfield, both with
the tempted and with the tempter, with humanity and with
the devil.

CHAPTER SEVEN

FINDINGS AND KEEPINGS

WE HAVE now met the pioneers of Lake travel, and have seen what they came for, what they were looking for. But what, in fact did they find? And in what way did the Lakes satisfy the romantic need which drew more and more people to the North-west?

First of all we must remember that in spite of the growing traffic the Lake tour still remained an adventure—to the Londoner, perhaps, it was a greater adventure than crossing the Channel, for Cumberland seemed remote in a way in which Paris and Florence were not. It was not so much a matter of distance as of history—the county did not belong to the civilization from which the eighteenth century drew its culture. Its names did not pluck at the strings of classical poetry; they were harsh, unfamiliar, barbarous. Moreover, though not distant, it was by no means easy to reach, being barricaded from the rest of Britain by mountain, marsh, and sea—the Border hills, the Pennines, the Solway, and Morecambe Bay.

For most travellers from the south it was Morecambe Bay which offered the most obvious line of approach, and its crossing gave an exciting and dramatic start to the tour, making a satisfying divide between the England the traveller knew and the strange kingdom to which he was going. The land was left behind at Lancaster, the stranger passed into an amphibian world that was neither earth nor water, and when at last he emerged from the sands and mists and mosses, the Lake mountains were staring down at him, the golden rod and bracken were glinting and gallivanting among the rocks, and the people spoke a dialect harder to understand for some than French or Italian. The visitor felt that he was opening his eyes on a new world, for the crossing gave an experience of forgetfulness, of oblivion, of detachment from the life of everyday. It was like

76

falling asleep and waking, like being buried and resurrected, like drowning and being revived.

The inner part of the Bay is shaped roughly like a letter M, the central V of the letter being the peninsula of Cartmel, while the upright wedges on either side are the Levens Estuary, on the left, and the Kent Estuary on the right. Beyond the boundaries of this inner M, the left leg of the letter slopes back and out to Barrow and Walney Island, while the right leg curves across, like the downstroke of an old-fashioned script, to Morecambe and Heysham. But by now we have reached the open Irish Sea, and there is no longer any possibility of a low-tide crossing. The practicable route, therefore, looking from the south, is from Hest Bank, between Morecambe and Carnforth, across the Kent Sands to Cartmel, and then by the Levens or Ulverston Sands to Conishead or some other part of the Furness coast.

The Bay route has a long history. In medieval times guides were maintained and endowed by the priories of Conishead and Cartmel, and on the Ulverston Sands, about a mile from the shore, there is a small island, known as Chapel Island, where, according to West,[1] the monks of Conishead said mass for the benefit of those crossing the sands. The guides, who were known as Carters (by tradition, because the first family to hold the office was of that name), continue to carry out their duties even today. The Bay route, indeed, remained the chief entrance into Furness until 1820, when the turnpike was completed through Levens and Lindale. And even after this date, right until the opening of the Ulverston and Lancaster Railway in 1857, public coaches ran a regular service across the Sands —both large carriages, holding a dozen or more passengers which were apt to get stuck fast because of their weight, and the lighter "diligences" holding, perhaps, no more than three. An advertisement for one of these latter appeared in the *Cumberland Pacquet* for 11th September 1781 : "... setting out from Mr. Stanley Turner's the Sun Inn, Lancaster, every Monday, Wednesday, and Friday, as the tide will permit, to Ulverston, over the sands", and returning from the King's Arms, Ulverston, every Tuesday, Thursday, and Saturday. The fare

---

[1] West: *Antiquities of Furness* (1774).

was five shillings (which seems cheap when one reckons that it cost two guineas to go from Carlisle to Manchester by stage-coach) and the proprietors assured the public that they had "procured a sober and careful driver, who is well acquainted with the sands".[1]

Moreover, the Bay was part of the old West Coast route from Lancaster to Whitehaven, which involved also the cross-ing of the Duddon Sands and of the triple estuary of the Esk, the Mite and the Irt at Ravenglass, though the Esk was usually forded some miles higher at Muncaster. These Cumberland estuaries, at Millom (Duddon) and Ravenglass, did not offer much difficulty to the traveller, but his journey needed careful timing if he was not to be continually held up by the tide. In-deed, it was usual for those travelling north, having crossed first the wide sands of the Kent, to wait a tide at Flookborough or Cartmel, perhaps spending a night there, and then to hurry across the Ulverston Sands and by Ireleth to the Duddon and so into Cumberland.

This was the way followed by John Wesley in 1759. He had been preaching at Liverpool and Bolton, and when he arrived at Lancaster in the evening of Friday, 11th May, he was told that it was too late to cross the sands. But Wesley, with his impetuous and imperious nature, could not bear to stand about doing nothing, so, ignoring advice, he started at once across the Kent, or as he calls them, the "Seven-mile" sands, and arrived at "Fluckborough" about sunset. Here he spent the night, departing the next morning so early that he had crossed both Ulverston and Duddon Sands and reached Bootle, eight miles north of Millom, by eight o'clock. But now the tides began to trip him up.

"Here", he writes, "we were informed, that we could not pass at Ravenglass before one or two o'clock—where as, had we gone on, (as we afterwards found,) we might have passed immediately. After we were directed to a ford near Man-chester (Muncaster) Hall, which they said we might cross at noon. When we came thither, they told us we could not cross; so we sat till about one: we then found we could have crossed

---

[1] Quoted from "Guides over the Kent and Leven Sands", by John Fell, *Transactions Cumb. and West. Ant. and Arch. Soc.*

at noon."[1] In spite of all these hindrances, he managed to reach Whitehaven before night, but was determined never to use the sands again. It was, he agreed, some ten miles shorter than the overland route by Kendal and Keswick, but if you got out of step with the tides, you had to face continual delays; "especially", he adds, "as you have all the way to do with a generation of liars, who detain strangers as long as they can, either for their own gain or their neighbours".

In many ways Wesley was a prophetic figure, looking forward to the nineteenth century and the great romantics, but in his attitude to the countryside he still belongs to the age of Defoe. As he waited, impatient as a horse in cold weather, beside the tidal Esk, or at Ravenglass, with its small smugglers' street and dune-locked harbour, he had no eyes whatever for the land. All the magnificence of the western dales was standing round about—Bowfell looking down Eskdale, Gable looking down Wasdale, Scafell between the two of them, and the Isle of Man across the water—but his thoughts were only for the souls he had to save at Whitehaven. When, two or three days later, he went to the Lorton Valley near Cockermouth, he comments that many of the people who came to hear him "found God to be a God both of the hills and valleys, and no where more present than in the mountains of Cumberland". It is a remark that might have been made some forty or fifty years later by another man from that same town, but how different, then, would have been its implication. To Wordsworth the fell country was the one place above all others in which to seek for God; to Wesley it was the last place where you would expect to find Him, so that the witness of Lorton was a much more than ordinary sign of His mercy.

To Wesley, to Defoe, and to most of the early eighteenth-century travellers, the Bay, like the mountains, was primarily an obstacle to be overcome, a nuisance to be endured as patiently as possible. Even to Pennant, who had learned to admire the mountains, the eleven-mile ride across the sands seemed long and melancholy—"the prospect on all sides quite savage, high barren hills indented by the sea, or dreary wet sands, rendered more horrible by the approach of night, and

[1] John Wesley: *Journal.*

a tempestuous evening, obscured by the driving of black clouds". But for later travellers, the crossing became one of the most exciting experiences of the whole tour.

There was every reason for this. They first saw the Bay from Lancaster, where, on the Castle Hill, they viewed the full scoop of it, round to Walney Channel, with all the folds and pleats of its creeks and estuaries.

"On the Castle tower", says Celia Fiennes, with that note of surprise in her voice as if she were finding words for what never could have been said or noticed before,

> On the Castle tower walking quite round by the battlements I saw the whole town and river at a view, which runs almost quite round and returns againe by the town, and saw the sea beyond and the great high hills beyond that part of the sea which are in Wales, and also into Westmoreland to the great hills there called Furness Fells or Hills being a string of vast high hills together; also into Cumberland to the great hill called Black Comb Hill whence they digg their black lead.

I don't know where Miss Fiennes picked up the idea that black lead was dug from Black Combe, unless it were from the associations of the name, but at least she puts the hill in the right county which is more than can be said of Anne Radcliffe. Moreover, in that curious manner of hers in which she is at one and the same time both garrulous and at a loss for words, she tells us just what she sees and no more; her vision is unsophisticated, unprepared, unperverted. But Mrs Radcliffe, looking out from the same point, was not content to see merely what was in front of her. She saw, at the same time, the paintings of Claude, the master of the Ideal Landscape, the great forerunner of the Picturesque.

In fact, it was beside the Bay more than anywhere else in the Lakes that the Claudian world turned from fiction into fact. For, from any of the hills along the shore, from Lancaster, but better still from Arnside Knott or from Hoad, Ulverston, the fells arranged themselves in their amphitheatre, the sea disappeared over the edge of the picture, and the rivers "serpentined" gently into the middle distance. The line of a beck among the fells is as hard as a steel wire—it may be alive and

LOWESWATER WITH MELBRAKE

WINDERMERE FROM BOWNESS FERRY by William Burgess

leaping and lissom, but it is always clear-cut and defined. But here, in the Bay, the waters dawdle and sidle, rivers seep up from the sands when the sea goes down, gulleys ebb and flow as if they don't know which way to run, and long pools of water are left on the mosses, with neither outlet nor inlet, stranded like fish till the next tide. Higher up the estuaries, where the turfed marshy lawns lie between the lower hills, the rivers hesitate and ponder, mooning from side to side. The mists simmer, accepting the sunlight, soaking it in, sopping it up, till the shallow slopes seem steeped in light, seem to hold it suspended or in solution, seem to melt and let it evaporate slowly into the air. So that if the sun were snatched away and the sky darkened, the fields themselves would go on lighting the world with their pale, distilled glow. Here, indeed, was Claude —his great semicircles, his lingering, linking distances, and his tender lyrical light.

Moreover, the limestone of the Bay was much more like the rocks of the Italian scene than was the slate of the fells. These latter were magnificent as backgrounds, and most impressive as side-screens, but the actual rocks that they were made of were curiously awkward to handle in a picture. None of the Lake artists seems even to have looked at the slate before William Green; Gilpin, for instance, always drew the rocks in the foreground lake scenes as if they were of sandstone. Here, in the Bay, the cliffs were not unlike those of the familiar Tuscan scene. They stood up, sheer as walls, from the turf; they broke easily into terraces; they shaped themselves naturally into pillars and parallelograms. They were never too assertive, never out of hand, yet like the rocks among which so many St Jeromes had knelt and prayed, they were always surprising and unpremeditated.

Here, where the salt marsh spreads like a weed so far up the valleys, one feels a perpetual recurring shock at seeing the line of the shore without a sign of the sea. It is not that the tide is far out—there is no glimpse of the place where the tide might be. We are surrounded by curving hills, and the open sea lies behind the highest of them, yet now and then the water comes nosing and sniffing its way like a dog, wetting the base of the cliff, scratching beneath the overhang and rubbing the corners smooth as pebbles.

These limestone rocks, more than any others in the Lakes, are ready to take their place in a human, and even a humanist, landscape. Their smooth, rubbed forms, the terraces and parapets, the colonnades and Fairy Steps into which they arrange themselves look as if they had been moulded, not only by weather, but by history. They would not have seemed strange in the classical world, in the wilderness without a city wall. The plants at the foot may belong to the sea and the salt—bladder-campion and buck's-horn plantain—but higher, in ledges and shelves of the rock, are scabious and salmon-coloured rock-roses, and, in the woods at the cliff-top, wild lilies-of-the-valley and herb Paris. It is indeed these woods that give the Bay its melancholy appearance in July and August when the shore is muffed and cuffed out of sight behind rolls of dark-green astrakhan. In autumn it turns back once again to the yellows and browns of the Italian painters—all the woods of Silverdale, Meathop, Cartmel and Baycliffe, variegated like marble or the skin of a leopard. Later in the year, when the woods are soggy with sepia, the marshes flare up in a brilliant, bitter orange, and the old limestone walls are like trickles of sour milk.

For the traveller who decides to cross the sands, however, all this detail must be left behind. Thomas West describes the shore rather as if he were sailing past it on a river steamer. There is Heysham Point, with the village hanging on its side; Wharton Crag to the right; "grounds bearing from the eye for many a mile . . . are terminated by cloud-topt Ingleborough". As you advance across the Bay, there are broken ridges of rocks and the two conical islands at the mouth of the Kent Estuary; in the distance, Heversham village and church, and then Whitbarrow, and next Cartmel. And so on. He is writing, one feels, more from his memory of the shore than from his experience of the sands. For once you are out among them, they make invalid all former conceptions of proportion and perspective. The shores and cliffs are now only chalkings of copper, ochre and olive, dimly seen beyond the immense stretches and stridings of sand. The fells that make up the inland horizon seem shallow and insignificant, paradoxically dwarfed by the enormous flatnesses of the Bay.

Moreover, as William Green hints in his *Guide*, these levels have for the traveller a dramatic suggestiveness, no less stirring than the rhodomontades of the fells. "As he persues his *often-trackless* way, he will recollect, that probably but a few hours before, the whole expanse was covered with some fathoms of water, and that in a few more it will as certainly be covered again."[1]

Green's style is not particularly happy, yet he touches here on that which gave to the crossing of the Bay its chief fascination. It was a journey through forbidden territory, a dash through no-man's-land, an expedition into a world that was not our world at all. Not even Wells's first men in the moon moved through a more strange, less human territory. Anne Radcliffe understood this very well. No one could evoke better than she could the tame terrors of her age—the shadow on the window, the silence in the ruined abbey. Yet when she came to the Lakes she left her ghosts behind her, turning instead to the tangible mystery of rock and tide. Her beautifully-written account of the return crossing, from Ulverston to Lancaster, reminds one of an eighteenth-century chalk drawing:

> We took the early part of the tide, and entered these vast and desolate plains before the sea had entirely left them, or the morning mists were sufficiently dissipated to allow a view of distant objects; but the grand sweep of the coast could be faintly traced, on the left, and a vast waste of sand stretching far below it, with mingled streaks of gray water, that heightened its dreary aspect. The tide was ebbing fast from our wheels, and its low murmur was interrupted, first, only by the shrill small cry of sea-gulls, unseen, whose hovering flight could be traced by the sound, near an island that began to dawn through the mist; and then, by the hoarser croaking of sea-geese, which took a wider range, for their shifting voices were heard from various quarters of the surrounding coast. The body of the sea, on the right, was still involved, and the distant mountains on our left, that crown the bay, were also viewless; but it was sublimely interesting to watch the heavy vapour begin to move, then rolling in lengthening volumes over the scene, and, as they gradually dissipated, discovering through their veil the various objects

[1] William Green: *The Tourist's New Guide* (Kendal, 1819).

they had concealed—fishermen, with carts and nets stealing along the margin of the tide, little boats putting off from the shore, and, the view still enlarging as the vapours expanded, the main sea itself softening into the horizon, with here and there a dim sail moving in the hazy distance. The wide desolation of the sands, on the left, was animated only by some horsemen riding remotely in groups towards Lancaster, along the winding edge of the water, and by a muscle-fisher in his cart trying to ford the channel we were approaching.[1]

As the route increased in popularity, the strange case arose that here, on the loneliest road in England, it was never possible to be alone. For when the tide receded there were often forty, fifty or more carts, chaises, and gigs, with foot-travellers, horses, and dogs, all waiting on the shore for a carter to guide them across. The sands, for the most part, were firm and smooth—hard as "stucco", as one writer[2] says, "upon which the horses' hoofs scarcely make an impression"—and many people enjoyed the swift, easy, silent motion of the carriage, though others were disappointed because they could see so little of the shore. In winter, especially, with the light half-gone and a heavy mist scarfing the marshes, it must have been very like flying blind in an aeroplane. Yet even to the least imaginative traveller, there were incidents to break the monotony of the journey. The crossing of the main channels, for instance:

"Now," said my sister, "we must either go back or swim over." But judge my surprise, when we drove right into the stream; I own I felt afraid, for a moment. But my sister's vivacity soon dissipated my fears. A more picturesque, grot-esque, *touresque*, or whatever other *esque* you may think fit to call it, I think I never saw.[3]

It is a subject that would have suited Rowlandson—dozens of carts and traps toppling over the kerb of the channel, flop-ping down the short steep chutes of wet sand, splashing in the water; horses floundering on the opposite bank; riders up to

[1] Anne Radcliffe: *Observations during a Tour to the Lakes* (1795).
[2] The Hon. Mrs Murray: *A Companion and Useful Guide* (third edition, 1810).
[3] John Briggs: *Letters from the Lakes*, etc (1825).

the thighs; dogs swimming, or barking and running in circles; wretched foot-passengers begging a lift or at least a hand-hold on a cart or carriage; men wading and swerving as the floor shelved deeper than they expected; women shrieking and pulling their skirts about their knees. Yet all around them was the endless disregard of the sands, under a damp cuticle of reflected light. What danger there might be was easily forgotten in the bustle, and even the discomfort was well paid for by the sight of others in a worse fix, and it is hard not to think of the crowds who would enjoy the same sort of mock-perils and horseplay among the big-dippers and helter-skelters which later were to be built along the shores of the same Bay.

When it was all over, it was the danger, the loneliness, which remained in the mind. Often the travellers found their memory returning to the cockle-gatherers of Kent's Bank, Allithwaite and Flookborough—men, women and children, desperately poor and often prematurely aged, who prodded the sands in the cold half-dark between the tides, and carried home their catch in sacks on their backs. Gray, who prudently avoided the crossing, has a story of a cockler who was out on the Kent Sands with his wife and two grown daughters. The fog descended and the water in the channel seemed much deeper than he had expected. The old man was puzzled: he had crossed the sands many times before, but now he was not certain of the way. He stopped and began to scratch about in the sand trying to find some spar or rock or similar mark which he could recognize. His wife and daughters waited by the cart. The old man did not return. They called to him, but no reply came from the mist. The tide began to rise and the two girls tried to persuade their mother to turn round and trust the horses to guide them to the shore, but she would not listen to them and remained wandering about on her sandbank while the others, clinging desperately to the cart, waded and floundered and swam back to Bolton-le-Sands. "The bodies of the parents were found the next ebb," says Gray, "That of the father a very few paces distant from the spot where he had left them.[1]

Gray's account, written in 1769, has the true eighteenth-century melancholy and sentiment, but by the time that the

[1] But how could anyone know it was the same spot?

Lake Tour had become popular, people were beginning to look on danger less as a warning than as a challenge. The young turned now, not to the moralizings of Gray, Young and Blair, but to the vigour and optimism of Scott—the peril of the Solway, with all the dash and devil of the rescue. From this time the stories of the crossing became robust, unsentimental, even slightly sardonic. People still got drowned, of course, but, instead of pitying them, the survivor congratulated himself on his own courage. There was the visitor who asked the carter if any of the guides had been lost on the sands. "Nay, I nivver knew any *lost*," replied the man. "There's yan or two been drownded, but they're usually foond agean when t'tide gaas oot."

But the prize story of this sort belongs to Adam Walker, the Natural Philosopher, who was himself a native of the Lakes, because of which he may claim the privilege of telling it in his own words:

A Gentleman's horse was some time ago drowned in crossing one of these rivers too late. The horse floated, and the Gentleman stuck to him, as a wretched seaman would do to a plank. The Man and Horse were carried up by the tide a considerable way inland, and so near the shore that he tried by the long tail of the Horse if he could touch bottom. No bottom was to be found! The tide turned and the Man and Horse began to move towards the main sea! His heart sunk within him, though he still swam by the assistance of the Horse's tail. Several miles was he carried by this uncouth navigation, when once more he was determined to try if he was within soundings. Having fastened one hand on the Horse's tail, he plunged into the sea, and think what must have been his feelings when he felt the bottom!—PROVIDENCE had placed him on a sand-bank! He stood up to the chin—the waves went over him—he disengaged himself from his good friend the dead Horse, and waited there till the tide forsook the Sands, and got safe home.[1]

This bravado, this sense of adventure, managed to combine itself even with the quasi-scientific curiosity of the time. The early tourists had an insatiable interest in natural phenomena of all kinds, but they preferred those which held implications

[1] A. Walker: *A Tour from London to the Lakes*, (1792).

of danger and excitement and strangeness. The word "phenomenon" was already taking on its popular, debased meaning. The scientist was confident that soon he would be able to understand and· explain the whole workings of Nature, to take the world to pieces like the wheels of a watch. Yet, in a dark, irrational corner of his mind he hoped that he would not succeed, hoped that there would be at least one wheel left over. Therefore it was when Nature puzzled him, when she astonished him, and even when she half-scared him, that he delighted in her most.

Now of all Lake curiosities it was the weather which most obviously suggested terror and tumult. We may reflect, ironically, that it still does, but while the modern holiday-maker grumbles about the rain, the Picturesque traveller gloried in tales of gigantic storms, floods, water-spouts and prodigious winds. It was the mild and temperate William Gilpin who set the fashion. In his *Observations* he tells the story of two storms —one at Brackenthwaite in the Lorton–Buttermere valley, and another at St John's-in-the-Vale—which have since gone roaring and rumbling through journal after journal and guide-book after guide-book. That at St John's-in-the-Vale, in 1749, had already been described by a Mr Smith in *The Gentleman's Magazine* in a manner suited to this spot where the very crags took on the shape and similitude of a medieval castle—turrets, buttresses and crenellations materializing like a geological ectoplasm out of the bare rock.[1] There had been, he says, much thunder and lightning in the hills beyond Skiddaw and at last "the cloud from which the tempest proceeded" came against the mountain, splitting on it like a wave against a rock. The cloud divided into two halves, one of which "discharged a great quantity of water" on the Carlisle plain, while the other passed over Threlkald into St John's-in-the-Vale. Here it broke into a violent thunderstorm, or cloud-burst, which ravaged down the side of the fells, turning all the little becks into cataracts that swept rock, scree and débris before them, uprooted trees, battered down walls, crushed cottages, and tore up the valley bottom like a bulldozer run mad. "The inhabitants," says Smith, "who were scarce less astonished and terrified, than they would have been at the sound of the last trumpet, and

[1] This is the foundation of Scott's poem *The Bridal of Triermain*.

the dissolution of nature, ran together from under the roofs that sheltered them, lest they should be beaten in upon their heads, and, finding the waters rush down all round them in an impetuous deluge . . . such of them as were able climbed the neighbouring trees, and others got on to the tops of haystacks."[1]

The inundation at Brackenthwaite in 1760 was similar, but the celebrated "Irruption" of Solway Moss, though rather out of our route, was a much odder affair, truly deserving to be called a curiosity, and we are lucky to have a dispassionate account of it from Pennant, who visited the district in 1772, the year after it happened. The Moss, as he describes it, consisted of some sixteen hundred acres, most of it quagmire or peat, and according to his theory it was really an under-surface lake of water or liquid mud covered by a crust of turf and moss which had grown thin because of continual digging for fuel. Then, in November, after several weeks of heavy rain, the lake swelled up and the crust broke. The flood seems to have advanced in a great slow-moving wave of mud, like the slow spread of lava from a volcano. A farmer, who discovered it, at night, thought at first in the darkness that his dunghill was moving. Then he realized what it was and warned his neighbours. The disgusting black flood slimed itself over four hundred acres, gurgling and growling as it crawled along, so that families trapped in their upper rooms were left bewildered and terrified until morning. No human lives were lost, though numbers of farm animals were smothered, and one cow was saved only after having stood for sixty hours up to the neck in mud. "When she was relieved," says Pennant, "she did not refuse to eat, but would not taste water; nor could even look at it without showing manifest signs of horror."

It was not merely the strange and rare which attracted the attention of the tourists. They were curious also about the regular climate; about the helm wind which blows on Cross Fell; about the small local storms which belonged to a particular lake, the sudden gusts and eddies, the "Bosom winds" and "Bottom winds". For a long time people discussed the weather in Cumberland as if its sole purpose was to make the scene practicable for a painter. When the guide-books consider the

[1] Quoted from Hutchinson's *History of Cumberland* (1794).

best time of year for visiting the Lakes, they nearly always recommend a rainy month rather than a dry one. The clouds, mists, and moving vapours gave to the landscape a softness and luminosity like that of wash drawings or an aquatint, and it was in the form of an aquatint that many of the travellers imagined their ideal landscape.

Hutchinson tells how, on Ullswater, on a hot summer day when evaporation is great, the heads of people leaning from a boat over the surface of the lake are seen to be surrounded by "a faint halo, with a slight mixture of prismatic colours". He tells, also, of luminous peat, a sort of putrefied earth, which in the night resembles fire, when it is agitated, by being trod on. And he goes on to paint a scene which would surely have delighted Coleridge:

> A similar appearance is observable on what is called *benty ground,* (i.e. where the vegetation is chiefly *rushes*) when a slight rain comes on after a long continuance of drought. Every rush or blade of grass, if trod or touched, is instantly illuminated, and remains so during the night, if moist. . . . Strangers are surprised, and often frightened, to see their horses' legs besprinkled, to all appearance, with fire, and sparks of it flying in every direction.[1]

These, however, are merely isolated incidents and discoveries, stories to tell at home, little adventures collected like ferns or shells, the experimental bric-à-brac of the visitor, the stranger. It was not till Wordsworth came that we had one in whose mind all such findings and keepings could cohere into a multi-seasonal whole. In his memory a lifetime of similar discoveries and observations was so arranged and ordered that the picture which appeared was more than a picture. No painter has analysed the atmosphere of the Lakes as carefully and perceptively as Wordsworth, yet for him the visual experience was by no means an end in itself, but a means to a more complete understanding. The mists do not obscure what they cover, but seem, in some strange way, to reveal it more clearly:

> The country is, indeed, subject to much bad weather, and it has been ascertained that twice as much rain falls here as

[1] Hutchinson: *History of Cumberland.*

in many parts of the island; but the number of black drizzling days, that blot out the face of things, is by no means *proportionately* great. ... The rain here comes down heartily, and is frequently succeeded by clear, bright weather, when every brook is vocal, and every torrent sonorous. ... Days of unsettled weather, with partial showers, are very frequent; but the showers, darkening, or brightening, as they fly from hill to hill, are not less grateful to the eye than finely interwoven passages of gay and sad music are touching to the ear. Vapours exhaling from the lakes and meadows after sunrise, in a hot season, or, in moist weather, brooding upon the heights, on descending towards the valleys with inaudible motion, give a visionary character to everything around them; and are in themselves so beautiful, as to dispose us to enter into the feelings of those simple nations (such as the Laplanders of this day) by whom they are taken for guardian deities of the mountains.[1]

It is much more than a matter of accident that this northwest part of England has come to be known as the Lakes rather than the Mountains. Yet, to those of us who live there, it is the mountains rather than the lakes which determine its character. To us, the lakes, attractive as they may be, are passing floods, older than man, no doubt, but almost temporary compared with the enduring fells. To the visitor, on the other hand, the lakes have an immense fascination; no valley, they feel, is complete without one. The Picturesque traveller gloried in water—lakes, ponds, rivers, cascades, clouds, floods, water in the sea, water on the land, water in the air. He loved islands, especially the Floating Island of Derwentwater which, of all the water fancies, was the most exciting. I say "fancy" deliberately, because, as the island appeared only for a week or two at a time and sometimes not for years at a stretch,[2] few of the travellers ever saw it at all. For the majority it rose and fell only in imagination, drawing about it the mists and mystery of all those strange islands that float through the legend and history of the world, from Circe's Isle to Prospero's, from the Isles of the Blest to Juan Fernandez. To them it was a magic

[1] Wordsworth: *Guide to the Lakes.*
[2] G. J. Symons in *The Floating Island of Derwentwater* (1888) estimates that the island rose about forty times between the years 1753 and 1888.

island, an island of fancy, and it is with this fancy that I am now concerned, rather than with the observable facts.

Of the few tourists who did see the island, William Hutchinson, in his excursion of 1773, was the first. He writes:

> We next visited a very extraordinary phenomenon, an island about 40 yards in length and thirty in breadth, grown over with rushes, reeds, grass, and some willows.—We would have landed upon it, but as the water was said to be forty fathom deep in that place, and the attempt rather hazardous, we desisted, and had not the means of enquiring particularly as to its nature.—This island rose about 4 perpendicular feet above the surface of the water, on which we were told it floated;—from its magnitude we were not able with one boat to try whether it would move, from the perpendicular line of its then station, or whether it was bound to and connected with the bottom of the lake by the roots of any aquatic plants which appeared upon its surface.[1]

That has a completely authentic sound. There are the measurements, and the presence of those amazingly quick-growing willows. There is the Defoe-like touch of the attempt to move the island, to make it swing round on its anchor, as it were. That, surely, would convince anyone. But oddly enough it did not convince Hutchinson himself. When he visited Derwentwater the year after that, the island had not risen, and he concluded from this that it did not float at all, but merely rose above the surface of the lake when the water-level was low. It is strange that this writer, who rarely hesitates to exaggerate, should be so cautious when he had the evidence of his own eyes. Indeed one feels that many of the travellers wrote of the Floating Island as if they were afraid of being laughed at when they returned home, so that it was not till the time of Jonathon Otley that anyone made a systematic study of the island, or tried to reason a way through the many theories which had been put forward to explain it.

Below all that water music the solid earth sang its own steady bass. To the visitors this seemed less exciting, for to them the rocks were not so much the foundation of the landscape as the frame. One rock, however, never failed to rouse their wonder

[1] William Hutchinson: *Excursion to the Lakes* (1776).

—the Bowder Stone of Borrowdale. This stone is a large boulder, deposited by a retreating glacier at the end of the Ice Age. There are many such in the Lakes and, compared with others, the Bowder Stone is less spectacular in its situation, being in the dip of a valley instead of the brow of a hill, but it is by far the daddy of them all in size, balanced on its narrow base, as Mrs Radcliffe says, "like the roof of a house reversed". As a stone it is no more remarkable in shape or substance than the millions of smaller stones in all the becks of Cumberland. The early travellers did not look at these stones, but they *did* look at this one and so were able to see, magnified till it was big enough to attract their attention, something of the beauty of form, colour and texture which was lying around them everywhere in the dales.

At first glance, the stone seems a freak of perspective. You see what might be a perfectly ordinary fragment of volcanic rock, but you see, as it were, a rabbit's-eye view of it. It blocks the entire mouth of the burrow along which you are walking. The boulders and rocks round about are like gravel or the most minute shiverings of scree, and the birches are like summer grasses, glossy and lish in the stem and flecked and feathery with seed.

When we read the eighteenth-century accounts of the Bowder Stone, we are entertained again and again by attempts to explain it. Obviously it was much too heavy to have been moved by human means, nor could one imagine any flood which could sweep it along the river-bed. Henry Kett, a contributor to Mavor's *British Tourist*, thought that it had fallen from the rocks above, and managed to persuade himself that he had spotted the "large vacant place from which it had broken off". Yet even if one admitted this, it seemed hard to believe that the stone could have rolled so far, to say nothing of its finishing perched on one point like a gigantic top. How, then, could it have come where it was? Their answers, as unscientific as Old Moore's Almanack, seem to me oddly imaginative. They did not say that the stone had grown out of the ground, as had been said of Stonehenge; but they did say that it had always been there, had never been anywhere else; that it was by itself and of itself; that it was, in fact, "a separate creation". Clarke, speaking of this and other similar boulders, called them "self-stones", a phrase which hangs about the memory as a cat hangs about a house after its owners have left. Unscientific it may be, geologically absurd, astronomically preposterous, but I cannot help feeling that in some strange inexplicable way it may yet be true.

In early prints of the Lakes it is common to find the people treated as merely part of the scenery. Raiders in Highland dress light bonfires beside Derwentwater; bandits or robbers assemble on Kirkstone; vague, draped figures, melancholy as the mist, pause and ponder over the sands of Morecambe Bay. The landscape becomes a landscape with figures, but it would not do for these to be the solid, shrewd, independent people who could be met at every farm and in every inn. Such people did not really suit the scene as the tourists saw it. They required figures less substantial, more shadowy. They were in search of the sentimental primitive, of simplicity and innocence, and they preferred a simplicity that was rather obviously naïve, and an innocence that was easily betrayed. For, while they enjoyed searching for a lost Eden, they did not really want to find it. They would contemplate with pleasure the *idea* of Eden, of a rural community free from the vices of the town, but they did not really want this idea to disturb their pride in their own urban way of life. Eden, like Sunday school, was charming, but essentially for the children, and they themselves, they felt sure, were completely adult.

From their point of view, therefore, the story of Mary Robinson of Buttermere was just what was required, though Mary was by no means the only forlorn girl in the Lakes.

Indeed, Briggs, in his semi-ficticious *Letters from the Lakes*, introduces a girl's attempted suicide in the river at Lancaster as if this were the sort of thing the tourists must be prepared to expect. Wordsworth's preoccupation with tales of girls and women deceived and deserted may have sprung from his conscience, but he was drawing from a local tradition which was very strong. Nor were the unhappy ones always women. There is, for instance, Clark's Leap on Thirlmere, the story of which is told, not by a visitor, but by the sardonic surveyor of Keswick:

A man of the name of Clark was jealous of his wife to that degree that he was resolved to put an end to his own existence. He communicated his resolution to his wife, and told her at the same time, that he was determined to hang himself : to this she objected for fear that it might prove too painful : he then said he would shoot himself, but from this she likewise dissuaded him, for fear he might not kill himself outright, and so suffer extreme pain to no purpose; he next proposed to drown himself; this pleased her, and they went lovingly together to the water's edge: he then proposed to wade in, but she said the water was so cold, that he would suffer much needless pain; they then walked by the waterside till they came to this rock, which she told him she thought was fit for his purpose, as the water was deep enough at the edge to drown him; He was then going to throw himself directly in, but she told him he might hurt himself against the rock before he reached the water, so that he had better take a run and leap as far as he could : He followed her advice, very calmly put off his coat and took his leap; she staid till she saw him drowned, and then returned, fully satisfied that she had done her duty in giving him the best advice she could.[1]

The tourists were in search not only of the sentimental but of the eccentric. Now the mountains have always been rich in characters as grotesque and individual as the crags they live among—from the two Quakers of Kendal who called themselves Adam and Eve and went naked in the streets, to the old man of next door to living memory in my own town, who used to carry his Sunday dinner each week to a certain spring below Lowscales near the Duddon Estuary, saying that the water there was better than anywhere else. The little fell farms, ten acres of ploughland and a warren of bracken and rock, bred such men as naturally as it bred foxes, though, with the disappearance of the "statesman" holdings, they were growing rarer by the end of the eighteenth century. One, however, survived and was a continual joy to the tourists—John Mounsey, the King of Patterdale. His very title fascinated them. It had a faint suggestion of the Scottish clans, of ancient allegiance and patriarchal pride; it corroborated their conception of

[1] James Clark: *A Survey of the Lakes* (1787-9).

Cumberland as a little world apart, appealing both to their sentiment and their sense of humour. Budworth represents the old man as a miser, gradually putting together a fortune by the most fantastic means. He grazed ponies on the common land, and worked them till they had not an ounce of strength left; he let out fields for a rent of dinners and suppers to save having to feed at home; he always carried bread and cheese in his pocket to avoid having to pay at an inn. Once, says Budworth, when he was transporting a load of slate by boat on Ullswater, he was wrecked on an island in a storm and remained there for two days with one labourer for companion. This other man had brought no food, so when the King felt hungry he would go to the other side of the island and there eat his bread and cheese while pretending that he had only gone to see if the weather were likely to change. It is a story compounded obviously enough of gossip and leg-pulls, but it carried here and there a genuine stamp. "He sometimes has been heard to complain", says Budworth, "that a man should be cut off in the prime of his life, at eighty or ninety years—for if he could live to the age of Methusalem, he might save a little money." Here surely is the voice of a true dalesman, more subtly ironic and more profoundly content than Captain Budworth could ever guess.

Of the many legends and the like, I need mention only one, the Phantoms of Souter Fell. Here is a tale which contained much for which the travellers were seeking. To begin with, though it had the tone, the timbre, of a medieval romance, it was set in the near-present, the mid-eighteenth century, and because it was founded on evidence at no more than second-hand, it seemed almost contemporary, almost subject to verification, belonging among the curiosities rather than the folk-lore. There were good reliable-sounding names like that of William Lancaster to witness for the event, and even that of Daniel Stricket, who—and this should dispose of any further doubt—was an auctioneer.

It is not likely that any of the tourists really believed the story, but it had just that apparently objective, quasi-scientific sound which made it plausible in that quasi-scientific age. There was a queer suggestion of mirage, perhaps a time-mirage, by which the people of Souter Fell had been able to see an event that had not then taken place. Again, the fact that the last recorded appearances were in 1745 linked them with the Rebellion, and therefore with Scotland and the wild Highlanders and all the romantic lawlessness which Hanoverian England could now afford to regard with condescending pleasure. But these figures were prophetic of much more than the invasion of the Young Pretender. They were prophetic of new explorings of the imagination, of the reappearance of half-forgotten symbols, of movements in and out of consciousness on strange un-turnpiked regions of the human mind. Some of that exploring was to take place among these very hills, and the mist in which the phantoms precipitated and dissolved like a sediment was soon to surge and simmer through *Christabel* and *The White Doe of Rylstone*, to mingle with the opium-fumes of De Quincey's dreams, and to ascend like prayers to the adolescent saints who dropped roses into the delirium of the aged John Ruskin.

Here is Hutchinson's version of the story:

On Midsummer eve 1735, William Lancaster's servant related that he saw the east side of Souter Fell, towards the top, covered with a regular marching army for above an hour together; he said they consisted of distinct bodies of troops, which appeared to proceed from an eminence in the north end, and marched over a nitch in the top, but as no other person in the neighbourhood had seen the like, he was discredited and laughed at. Two years after, on Midsummer eve also, betwixt the hours of 8 and 9, William Lancaster himself imagined that several gentlemen were following their horses at a distance, as if they had been hunting, and taking them for such, paid no regard to it, till about ten minutes after, again turning his head towards the place, they appeared to be mounted, and a vast army following, five in rank, crowding over at the same place, where the servant said he saw them two years before. He then called his family, who all agreed in the same opinion; and what was most extraordinary, he frequently observed that some one of the five would quit rank, and seem to stand in a fronting posture, as if he was observing and regulating the order of their march, or taking account of the numbers, and after some

HEAD
OF WASDALE

CASTLE CRAG
AND
BOWDERSTONE
by J. Farrington

time appeared to return full gallop to the station he had left, which they never failed to do as often as they quitted their lines, and the figure that did so, was generally one of the middlemost men in the rank. As it grew later, they seemed more regardless of discipline, and rather had the appearance of people riding from a market, than an army, though they continued crowding on, and marching off, as long as they had light to see them.

This phænomenon was no more seen till the Midsummer eve, which preceded the rebellion, when they were determined to call more families to be witness of this sight, and accordingly they went to Wilton Hill and Souter-Fell-side, till they convened about 26 persons, which all affirm they then saw the same appearance, but not conducted with the usual regularity as the preceding ones, having the likeness of carriages interspersed; however, it did not appear to be the less real, for some of the company were so affected with it as in the morning to climb the mountain, through an idle expectation of finding horse shoes, after so numerous an army, but they saw not the vestige or print of a foot.[1]

[1] Hutchinson: *History of Cumberland.*

CHAPTER EIGHT

THE FUN OF THE FAIR

UNTIL THE seventeen-nineties the tourists confined them-selves largely to the centre of the district, though Arthur Young, one of the very earliest, discovered Haweswater, a lake which is unknown to the vast majority of Lake visitors even today. But soon they were to explore further. The Hon. Mrs. Murray, who came in 1794 and 1796, gained herself the hon. title of "The First Lady of Quality to cross Honister Pass". She also ventured as far as "Innerdale", and recommended a visit to Wasdale. By the time of Green's comprehensive *Guide* of 1818, the lakeless dales had been added to the itinerary, and at last people began to leave the main roads, to turn their backs on the valleys and passes, and to step in among the hills. The glass was broken, the frame thrown away, and now the specta-tor could carry himself into the heart of the picture.

This change revealed itself very clearly in Wilkinson's *Tours to the British Mountains*, published in 1824, but written about twenty years earlier, at the time when a new intellectual society was beginning to spring up among the Lakes. To this society Thomas Wilkinson both belonged and did not belong, for he was a Quaker, owning and farming his forty acres at Yanwath on the banks of the River Eamont—a man of courage and insight, but of simple manners, who must have seemed strange and out of place among the fashionable settlers. Yet he was years ahead of most of them in appreciating the genius of the young Wordsworth, and, as a reward, was given a clod-like immortality in the poem beginning:

Spade! with which Wilkinson hath tilled his lands.

His true memorial, however, should not be in this poem, but in the lovely and familiar *Solitary Reaper* which was suggested by a sentence in his Journal of a tour in Scotland,[1] which Wordsworth read in manuscript. He stands out among his Lake contemporaries as plain and solid as a rock—a friend of Clarkson, a supporter of Wilberforce, an uncompromising pacifist who would let his carts be seized and sold rather than agree to pay the military tax for the war with France. Yet there is little of the Quaker to be seen in his *Tours to the British Mountains*. Admittedly, in the course of a climb he will pause and speak of the grandeur of the Creator as often as another man will pause for breath. And since he accepted a literally scriptural estimate of the age of the earth, he was sometimes curious to know how long it took the rest of the world to discover the Lake Mountains—perhaps Scafell had existed a thousand years before the first birds came across it; perhaps two or three thousand before the first men arrived. In other ways he is curiously modern, the forerunner of the holiday-walker of today. He was not confined to lake-level, but enjoyed the exhilaration of the uplands, the spaciousness of the tops, the silences and even the storms. He had eyes of his own and did not need West or Hutchinson to tell him what to look at, and he could get as much pleasure from the ascent of a little-praised hill like Black Combe as from that of Helvellyn or Skiddaw. When he travelled about the country visiting his friends and perhaps staying a night or two at Po House in the Whicham Valley, or with the Greenhows at Riggindale or the Smiths at Coniston, he would try to climb whatever fells were within reach. In this way he got to know them in all sorts of weather, rain, fog, frost and snow, relating his adventures with a curious matter-of-factness, an unemphatic but detailed realism which is quite new in Lake writing.

"... The particles of snow," he says, describing a crossing of the Shap fells, "flying from the furious winds, strove who should first enter my eyes, ears, mouth, button-holes, boot-tops &c. If I put my hand into my pocket for warmth, it was rather provoking to find my pocket full of snow, &c." That "pocket full of snow, &c." is the most tangible thing we have

---

[1] "Passed by a female reaping alone and singing in Erse as she bent over her sickle, the sweetest human voice I ever heard; her strains were tenderly melancholy, and felt delicious long after they were heard no more."

yet met with. Wilkinson, indeed, relied on the senses of touch and of hearing almost as much as on that of sight for an understanding of the external world:

On entering a thick and solitary wood the night was uncommonly dark; and though I was well accustomed to the way, I was soon out of my path, and found myself entangled in the bushes; when, partly to make an experiment, and partly to amuse myself with my forlorn situation, I formed the resolution to make my way through the wood (between half a mile and a mile) with my eyes closed. Accordingly I winked and went on, with my staff in my hand, enjoying my fancy, and met with no interruption, save once coming down on a knee, till I nearly got through the wood; when, lo! I suddenly heard the tread of a man's foot, which instantly occasioned a singular sensation, and threw my musing tranquility into a kind of thrill, or even a chill. I instantly opened my eyes, and saw the man and I were passing one another. I spoke to him:— he replied:— and I found by his accent he was an Irishman. I before mentioned I wanted to make an experiment; which was to ascertain the difference, if any, in perception between a very dark night, and having one's eyes fully closed. I now found the difference was most manifest. I clearly distinguished the trees around me, as by a faint moonlight, and I had not the least difficulty the rest of my way home.

Again, from Wilkinson's book we see how the country-folk were beginning to get used to the tourist. Nobody was surprised that he wanted to climb the fells; nobody warned him of terrible dangers or insisted that he needed a guide. Of course, he was a Cumberland man himself, and people realized that he had the sense not to get lost or crag-fast, but it is obvious that the new habit is now established and accepted. We learn, for instance, of three ladies (probably Mrs Smith of Coniston and her two daughters) who had climbed Helvellyn without a guide and in the middle of winter. We hear also of the ascent of Blencathra and Skiddaw by a party of six, one of whom was lame, with a crutch, and another blind. The lame man was the first to reach the top of Blencathra, though, after climbing the second mountain, he collapsed from the exertion and needed a horse to help him on the last part of the descent. But the blind man lost his nerve through Wilkinson's account of the precipices he could not see, and threw himself to the ground shaken by a terrifying vertigo of the fancy. Nevertheless, when the others tactfully moderated their descriptions, he climbed the rest of the way as well as any. One wonders if he may have been John Gough, the blind botanist of Kendal.

It is surprising to find that a plain and practical Quaker like Thomas Wilkinson should have been attracted to one of the most shadowy aspects of the Picturesque—the daydream of the Gothic. Yet on his estate on the banks of the River Eamont, he had constructed his own small version of Pope's grotto of Twickenham. Here you could see a hermit's cell, roofed with thatch, lined with moss, and equipped with hour-glass, crucifix, beads and skull—"all very pretty," says Wordsworth, rather patronizingly, "as not spreading very far". But Wilkinson was no Stephen Duck in his Merlin's cave, and the true character of the man can be heard in the lines inscribed on the wall;

> Beneath this moss-grown roof, this rustic cell,
> Truth, Liberty, Content, sequester'd dwell:
> Say, you who dare our hermitage disdain,
> What drawing-room can boast so fair a train?[1]

Surprising as this hermitage may be, it was not the only one in the district. At Conishead near Ulverston, the modern house built on the site of a medieval priory, Col. T. R. G. Braddyll had constructed a cell out of what he claimed was the ruins of a priory chapel. And, as Braddyll was a richer man than Wilkinson, he was able to provide not only a hermitage but a hermit, paying him to be in attendance whenever guests were shown round the garden. He is said to have held the post for twenty years during which his hair and nails were never cut.

None of the larger and more imposing experiments in the Gothic pleased the travellers quite as much as these. Wray Castle, that immense piece of stage scenery at the upper end of Windermere, was not yet built. Lowther, because of its aristocratic associations, was too imperious to become a joke. And anyway, those odd farms on the estate, with a castellated

[1] John Housman: *A Topographical Description* (1800).

tower on one side and a cowshed on the other, can scarcely have been a joke to live in. Yet there remained Conishead Priory, a house that, in the end, became worthy of its own hermitage. It had the most Claudian situation in the Lakes; a backing of fells to the north and east, the limestone scars of Birkrigg close behind it, and, in the front, the Levens Sands with the Cartmel Peninsula and the open sea. Everywhere around was the collusion of limestone and turf, silver and green, grey and brown, and the traffic of tides in the estuary, and the solid clouds quarried by the wind; and in autumn the yellow mists, the intangible sands, the far shores hesitating like a mirage, and the platitudinous texts of the drifting leaves.

It was a site, too, which held its associations as an old hymn-book holds its smell. The house was founded as a hospital in the reign of Henry II, and after having been elevated into a priory it drew revenues from iron-ore mines, from bloomeries for smelting, from fishing rights and pasturage. Like most religious establishments in the district it was demolished at the Dissolution, and soon afterwards a dwelling-house was built in the ruins.

This building was pulled down in 1821, and was replaced by a structure which is the most ambitious romantic invention in the district. It came somewhat later than the main phase of the Picturesque, and in it the Gothic fantasies congealed into stone, and the daydream stiffened into the life of the waking day. Its style, unlike Lowther, Wray, and Muncaster, was not that of the fortress but that of the monastery. It drew less from history than from literature, and the architect had let the word "priory" echo among all the ruined aisles and empty corridors of Mrs Radcliffe and Scott. . . . From a distance it holds to the sky a roof-line as cluttered and complicated as a fretwork pipe-rack—square towers, crochet-worked turrets; spikes, pinnacles and pimples; crenellated balustrades, crow-stepped gables, twisted and twiddly chimneys.

The great entrance hall poses above the courtyard, like the west end of a monastic church—flanking towers, with slotted windows, fretted gable, a great pointed window with a rose window above it. Inside the hall, the charade is played still further. There are seats like choir stalls, or sedilia, along the wall, the life of Christ in stained glass in the windows, and an organ gallery walled in by a screen stolen from a Yorkshire church. There are even niches left blank of their statues to suggest the work of the Reformation.

Beyond the hall are corridors, designed like cloisters, cold, groined and gloomy enough to give the horrors to any maid who had to answer a bell at night. And in one room the abbot turns suddenly into a seventeenth-century squire, with a library or smokeroom panelled, or seeming to be panelled, in oak, part of it a genuine carving of 1623, and part a plaster moulding painted to look like wood.

Colonel Braddyll's fancy cost him £140,000 and he did not enjoy it for long, as he lost most of his money in the Durham coal-mines and had to sell the house in 1850. Ironically enough, after having been for a time a hydro, it then returned to the coal and became a convalescent home for the Durham miners. Today, patched and plastered in the sour yellow that is usually kept for the gates of country railway stations, it looks grotesquely incongruous—the back-cloth of the ball-scene in *Cinderella* lying on a lorry, waiting to be moved to the next theatre, or a fancy dress hanging on the clothes-line beside the pyjamalegs, the panties and the handkerchiefs. Yet here and there, the dream still sticks like an unswept cobweb—in the pillared recession of the corridors and the bat-wing shadows of a groined roof, in a niche or crook or corner that is now perhaps only a cupboard or a lavatory. It was worth the money to have the feeling that something might say "Boo" on the stairs. For in the mid-nineteenth century, when the mines were paying, and the railways were booming, and society seemed as solid as mahogany, it was only by being half-frightened to death that a man could be quite sure that he was alive.

This dream of the Gothic, of ballads and Border warfare, of the pride and independence of mountain clans, was able to reveal itself in a special way in the Lake islands. For islands appeal not only to man's sense of the romantic but to his love of possession. When there was some talk of a plan to drain the lower end of Derwentwater, Mr Pocklington, owner of the largest island, objected on the grounds that "it would join his

kingdom to England". Now if we examine the place-names of
the district we find, as might be expected, that the settlers often
gave their own names to a farm or a clearing, so that vast numbers of villages, hamlets and fields bear a Norse cognomen plus
"seat" or "side" or "thwaite" or "by". The lakes, too, often
bear the names of their ancient owners. Ullswater, Devoke
Water, Bassenthwaite, Ennerdale (in its earlier form of Anen-
derdale) and Thurston Water (the name once given to Coniston)
all contain, or are thought to contain, proper names. And in the
time of the tourists, Thirlmere was known as Leath's Water,
sometimes contracted to Layswater, after the proprietor, while
the largest islands of Derwentwater and Windermere carried the
names, respected and respectfully, of Mr Pocklington and Mr
John Christian Curwen.

Curwen's Island or Christian's Island is the large low whale-
back of land which lies almost opposite to Bowness Bay, and is
known today as Belle Isle instead of by its old name of Long
Holme. The first attempt to "improve" the island (made by a
Mr English in the middle of the century) provoked much censure, but in 1789 the ownership passed into the hands of the
Curwen family, who planted with discretion, and built the odd,
but rather amusing, circular house which evoked much praise
from those who were not yet converted to the Gothic. The gardens remained, but, as Clarke pointed out, it was ridiculous
to expect the owner to row over to the mainland every time he
wanted a cabbage.

The unfortunate Mr Pocklington, however, came in for
practically no praise, perhaps· because he had no powerful
Cumberland family behind him, like the coal-owning Curwens.
It is true that the man had no taste at all. His buildings were
laughably ugly and were stuck all over the place like decora-
tions on a Christmas cake. He did not even confine his embel-
lishments to the island. At one place he cut off the branches of
an oak, shaved the bark and whitewashed the trunk, so that
it stood in the meadow like the ghost of a tree. While at the
Bowder Stone, says Don Espriella, he "erected an ugly house
for an old woman to live in who is to show the rock, for fear
travellers should pass under it without seeing it, . . . [and] dug
a hole underneath through which the curious may gratify them-

selves by shaking hands with the old woman".[1]

Yet in spite of this, it seems surprising that he provoked such censure from the tourists, for he entered so whole-heartedly into their own game, getting far more fun out of his island than did Curwen at his sedate seat on Windermere. Derwent Island, as it is now most unimaginatively named, is at the lower end of the lake, side by side with Friar's Crag, and so close to the town of Keswick that one feels it ought to be under the jurisdiction of the Parks Committee. It has had several names. In the late eighteenth century it was known not only as Pocklington's Island but as Paradise Island, though the sight of Mr Pocklington himself, naked as Adam and with a suitable Eve, is one of the few possible attractions which he does not seem to have thought of. Before this it was Vicar's Island, from a presumed connection with Furness Abbey; and earlier still it held the splendid Norse name of Hestholm, "stallion island".

In spite of Pocklington's silliness, there seems to have been a childlike charm about his doll's village during the few years that it lasted. For the house itself, there is little to be said, but half-hidden away at various points on the island were several more entertaining contrivances. First of all, there was the church, built, as Budworth says laconically, "as an object"; a fort and a battery, fitted with cannon for echoes; a boat-house looking like a Primitive Methodist chapel; and, most endearing of all, a Druid Circle fifty-six feet in diameter, planned on the model of Castlerigg.

With all this to choose from, what right had the tourists to be ungrateful? Pocklington's fancies might be naïve, but at the bottom they were no more ridiculous than the attitudes and cadenzas of many more learned and more respected men. He was, moreover, curiously uninhibited and generous both of enthusiasm and of money to a project like the Keswick Regatta which he helped to establish during the 1780s.

The first attempt to organize an entertainment of this kind was made at Ouzebridge on Bassenthwaite in 1780, when ducks were chased by water-spaniels and a number of horses were taken out into the middle of the lake in a flat boat fitted

[1] *Letters from England*, by Don Manuel Alvarez Espriella [Robert Southey] (1807).

with a plug—the plug was pulled out, the boat sank, and the first horse to swim ashore was the winner. Pocklington's Derwentwater regattas were both more spectacular and more humane. In 1782, for instance, according to the account in *The Cumberland Pacquet* (a weekly paper published at Whitehaven), a large gathering of people assembled on the shore of the lake as early as eight o'clock on the morning of the event. There were marquees in the fields and boats and barges on the water, many of them decked with bunting. At noon, Mr Pocklington's personal friends rowed out and were greeted by a salute of guns from his battery, while, at the same time, five boats set off on a race round the four islands. At three o'clock there was a sham attack on the main island, the besieging fleet coming from behind Friar's Crag, and after two attacks, "a great variety of beautiful manœuvres", and a whole *Sacre du Printemps* of guns and echoes, the garrison capitulated. By this time it was dark. The visitors were guided back to Keswick by a string of lamps stretched from the water's edge to the town, and the day ended with fireworks and a dance—"a chain of amusements", claimed the paper, "which ... no other place can possibly furnish, and which wants only to be more universally known, to render it a place of more general resort than any other in the Kingdom."

The commercial note sounded in *The Cumberland Pacquet* was to grow louder and louder from now on. Mr Pocklington's fleet on Derwentwater, the Duke of Norfolk's pleasure barges on Ullswater, and Mr Curwen's seventeen vessels with rowers in scarlet were reserved for friends of the owners; but soon everyone could find water-transport at a modest cost. Hutton, the museum-keeper, plied a boat for hire at Keswick; the White Lion at Bowness and the New Inn at Coniston each had boats for the use of residents. The King's Arms at Patterdale provided not only a boat but a small cannon for the echoes, which was discharged "at trifling expense". Nor did you need to be a nobleman to be received with a military salute. You did not need even to be rich, for Lodore tactfully provided two cannons, one for four shillings and one for half a crown ... though, as Don Manuel Espriella very understandably said, "when one buys an echo, who would be content, for the sake of saving eighteen pence, to put up with the second best, instead of ordering at once the super-extra-double-superfine?"

Gradually the towns began to adapt themselves to the new industry. Penrith had a start on the others, for it was on the main route to Scotland, and the last stop before Gretna, so that the inns had always to be prepared to put up runaway couples. In winter there was a regular Card-Assembly together with many private parties; and in summer there were bowling-greens which, as Clarke says, afforded "exercise and amusement to such of the males as have no better employment".

In contrast, Keswick and Ambleside and to some extent Kendal catered not so much for the passing traveller as for the true Lake tourist. Ambleside, early in the nineteenth century, had Green's exhibition of drawings and aquatints. Kendal had one museum, Mr Todhunter's, and Keswick two, Hutton's and Crosthwaite's, of which the latter was on much the larger scale. It was housed in a lofty, imposing building, fitted with "a number of little reeds fixed to the foot of the window-sash, through each of which, by applying your eye, you are directed to principal objects on the lake". Inside was an astonishing assortment of oddments and oddities[1] gathered rather as a sheep gathers bits of briar and twig and barbed wire in its wool. There were fossils, shells, stuffed birds, petrifactions, local antiquities, and various curiosities and monstrosities scraped together from all over the world—including a set of musical stones collected from the River Greta, the straw hat of a sailor who was with Bligh on the *Bounty*, two barnacles from the bottom of Captain Cook's ship, a piece of bamboo brought back from India by Captain John Wordsworth, and a lamb with claws instead of hooves and with wool of three colours. ("a racoon broke loose from Mrs Bradyle of Conniside [Conishead] Priory, and was missing a fortnight, he was seen amongst the ewes, and it is the general opinion that he copulated with them.") In spite of the sniffs of the virtuosi, the museum was extremely popular, and in 1793 could claim to have been visited by "1540 persons of rank and fashion". Each week their names were printed in

[1] See Appendix C.

The Cumberland Pacquet, and throughout their stay in Keswick they were greeted by Crosthwaite's barrel-organ whenever they passed down the street, while strangers had their attention drawn to the museum by the sound of an enormous brass gong.

Peter Crosthwaite, one of the most extraordinary characters in the Lakes at this time, was the son of a farmer of Dale Head in the parish of Crossthwaite, and as a boy had been apprenticed to a weaver. Later he went to sea, and served with distinction but little reward in the gunboats of the East India Company which later became the Indian Navy. He left the Service when he was thirty-one, and after twelve years or so as an excise officer he decided to retire to Brown Beck, in the Naddle Valley, where his father had given him a small estate. The solitude of Saddleback and the Naddle fells, however, did not suit his enterprising and ingenious spirit, and within a year he had moved to Keswick and began to assemble his museum. It was a venture which he tackled with an obvious opportunism and a batty enthusiasm which must have made him quite the most intriguing curiosity in all his collection. Nor were his activities confined to his own house. By right of his naval experience he was promoted admiral of Pocklington's fleet, he made surveys of the Lakes, and kept detailed observations and measurements of rain, wind, and weather. When a canal was contemplated to link Bassenthwaite Lake with the sea, he surveyed the whole route at his own cost. He was continually spying out the needs of tourists and anticipating their demands. In 1786, for instance, he made a zigzag path to the top of Latrigg, doing most of the work with his own hands or with the help of his son. About this time, too, he arranged for three men to build the first beacon on Skiddaw, and in 1796 he persuaded Mr Robinson of Buttermere (the father of Mary) to construct steps in the rock for the convenience of tourists visiting Scale Force. Today, however, he is known chiefly for his maps of the Lakes, sold at the museum along with prints, guide-books and an improved Æolian harp of his own design. These maps, with their undoubted charm, are a revealing memorial of this second phase of Lake travel. In their proportions they are reasonably accurate, marking the sites of West's "stations", the inns and the farms, and giving also depths of the lakes, direction of the current and the like. Again, they are decorated, after the manner of an old sea-chart, with drawings of antiquities and gentlemen's seats, and views of the fells which look exactly like municipal flower-beds piled high with shrubs. Yet the old adventure is gone. The mountains no longer contort themselves into strange shapes, the rocks do not "impend"; the lakes and becks do not disappear into dark, unknown dales and ghylls of deep and dubious hachuring. All is now mapped and measured. There is no more mystery in the Lakes, but only a calculated curiosity, a polite and paid-for pretence.

And what was the attitude of the inhabitants to all this? If we are to believe the first visitors, they were amazed at the strange interest in their county. "Ith' neome oh fackins," said Budworth's young guide in pure Cockney Cummerset, "wot a broughton you here?" There is the story of a man who bought a plot of land at Grasmere. "He paid too dear for it, Sir," said a "poor unrefined rustic" to Mr Grant. "Had I been in his place, I would have bought another estate among the mountains, at the same price, and twice the value; but Mr Olive is a neat nacky man like, and thinks it fine diversion to look at the water coming down the fells, when there's a flood like, and that's all he has for his money."

This point of view did not last long, and if there were few like Wilkinson of Yanwath who felt a deep and lasting love for mountain scenery, there were many who saw that there was gold in the hills. Very soon the children were waiting to open the gates for carriages as today they do for cars, and we hear of one lad running indignantly after the gentry to demand change for a bad ha'penny. Moreover, the dale folk had a shrewd eye for the affected response, the pretended ecstasy. The very name by which the tourists were known, the "Lakers", has an underlying irony, since "laking" or "laiking" is the dialect word for "playing", and, more particularly, for playing as children play. Already, Picturesque travel was beginning to look rather naïve; sometimes there was seen a rather sophisticated smile among the tourists. And long before Peacock that smile found its way into literature, in the curious work from which I have taken the title of this book. *The Lakers,*[1] a comic opera in three acts, was published anonymously in 1798, but is known to have been the work of James Plumtre (1770–1832), the vicar of Great Gransden in Huntingdonshire, and a relative of the John Plumtre with whom Jane Austen's niece, Fanny, was once in love.

The story centres round Miss Beccabunga Veronique, a lady botanist who writes Gothic romances after the style of Radcliffe and Walpole. "I think I shall lay the scene of my next upon Derwentwater," she says, "make St Herbert to have murdered a pilgrim who shall turn out to be his brother, and I shall call it *The Horrors of the Hermitage.* I shall introduce a mysterious monk of Borrowdale, and shall have fine opportunities of describing groves and bowery lanes, in all the pomp of beech, birch, mountain-ash and holly. The castle upon Lord's Island is to be haunted by an armed head. Horror is to be piled upon horror." That novel, unfortunately, was never written—neither by Miss Veronique, Mrs Radcliffe, Miss Charlotte Smith, nor any other of the fashionable novelists who turned their eyes to the hills. But Miss Veronique was more persevering as an artist than as a writer. She examines the landscape through her Claude-glasses—first the gold-tinted glass ("How gorgeously glowing!"), then the dark one ("How gloomily glaring!"), then the blue ("How frigidly frozen!"). Till at last the picture is finished.

VERONIQUE. I feel myself peculiarly happy in my little sketch. Pray look at it, and give me your opinion.

SAMPLE (*a bagman*). Why, it's no more like the thing than —Why you've made the hills more like sugar loaves,—

VERONIQUE. If it is not like what it *is*, it is like what it ought to be. I have only made it picturesque. . . . I have only given the hills an Alpine form, and put some wood where it is wanted, and omitted where it is not wanted; and who could put that sham church and that house into a picture?[2] It is quite antipathises. I don't like such meretricious ornaments. . . . I have made the church an old abbey, the house a castle, and the battery a hermitage. I have broken

---

[1] I am indebted to the late Mr Frank Warriner of Beck Foot, Duddon Bridge, for much information about *The Lakers.*

[2] This obviously refers to Pocklington's Island.

the smooth surface of the water with water-lilies, flags, flowering rushes, water-docks, and other aquatics, making it more of a plashy inundation than a basin of water: then I have put in for a foreground the single tree they ought to have left standing ... and have sprinkled some ferns and burdocks, and gorse, and thistles, over the turfy slope. I must, I think, do this in colours; an orange sky, yellow water, a blue bank, a green castle, and brown trees, will give it a very fine aspect.

SAMPLE. I can make neither head nor tail on't. Why, Miss, you might as well draw a head with a goggle eye and a hooked nose, a wide mouth and a double chin, and give it a beard and a wig and call it my picture.

But a flute is heard and Veronique sings her own Ariette:

> "A lady once her lap-dog lost,
> Bow, wow, wow."

It is not surprising that such heavy-handed dialogue was rejected by both Covent Garden and the Haymarket, but it is interesting, nevertheless, to find so many aspects of the fashion satirized at so early a date.

CHAPTER NINE

THE LAKE POETS

THERE ARE two sorts of tourists: those who return home and those who stay, and the latter are the more destructive. There is a sort of man who can come into a district that is new to him and can take root there; can learn to accept its tradition, to adapt himself to its people, to assume, like the birds and the lepidoptera, a protective colouring. But there is another who remains all his life a stranger, a foreigner, looking on from the outside, trying, perhaps unconsciously, to make the people and the land adapt themselves to him. And of such a sort, except for Wordsworth, were the Lake Poets. They were not indigenous. They were never acclimatized, they never really established themselves. They caught and flourished for a while like the seeds of an exotic plant brought accidentally in the packing-straw of a merchant steamer. Then, after a prodigious season, they withered and died. They remained always separate, alien, self-conscious, and they bequeathed this self-consciousness to the generation which followed. From this time onwards, the Lakes began to change. The main tourist centres became cosmopolitanized, mongrelized. The clean slate of the dale villages was smarmed up with a coat of Victorian paint. The voices were different, the smell new; and slowly, almost imperceptibly, hotels and shops and boarding-houses began to be touched up, faked and frilled into a faint resemblance of seaside promenades, hydropathic spas, or continental health resorts. The dalesman skulked back to his farm; the quarryman migrated to the mines on the coast. A new race colonized the Lakes: the moneyed intellectuals, the professors, the retired clergymen, the not-quite-so-retired business men. They gave us some of our most brilliant figures of the last century, but they changed the character of the district more drastically than any factory or dam.

There is something false about the very term "Lake Poet". It began as a sneer, and it has ended as a vague proprietary title, a trademark, by which certain writers attain the rank of local worthies without one's needing to read them. And on none of them does the name ring more falsely than on Robert Southey. You might almost say that his only 'claim to the title was a residential qualification. For he was never a poet, and very little of his long and honourable labours had anything to do with the Lakes. Yet, of that group of literary settlers, he was—oddly enough—the central figure. No doubt it was the presence of Wordsworth which drew them in the first place, but it was Southey, more than Wordsworth, who took on himself the position of Literary Host, Lord High Admiral of the Water Poets. Southey, in fact, became himself one of the picturesque features of the district, and helped to add a new brash of colour to the banks of the Greta.

Yet his coming to Keswick was almost an accident. It was Coleridge who arrived first. During the winter of 1799–1800 he had been living in London, with his wife and son, trying to scrape a living from political journalism, and all the time aching for the company of Wordsworth, who had just settled in Grasmere. He was consoling himself among this drudgery with thoughts of escaping for a year or two to the Mediterranean, but the dream had to be abandoned when he found that his wife was expecting another child. Characteristically, he threw up everything and bolted for Grasmere, and three months later moved over Dunmail Raise to Greta Hall near Keswick.

The house he had discovered was really two houses under one roof, one half being occupied by the landlord, Mr Jackson, who had just retired on the profits of a small carrier business. His was the wagon which Wordsworth used to see on its regular route through Rydal and over the Raise to Thirlmere and Keswick—the horses, guided by their beloved drunkard, straining against the hill:

> And the smoke and respiration,
> Rising like an exhalation,
> Blend with the mist—a moving shroud
> To form an undissolving cloud.

As soon as Coleridge was settled at Greta Hall with his family he set about trying to persuade his brother-in-law to join him. The house was large; there were plenty of rooms for study, for visitors and for the children; and Sara Coleridge (heaven pity her) needed the company of her sister. He wrote to Southey in April, 1801 :

> Our house stands on a low hill, the whole front of which is one field and an enormous garden, nine-tenths of which is a nursery garden. Behind the house is an orchard, and a small wood on a steep slope, at the foot of which flows the river Greta, which winds round and catches the evening lights in the front of the house. In front we have a giant's camp—an encamped army of tent-like mountains, which by an inverted arch gives a view of another vale. On our right the lovely vale and the wedge-shaped lake of Bassenthwaite; and on our left Derwentwater and Lodore in full view, and the fantastic mountains of Borrowdale. Behind us the massy Skiddaw, smooth, green, high, with two chasms and a tent-like ridge in the larger.

His neighbour, he went on to say, was kind, generous and affectionate, and had waived claim to the first half-year's rent. He had earned his money "by hard labour, and by pennies and pennies", yet he had a genuine love of books and learning, and gave Coleridge the use of his not inconsiderable library. Sir Guilfred Lawson's library was also available, and, if necessary, books could be borrowed from the cathedral at Carlisle. In addition, for society there was Wordsworth.

This latter inducement would mean little to Southey who, at that time, was no admirer of the new poet and resented his influence over Coleridge. He thought that the latter had been rash and selfish in dragging Sara into the cold and damp of Cumberland, so remote both from relatives and from London. Nevertheless, as he had just returned from Portugal and had not seen his brother-in-law for some time, he accepted the invitation and travelled north with his wife in August 1801.

He stayed only a fortnight, during which time his head was too full of memories of Portugal to take much notice of the Cumberland fells. As for Greta Hall, it does not seem to have made any impression at all.

In the next few years, however, it became more and more urgent that he should find somewhere to settle down. He was working on a history of Portugal, on translation, and on his epics. His mother died; his wife gave birth to their first child. He began to look round, almost desperately, for a suitable house, and all the time Coleridge was begging him to come to Keswick. Yet still he hesitated. He blamed the weather. He knew, now, that Coleridge's marriage was a failure, and as he himself had done all he could to bring about that marriage, he must have guessed that his presence at Greta Hall would not always be comfortable. But the house was waiting, rooms for the books, a garden for the children, and above all, it would be cheap. Then suddenly, Margaret, his baby daughter, took ill and died, and it seemed best that his wife should be with her sister in her grief. They arrived at Keswick in September 1803.

In the forty years that Southey was to spend in Cumberland, he became one of the most industrious, most conscientious and one of the most admired writers of his day—but he never became a Cumbrian. He was respected, trusted, honoured, but he had few local friends. His son, himself the vicar of a Cumberland parish, says that he scarcely got to know twenty of the ordinary Keswick people even by sight. In old age, he would walk the roads screened within himself by short-sightedness, surprised and bewildered if anyone spoke to him. He was always the off-come, always the new tenant.

The country never became part of his life as it did with Wordsworth. He never learned to take it for granted, to become part of it himself. He always felt that he needed to explain himself, needed to justify himself, he always felt obliged to show the sort of enthusiasm which is expected from a tourist when he has returned from a new holiday-resort. Wordsworth rarely tried to persuade people to visit the Lakes. If they came they were welcomed, but he did not really worry whether they came. But Southey was always persuading, one might almost say always advertising. As he grew older and more famous, he took to himself, in De Quincey's words, "the duty (for such he made it) of doing the honours of the lake". When friends or relatives came to stay with him, he would climb Skiddaw with them, or Great Gable, and there would be picnics, boating, and visits to the island that was now no longer Pocklington's. Sometimes the Coleridges, Southeys and Wordsworths would meet at some appointed place about halfway between Keswick and Grasmere. Sometimes there would be stately excursions to Lodore; sometimes the visitors were satisfied to play about in the garden, trying to build stepping-stones across the Greta. Among them were a good many of the famous. Samuel Rogers came before Southey settled there. So, too, did Charles Lamb, and was persuaded to forget his prejudices and admit that Skiddaw was "a fine creature" and that after all there was such a thing as the romantic, which he had doubted before. Hazlitt came soon after Lamb; Shelley called when he was in the district, and left Southey feeling as if he had seen the ghost of his younger self. Keats passed by, but did not call. The eleven-year-old John Ruskin, touring the Lakes with his parents and his cousin, attended Crossthwaite parish church solely in order to catch a glimpse of the poet:

> His hair was no colour at all by the way,
> But half of't was black, slightly scattered with grey;
> His eyes were as black as a coal, but in turning
> They flashed,—ay, as much as that coal does in burning!
> His nose in the midst took a small outward bend,
> Rather hooked like an eagle's, and sharp at the end;
> But his dark lightning-eye made him seem half-inspired,
> Or like his own Thalaba, vengefully fired.

To all of them, whenever they called, whether the time was convenient or not, whether he was idle or whether he was busy, Southey was always courteous, always hospitable, and (though he did not show it) nearly always glad when they went.

"You have now been reading the great book of Nature," he said to John Wilson, who was standing by the window looking at the view. "Here"—pointing to his library—"are the volumes of men."

There can be no doubt which he valued most. He described himself as "one, at the foot of Skiddaw, who is never more contently employed than when learning from the living minds of other ages." There were books collected from all over the world; books in many languages; one which was read by Lauderdale when he was a prisoner in Windsor Castle, and one given to his mother by a young nun; works of theology, politics, law, rare and obscure histories—"Ancient and Modern, Jew and Gentile, Mahommedan and Crusader, French and English, Spaniards and Portuguese, Dutch and Brazilians, fighting their old battles, silently now, upon the same shelf. . . . Fox's Martyrs and the Three Conversions of Father Persons, Cranmer and Stephen Gardiner; Dominican and Franciscan; Jesuit and *Philosophe* (equally mis-named); Churchmen and Sectarians; Round-heads and Cavaliers!"[1]

Books, in fact, were his environment; the view was merely an appropriate background for a professional writer. He lived, as he said, "as regularly as clockwork; indeed, more regularly than our own clocks, which go all paces". He rose at eight, breakfasted at nine, and worked on his histories and biographies till dinner-time, which was usually at five o'clock in the afternoon. The post came about six and from then until tea-time, at eight, he would read the newspaper, answer his correspondence, play with his many cats, or perhaps take a nap. After tea he devoted an hour to posterity by his daily stint on one of those epic poems on which his immortality was so surely to rest. Finally, there was a late supper, wine, conversation, and bed at half-past ten. He planned both for a present income and for future fame as thoroughly and as deliberately as, years before, he had planned the pantisocracy which he and Coleridge and the Fricker sisters and a few others were to set up in the backwoods of North America. Indeed, one cannot but suspect that, for Southey, the Derwent seemed the next best thing to the Susquehanna.

In all this there was little place for walking. He needed exercise, of course, but confesses that if a dose of physic would have done him as much good, it would have seemed the quickest, and therefore the least unpleasant, tonic. The natural world gave him peace, quiet, amusement, opportunity for work, and a means of keeping his liver in order; but it never became for him, as it did for Wordsworth, an essential part of his creative life. He says at one time (in 1804) that he has been kept indoors for a month by bad weather. Can one imagine Wordsworth missing his walks just because it was raining? He says at

[1] Southey: *Colloquies with Sir Thomas More* (1821).

another time that he has been confined to the house by the
dark evenings. Can one imagine De Quincey refusing to go
out at night? Indeed, Southey welcomed both the rain and the
long evenings because they freed him from distraction and left
him able to concentrate on his work, and if he had been the
genius he thought he was, we should be eternally grateful to
him for his devotion and determination.

As it is, his solemnity, his pretentiousness, his very virtues
seem cold and unamiable. The wide eyebrows, the abundant
hair, the pursed, self-satisfied mouth, the long nose pinched in
a perpetual sniff—none of them arouses affection. It is easier
to pity Coleridge for (to all intents) deserting his wife than to
admire Southey for protecting her. He lacks the very faults that
would make him interesting. His character is not so much admirable as exemplary:

> You are old, Father William, the young man cried,
>   The few locks that are left you are gray;
> You are hale, Father William, a hearty old man,
>   Now tell me the reason, I pray.
>
> In the days of my youth, Father William replied,
>   I remember'd that youth would fly fast,
> And abused not my health and my vigour at first,
>   That I never might need them at last.
>
> You are old, Father William, the young man cried,
>   And life must be hastening away;
> You are cheerful, and love to converse upon death!
>   Now tell me the reason, I pray.
>
> I am cheerful, young man, Father William replied;
>   Let the cause your attention engage;
> In the days of my youth I remember'd my God!
>   And he hath not forgotten my age.

The poem is Southey's own, and is quite serious, yet it sounds
to us like a parody of the parody itself.

But during those years of monotonously conscientious labour,
history before dinner and epic poetry after tea, Southey made
for himself a permanent place in English literature almost
without knowing it. For whatever one may say about his poetry,

his prose remains the most practicable, the most assured, the most readily readable of his time. Others could be more brilliant or more eloquent; none could write chapter after chapter with such ease, such comfort, such precision of movement. Only he did not know what to write about. He dug into books, produced enormous histories, massive criticisms, sound, well-shaped biographies. They all have merit—and one, at least—the life of Nelson—is a standard work, but they led him away from his true métier. He says in a letter to a friend that he suspects he has mistaken his talent and ought to have followed "the rich veins of gossip and garrulity". He was only joking, but he was quite right. For behind that long nose and the school-ma'am mouth was a mind alive, alert and witty—a little lacking in humanity, perhaps, yet with a real generosity when its sympathies were roused; lacking also the common touch, yet with an uncommon touchiness, that was not testiness, for everything that interested him. If, as seems likely, he often missed what was going on under his nose, he had an astonishingly quick eye for things farther off. The profound view, the long, cogitating stare, were not for him. He saw best when he was some distance away; thought best when he was a little outside his subject; wrote best when he was not altogether serious.

In this he was the spiritual antipodes of Wordsworth. Wordsworth's manner of thought was intensive; he prowled around the scenes of his boyhood till he had scratched up every bone that might be hidden in memory. But Southey was in spirit a traveller. He saw the most clearly at the first sight, and, as the view grew more familiar, it blurred and faded. Glimpses of Portugal remained vividly in his mind throughout his life, but the mountains of Cumberland were seen so often that he ended by not noticing them. It was only when he conversed with a stranger, with one to whom the view would be new, that he recaptured something of his former enthusiasm. He might be writing a letter about Spanish literature or Brazilian politics, and then suddenly he wants to persuade his friend to come to Keswick, so down goes a set piece of description: sunset over Derwentwater, or snow on Skiddaw. There are passages of more tender description, too, both in the letters and in *Sir*

Thomas More, where the scene is overlaid with the associations of many visits and many friends. Indeed, More's ghost chose to visit him in just those places where he would most often walk with the children or with visitors—Walla Crag, the Druid Circle, Applethwaite and Threlkeld Tarn, now known as Scales Tarn. Southey's best descriptive prose comes almost always when he is writing as a newcomer, a foreigner—curious, critical, excited by the novelty of it all, but not personally involved.

Now this is precisely the way he is able to write under the assumed character of Don Manuel Alvarez Espriella whose *Letters from England*, supposedly translated from the Spanish, appeared in 1807. This very lively work, with its wit, its excellent prose, and its brilliant picture of the time, does not deserve the neglect it has received. It seems that Southey first began to plan the book within a few months of coming to Keswick, and he went to a good deal of trouble to collect the material he needed. His brother Henry supplied an account of the Swedenborgian's chapel in London; his brother Tom answered questions about the Navy; while other friends provided information on cookery, prize-fighting and Westminster Abbey. Yet, in a way, he did not overstrain at the work, regarding it primarily as a means of raising money, and from this very unpretentiousness, this comparative irresponsibility, it has a lightness, an immediacy which is rare in his work. It takes the form of a journal written home by a visitor from Spain, and is ingeniously designed to cover those subjects and those parts of England with which Southey himself was best acquainted. Espriella lands at Falmouth in April 1802 and travels by Exeter and Salisbury to London, and after staying there for some time, sets off on a tour of the north, travelling by Oxford, Birmingham, Chester, Liverpool, Manchester and Lancaster to the Lakes. Then by York, Lincoln and Cambridge to London again, and finally by Bath and Bristol to Plymouth where he embarks. The character of the visiting Spaniard is admirably sustained throughout. He has his prejudices—his horror of the heresy of the English, his complete misunderstanding of anything connected with the Church of England, his neighbourly contempt of the Portuguese. He is continually making allusions to life in Spain (here Southey's own travels came in useful)

and his allusions have to be explained by the supposed trans-
lator. Again, after the manner of travellers, he frequently gets
hold of the wrong end of the stick, quotes from hearsay,
muddles what he has heard, and sometimes writes downright
nonsense—as when he asserts that a masculine type of woman
is known as a "horse-godmother", after the pattern of horse-
chestnut and horse-radish. All this adds reality to the impersonation, but still more cunning is the description of the view
from the top of Skiddaw where "the Scotch mountains appeared beyond like clouds, and the Isle of Man, we were told,
would have been visible had the weather been clearer". That
has an authentic clink about it; the failure to see Man (which
Southey himself must have seen many times) convinces us of
the truth of the story far more than the most detailed picture
of the island. It is the old Defoe touch once again.

Indeed, Southey's plain, direct, conversational prose is about
the nearest to Defoe's which could have been produced in the
romantic age. But his aim is rather different. His art is concerned not with the poetry of the matter-of-fact, but with an
ironic comment. He uses the prejudices of the Spaniard as a
means by which he can criticize English manners, English
society, and English religion, and at the same time he uses these
very criticisms as a comment on the prejudices from which
they arise. The irony is always two-edged, flashing backward
and forward, now at the complacency, the insularity of the
English, now at the intolerance, the one-sidedness of the
Spaniard, now at the latitude, the laxity of the Protestant, now
at the bigotry, the rigidity of the Catholic. Already some of the
standard jokes against the English are taking shape: we cannot make coffee, our coal-fires leave half the room stone-cold.
Again we are taunted with some of the very faults which we
ourselves continually detect in the foreigner: our streets are
never clean because of the coal-dust; we are credulous and
superstitious; we are a nation of the poor rather than of the
rich, for the industrial system has degraded the life of Lancashire factory-workers below that of the Spanish peasant; we are
cruel to animals, and the baiting of bulls would never be per-
mitted in a country where the bull-ring has taught men to
admire that noble beast. It is all both startling and salutary.

One catches, too, something of the bustle and bounce of travel at that time—a bustle which is perhaps missing from the Lake journals because so much travelling there was done on foot. There are the large, well-fitted, well-stocked inns of the south of England, an immense surprise to the Spaniard. There is the perpetual stir : doors opening and shutting, bells ringing, customers calling for the waiter, servants coming and going, the barber's boy with razors, the washer-woman with clean linen, the porter carrying luggage. On the roads themselves, especially those approaching London, there was the same hurry, the same sense of excitement, of accelerated rhythm, as the byways converged on the main route and the traffic increased in speed and in number, "...carriages of every description and every shape, waggons and carts and covered carts, stage-coaches, long, square, and double, coaches, chariots, chaises, gigs, buggies, curricles, and phaetons; the sound of their wheels ploughing through the wet gravel as continuous and incessant as the roar of the waves on the sea-beach". Then there were several modes of public transport : the post-chaise, its horses often worked to death in a few years from the savage way in which they were driven; the stage-coach, heavy and slow, sixteen passengers inside and more on the roof, with the coachman known to everyone along the road, dropping a parcel here, leaving a message there; and the mail-coach, the fastest and most expensive of all, with four passengers inside and two outside, its splendid horses, and the guard with blunderbuss to scare off the thieves and horn to warn all traffic to clear the way ahead. There was even a canal service from Manchester to Chester, with barges divided into two compartments at two prices, "the parlour and the kitchen", drawn by two horses at about a league an hour. The passengers, if they were agile, could jump on to the bank while the barge was moving, and walk alongside for a while, keeping pace with the horses. Everywhere there were people, everywhere there was curiosity, interest and excitement. For this was the heyday of picturesque travel, after the making of the turnpikes, before the coming of the railways, when a whole generation of gentlefolk took to the road. There were maps and road-books available for nearly every part of the country, with distances marked, and inns recommended, and all objects of interest noted by the way. The spas were at the height of their fashion, the seaside had been discovered, and both were crowded with visitors seeking cures for real, imaginary, or frankly invented illnesses.

"The English", says Espriella, "migrate as readily as rooks."

It seems fitting (and, of course, convenient for Southey) that Espriella should make the Lakes the goal of his country excursion, yet the section about them lacks something of the sparkle of the rest of the book. Nevertheless, it has a directness, an accuracy, and an unforced humour which are quite delightful. We see clearly the signs of the new commercialism. Ambleside has "the marks of the influx of money", and the inn at Patterdale is stocked and prepared for a succession of visitors. Already, too, the more knowing traveller has learned to raise an eyebrow at the cannons of Windermere and at the old woman beside the Bowder Stone, though Southey is not above mentioning some of the stock interests of his predecessors: the char, the single-horse carts, the waterfall seen through the window of a hut at Rydal. Espriella's route was quite ordinary, except that on a trip from Keswick he crossed Stye Head Pass and saw Wastwater and Ennerdale—his account of these lakes being among the first we have—but he is not at his best when he is attempting a large set-piece. At such times, though his prose is always graceful and his language restrained, he feels obliged to offer what he thought was expected. His best comes, on the other hand, when he is describing the scenes he knew really well—the roads, the cottages, the becks, odd nooks and notches of the dales round about. For even to Southey the new vision was beginning to show itself, the lesson of Wordsworth was not quite unheard, and the illusion of landscape was beginning to disintegrate into the scattered realities of rock and fern and water. The trees were beginning to separate themselves from the wood.

Here, then, in prose well-jointed, free-moving, and natural as a healthy body, is his account of Grange in Borrowdale:

This village consists of not more than half a score cottages, which stand on a little rising by the riverside,—built apparently without mortar, and that so long ago that the stones have the same weather-worn colour as those which lie upon the mountain side behind them. A few pines rise over them, the mountains appear to meet a little way on . . . and where they meet their base is richly clothed with coppice wood and young trees. The river, like all the streams of this country, clear, shallow, and melodious, washes the stone bank on which the greater number of the pines grow, and forms the foreground with an old bridge of two arches, as rude in construction as the cottages. The parapet has fallen down, and the bridge is impassable for carts, which ford a little way above. The road from the bridge to the village is in ruins; it had been made with much labour, but has been long neglected, and the floods have left only the larger and deeper rooted stones, and in other places the floor of the rock; the inhabitants therefore are relatively poorer than they were in former times. . . . I have never in all my travels seen a spot which I could recall so vividly; I never remember it without fancying that it can easily be described,—yet never attempt to clothe my recollections in words, without feeling how inadequately words can represent them.

If Southey was a Laker rather than a poet, Coleridge was a poet rather than a Laker. In the years which he spent among the Lakes he seems to have been aware of them only in flashes —flashes, indeed, of intense perception, but flashes which seem scarcely relevant to the workings of his mind at this period. Much of the time he could not really be bothered with the Lakes. He had come to them too late, for he no longer needed the continual stimulus of natural forms: indeed, the excitement they produced in him was only bearable in short spells, in holiday diversions. He had much else to worry about during those years at Keswick—the disruption of his marriage, his own ill-health, and the fear that poetry had left him. The greatest of his Lake poems, *Dejection*, is the expression of that fear and a lament for the loss of his lyrical genius.

His main contribution to Lake literature is seen less in his own work than in that of the Wordsworths. And more in Dorothy's than in William's. Of course it is impossible to measure the full influence of Coleridge on his friend, yet, on the whole, it seems to be a matter of stimulus and encouragement rather than of example or guidance. The main character-

istics of Wordsworth's style can already be seen in the poems
he wrote long before he made friends with the other poet. But
Dorothy was a more susceptible pupil. She learned to look as
Coleridge would look, and to feel as he would feel. Her journal
is full of glimpses seen as if through his eyes. In those wonderful months at Alfoxden, when she and the two poets were
"three persons with one soul", she shared with them the same
rapturous response to nature, "struck with deep joy", and
"silent with swimming sense". She let the wind blow through
her heart and across her senses as across the strings of an Æolian
harp, never caring, as the poets cared, what tune it might
play:

> ... she knows all their notes,
> That gentle Maid! and oft, a moment's space,
> What time the moon was lost behind a cloud,
> Hath heard a pause of silence; till the moon
> Emerging, hath awakened earth and sky
> With one sensation, and those wakeful birds
> Have all burst forth in choral minstrelsy....[1]

And when Alfoxden was over and all three of them were
living at the Lakes, it was Dorothy who preserved in its purest
and simplest form the rapture of the earlier days. Her brother
was preoccupied with poetry, while Coleridge was becoming
a strange, haunted, harassed being. Neither of them was unchanged as she was unchanged, so it was left to her to record
experiences which they too would have shared a few years
earlier. Her journal tells us what Coleridge missed seeing.

His first visit to Cumberland seems to have been made in
the late autumn of 1799. He was at Bristol during October
when he heard alarming reports of Wordsworth's health and
immediately set off north to find out what was the matter. The
Wordsworths, just then, were staying with the Hutchinsons at
Sockburn near Northallerton, and by the time Coleridge
reached them, William was better and the two of them set off
on a short walking-tour, accompanied part of the way by John
Wordsworth. First they visited Haweswater, Windermere,
Hawkshead, and Grasmere, spending several nights at Robert
Newton's. Then, by a curiously tangled route, they looped

[1] Coleridge: *The Nightingale.*

round the north-western lakes, including Buttermere, where
they probably stayed the night and presumably met Mary
Robinson, back to Wasdale and over Stye Head into Borrowdale, and by Matterdale to Ullswater.

Coleridge took notes of this journey and may have intended
to work them up into a Tour. He had read Gilpin, and perhaps,
like Southey, he may have read Celia Fiennes in manuscript.
But, at the time, he does not seem to have thought seriously of
settling in the Lakes. Wordsworth, however, did. While he was
at Grasmere he wrote to Dorothy telling her that he had seen
a small house which they might take. Two years later they
moved in, and the next year Coleridge followed them to the
north and made his home at Greta Hall.

At first he was happy and confident. We have already seen
his enthusiasm for the house and the view of the lake. In fact,
he could hardly leave the subject alone whenever he wrote to
Southey, or Thomas Poole, or Sir Humphry Davy. "The two
lakes, the vale, the river, and mountain mists, and clouds and
sunshine", he says at one time, "make endless combinations as
if heaven and earth were for ever talking to each other." And
at another, the lake is "a rich mulberry-purple", or the clouds
by moonlight looked as if they had been painted "and the
colours had run". Soon he began to look farther than the lake,
exploring Newlands and the Naddle Valley, climbing Skiddaw
and the Borrowdale hills, pottering about in the Stone Circle,
and sometimes calling at the cottages for a rest and a drink. At
such places, he made friends with the dalefolk far quicker than
Wordsworth did. Though he was a stranger, they seemed to
accept him almost as one of themselves and would rarely take
any payment for the bread and milk they gave him. One old
woman asked only for a cure for rheumatism, and Coleridge
promptly wrote to London to get one—and, heaven knows, he
needed it himself as much as she did. It was only the gentry
who were sometimes officious, as when Sir Michael le Fleming
of Rydal sent a servant to complain that Coleridge and Wordsworth should have passed *behind* the house and not in front of
it on their way to visit the famous waterfall. But there was an
easy reply to the discourtesies of one who went in for that
"damned whitewashing", and, anyway, Coleridge was too

excited to be worried by pinpricks like this. It was as if he had found a great pond or tarn, brimful of sensation and sensuous delight, but instead of diving in head first, as John Wilson would have done, he dipped himself, quickly, cautiously, and repeatedly, and then sat on the bank and recorded his impressions as the sun dried his skin. For though his response to nature was as complete and sensitive as Dorothy Wordsworth's, it was by no means so selfless or so unquestioning. He could always remain a little way outside the experience, could criticize and analyse, and this attitude showed itself partly in his interest in chemistry. William Calvert (the elder brother of the Raisley Calvert who had left Wordsworth a legacy of £500) had plans for setting up an experimental laboratory at Windy Brow, and Coleridge was eager to join in the project, and consulted Davy about the books and apparatus he would need. Nevertheless, his scientific speculations were induced by something very different from the curiosity of the eighteenth-century "virtuosi". To them, science was largely a method of classification, but to Coleridge it was an instrument to deepen his imaginative experience of the physical world. "If in Shakespeare we find nature idealised into poetry," he says, "through the creative power of a profound yet observant meditation, so through the meditative observation of a Davy ... we find poetry, as it were, substantiated and realised in nature, ... as at once the poet and the poem."[1]

His descriptions are as clean, as particular, as Dorothy Wordsworth's, but they have also the precision, the scruples, the method, of a scientist's notebook. Dorothy enumerates the details of a physical world as a lover repeats the name of his beloved to bring it closer to her. Coleridge, on the other hand, uses words primarily to define. Often, indeed, he avoids the accepted term, the common noun or names, seeking the exact and proper word:

> ... the impetuous gusts from Borrowdale snatch the water up high, and continually at the bottom of the lake it is not distinguishable from snow slanting before the wind—and under this seeming snowdrift the sunshine *gleams*, and over

[1] *The Friend.* Quoted from *Inquiring Spirit*, edited by Kathleen Coburn (Routledge).

all the nether half of the Lake it is *bright* and *dazzles*, a cauldron of melted silver boiling![1]

And again (of Ullswater):

> And now it is all one deep wall of white vapour, save that black streaks shaped like strange creatures seem to move in and down it, in the opposite direction to the motion of the body. And over the fork of the cliff behind, in shape so like a cloud, the sun sent cutting it his thousand silky hairs of amber and green light.[2]

He realized, indeed, that the stock romantic phraseology produced in the mind an effect as blurred and generalized as an engraving in *The Gentleman's Magazine*. So he was not content with a term like "waterfall", but felt impelled to dissect the shapes, colours and movements that he saw, describing them as minutely as if they were a rare discovery. Here, for instance, is his account of a waterfall at Buttermere:

> It is a great Torrent from the Top of the Mountain to the Bottom; the lower part of it is not the least Interesting, where it is beginning to slope to a level. The mad water rushes through its *sinuous* bed, or rather prison of Rock, with such rapid Curves as if it turned the Corners not from mechanic force but with foreknowledge, like a fierce and skilful Driver; great Masses of Water, one after the other, that in twilight one might have feelingly compared them to a vast crowd of huge white Bears, rushing, one over the other, against the wind—their long white hair scattering abroad in the wind. The remainder of the Torrent is marked out by three great Waterfalls, the lowermost Apron-shaped, and though the Rock down which it rushes is an inclined Plane, it shoots off in such independence of the Rock as shews that its direction was given it by the force of the Water from above. The middle which in peaceable times would be two tinkling Falls formed in this furious Rain one great *Waterwheel* endlessly revolving, and double the size and height of the lowest. The third and highest is a mighty one indeed. It is twice the height of both the others added together, nearly as high as Scale Force, but it rushes down an inclined Plane, and does not *fall*, like Scale Force; however, if the Plane had been

[1] Letter to W. Sotheby, September 1802.
[2] *Diary of Tour to the Lake District*. October–November 1799.

ESKDALE WITH
BOWFELL

BLEA TARN
by T. H. Fielding

smooth, it is so near a Perpendicular that it would have *appeared* to fall, but it is indeed so fearfully savage, and black, and jagged, that it tears the flood to pieces. And one great black Outjutment divides the water, and overbrows and keeps uncovered a long slip of jagged black Rock beneath, which gives a marked *Character* to the whole force. What a sight it is to look down on such a Cataract! The wheels, that circumvolve in it, the leaping up and plunging forward of that infinity of Pearls and Glass-Bulbs, the continual *change* of the *Matter*, the perpetual *Sameness* of the *Form*—it is an awful Image and Shadow of God and the World.[1]

To read that passage with care is to *see* a waterfall as you have never seen it before: in parts, it is almost to BE the fall. The vividness, the originality, of the imagery dazzles and takes the breath away. You are dizzy with the swirl and dash of the words; you feel the force and flow, the weight and pressure of the water. For one moment, he seems to fall back on a cliché— "so fearfully savage"—but immediately he gives the sentence a twist, and turns the conventional savagery into a living image. If only Coleridge could have written like this more often there would have been no need for another guide to the Lakes.

But during the years he spent at Greta Hall, it was not every day that he could achieve such happy athletics of perception. For during those years, a change came over him. When he arrived at Keswick, his greatest period of poetry was just behind. *The Ancient Mariner, Kubla Khan,* the first part of *Christabel* had been written—or perhaps one should say, had been born—for whatever may have been the labours of parturition, the poems were as strange, as individual, as completely and mysteriously *themselves* as any newborn child. He came, confident that he would soon be able to finish *Christabel,* and ready also to plan enormous Wellsian encyclopædias, like that history of British literature which was to include the Welsh, Saxon and Erse as well as English, and for which he was cheerfully prepared to learn Welsh and Erse. He came eager for Wordsworth's company and ready, also, for Southey's.

[1] Notebooks, dated Keswick, August 25, 1802. Quoted from *Inquiring Spirit.*

His marriage, though already something of an embarrass-
ment, was not yet a failure, and he still delighted in the precocious sensitivity of his elder son. But by the time he left in
1803, making his way eventually to Malta, he was ill and
disappointed. Poetry seemed to have failed him. He felt that
he would never find the rock on which he could build the many
mansions needed by his multi-perceptive soul, and already he
had resorted to the slow spiritual suicide of opium.

It seems that at least part of the blame for this tragic and
pitiful disintegration can be attributed to the Cumberland
climate. Coleridge, as a boy, had suffered a severe attack of
rheumatic fever, and from that time his general health, his
spirits, his creative energy had all been peculiarly dependent
on meteoric conditions. "My health", he said in a letter to
Poole, "is as the weather". He claimed to be in himself a perfect barometer, becoming "asthmatic and stomach-
twitched" whenever atmospheric pressure was low, and, unfortunately, as John Dalton, the chemist, had convinced him,
there was five times as much "falling weather" in Keswick as
compared with the Midlands, and more than twice the amount
of rain. It was this, according to his own account, which first
persuaded him to turn to opium, the "Kendal Black Drop",
probably in 1801 or 1802, so that by 1804 the drop had become a confirmed habit.

With ill-health and opium there came alternate restlessness
and lassitude, jerky energy and black depression. In the summer
of 1802 he was walking on his own to St Bees and the western
dales. In the autumn he was in Wales with Thomas Wedgwood
and in January at Bristol with Southey. In August he set off
with the Wordsworths for their tour of Scotland, but the rain
and his own wretched condition forced him to abandon the
journey after about a fortnight and to return at once. One
feels, too, that he had more than the rain to discourage him,
for the once-beloved Dorothy, all unknown to herself, had become a reproach, and, one suspects, at times a bore. Her spring-
ing enthusiasm, her infinitely fresh, youthful, inexhaustible
enjoyment of nature, the quickness of her senses, the resilience
of her spirit—all reminded him of the days at Alfoxden, and of
powers which he thought he could never recapture, or, if re-

captured, could no longer sustain. Of course, there was much
else that his mind could take delight in. No other man of his
time, and perhaps none since, looked with such passionate
understanding on so many things visible and invisible, turning,
with the inquisitiveness of a scientist and the insight of a poet,
to so many aspects of the physical world and of the mental and
spiritual life of man. Literature, semantics, theology, philosophy, politics, sociology, education, chemistry, natural history—all these were waiting like new continents for his exploring mind. But in the Lakes, these were not the interests
which were required of him. Instead, he was continually asked
to look at this scene and that, and he was painfully and almost
guiltily aware that he could not always share with Dorothy
that tremulous sensitivity of earlier days. Yet, though he did
not realize it, there was no loss, but rather a development. For
that nervous, sensual, animal response of Dorothy's—a thing
as involuntary as a moth's sense of smell or a bat's sense of
hearing—belonged to the age of immaturity, the age of just
after adolescence. It was dependent too much on a negative
state—on unfulfilled sex, on untasted experience—to last into
maturity. Dorothy preserved it, certainly, but only at the cost
of never growing up. With Wordsworth it became a tool which
he could call on when needed—often at the price of a head-
ache—but at other times could put aside. With Coleridge it
changed its nature, becoming less physical, more intellectual,
less a matter of the nerves, more a matter of the imagination.
But at the time, he did not understand this, and was aware
mainly of physical loss:

> O Lady! in this wan and heartless mood,
> To other thoughts by yonder throstle woo'd,
>   All this long eve, so balmy and serene,
> Have I been gazing on the western sky,
>   And its peculiar tint of yellow green:
> And still I gaze—and with how blank an eye!
> And those thin clouds above, in flakes and bars,
> That give away their motion to the stars;
> Those stars, that glide behind them or between,
> Now sparkling, now bedimmed, but always seen:
> Yon crescent Moon, as fixed as if it grew

In its own cloudless, starless lake of blue;
I see them all so excellently fair,
I see, not feel, how beautiful they are!

There was a time when, though my path was rough,
    This joy within me dallied with distress,
And all misfortunes were but as the stuff
    Whence Fancy made me dreams of happiness:
For hope grew round me, like the twining vine,
And fruits, and foliage, not my own, seemed mine.
But now afflictions bow me down to earth:
Nor care I that they rob me of my mirth;
    But oh, each visitation
Suspends what nature gave me at my birth,
    My shaping spirit of Imagination.
For not to think of what I needs must feel,
    But to be still and patient, all I can;
And haply by abstruse research to steal
    From my own nature all the natural man—
    This was my sole resource, my only plan:
Till that which suits a part infects the whole,
And now is almost grown the habit of my soul.[1]

Yet this pathetic elegy for lost powers was written by a man who was still, in many ways, the most astonishing genius of his time. He could not now long sustain quite the kind of sensitive experience he had once shared with the Wordsworths, but his powers of observation were still almost unique. One suspects that the very company of the Wordsworths, at this time, unconsciously depressed him—made him aware of his comparative failure, or, at least, of his failure in their eyes. He needed to be away from them, away also from Southey and from his wife, away from all those people whose very loyalty and sympathy seemed to him to be a criticism. "I must be alone," he said, after a walk to Watendlath with Southey and Hazlitt, "if either my Imagination or my Heart are to be excited or enriched."[2]

In the Lakes, of course, it was very hard for him to be alone, yet sometimes he managed it. Sometimes he found himself free

[1] *Dejection: An Ode.*
[2] Entry for 24 October 1803, in unpublished notebook.

and unwatched. In the first week of August 1802, for instance, he slipped away on a walking-tour, the journal of which is one of the most delightful, yet also one of the least known, of all Lake writings.

He set off from Keswick on Sunday the 1st of August, taking with him a shirt, two pairs of stockings, tea, sugar, pens and paper, and a book of German poetry wrapped in oilskin and carried in a knapsack. One of the aims of this journey seems to have been to examine the library presented to St Bees School by Sir James Lowther, so he made towards the coast, by Gilpin's route of Newlands and Keskadale to Buttermere:

> Conceive an enormous Bason mountain-high of solid Stone, cracked in half and one half gone; exactly in the remaining half of this enormous Bason, does Buttermere lie, in this beautiful and stern Embracement of Rock. I left it, passed by Scale Force, the white downfall of which glimmered through the Trees that hang before it like bushy Hair over a Madman's Eyes, and climbed 'till I gained the first level.

He made next by Floutern Tarn towards Ennerdale. Red Pike, above Crummock, was "a dolphin-shaped Peak of a deep red"; Great Borne on Herdus was "a roundish-headed green hill"; while in the country below Melbreak, which looks down towards Loweswater, he found ". . . a wild green view all around me, bleating of Sheep and noise of Waters".

He moved on, passing the precipices of Herdus Scaw, and noting every shape with the greatest precision. Ennerdale Lake, seen from above at the lower end, is "shaped like a clumsy battledore—but it is in reality fiddle-shaped"; Burnmoor Tarn, between Wasdale and Eskdale, is "flounder-shaped"; on Buttermere Hause the ridges are "long arm-shaped and elbow-shaped".

He spent the night at a farm near Ennerdale, and next day went on to Egremont and St Bees, where he found wretched lodgings in a pot-house, sleeping in his clothes, and paying elevenpence for gin and water, bed, and breakfast. Even the library turned out to be of no value (which was hardly surprising considering whose gift it was), and the next day, "a

wet woeful oppressive morning", he trudged back rather miser-
ably to Egremont. But after a better night there, he moved on
to Calder Abbey, noticing the "red freestone, which has the
comfortable warm Look of Brick without its meanness", and
then on by Gosforth to Wasdale, where he had been before,
with Wordsworth. Excited as a boy playing truant, he turned
his visit into a high adventure.

He approached the dale this time from the right direction—
that is, from the bottom, and not from Stye Head. The lake itself was too regular, "exactly like the sheet of Paper on which
I'm writing", but beyond it was that fantastic rubble cliff:

. . . two-thirds of its height downwards [i.e. from the top to
two-thirds of the way down.—N. N.] absolutely perpendicular, and then slanting off in *Screes*, or Shiver consisting of fine
red streaks running in broad Stripes through a stone colour
—slanting off from the perpendicular, as steep as the meal
newly ground from the Miller's spout. So it is at the foot of
the Lake; but higher up this streaky Shiver occupies two-
thirds of the whole height, like a pointed Decanter in shape,
or an out-spread Fan, or a long waisted old maid with a
fine prim Apron, or—no, other things that would only fill
up the Paper.

We can see here exactly how his mind worked in observation.
First the fact, the accurate defining image—then, as he grows
more excited, the image is touched with fancy, and then, at
the very moment when fancy threatens to overthrow the fact,
Coleridge breaks off. Fancy may explain and elaborate fact,
but it is not allowed to usurp.

Wasdale seemed to bring energy and youthfulness to
Coleridge. He spent the night at Thomas Tyson's, below Kirk
Fell, and the next morning, Thursday, the 5th of August, set
off to climb Scafell. As he climbed, he looked along the three
western dales, Eskdale, Miterdale, and Wasdale, to where the
three dale rivers joined at Ravenglass in "the *Trident* of the
Irish Channel". It was a new experience for him, in Cumberland, this close cousinship of mountain and sea, and perhaps
it reminded him of Somerset. His temperature rose with the
altitude instead of falling with the barometer. He climbed

almost to the summit and then found a wind-break among the
rocks, where, like a painter, he jotted down shapes and sizes
while he could still see them :

> And here I am *lounded* [i.e. sheltered. N. N.]—so fully
> lounded—that tho' the wind is strong, and the Clouds are
> hasting hither from the Sea—and the whole air Seaward has
> a lurid look—and we shall certainly have Thunder—yet
> here (but that I am hunger'd and provisionless) *here* I could
> lie warm, and wait methinks for tomorrow's Sun, and on a
> nice Stone Table am I now at this moment writing to you—
> between 2 and 3 o'Clock as I guess—surely the Ist Letter
> ever written from the Top of Sca' Fell!

So far as Coleridge was concerned, it might easily have been
the last he wrote anywhere. He was, he admits, something of a
gambler, and when he had climbed a hill by the circumscribed
route, he liked to abandon that route on the way down, following wherever his fancy led, and trusting that he would reach
the bottom safely. This was what he did on Scafell, and was
led into a breakneck descent which set up tremulous agitation
in his plumpish and ill-conditioned body. And Coleridge conveys so well the breathlessness, the perturbation, the shock and
shake and shiver of it all, that his prose takes us down with
him, bumping and bouncing, slithering and sliding, in what is
perhaps the earliest recorded rock-scramble in the Lakes. There
is little description here, and no horror-mongery. Coleridge's
ambition did not aim higher than a chatty journal to be read
by the Wordsworths, who, at this time, were in France on a
visit to Annette and the poet's daughter. Yet in no other passage of Lake prose is physical sensation evoked so tangibly. Nor
is it sensation merely for its own sake—as it is in Hutchinson
and perhaps in Gray. It revels in its own self, yet it acknow-
ledges its debt (almost, one might say, its respect) to the external
world which brings it into being. There is, throughout this
section, a wonderful *rapprochement*, reciprocation, co-operation, between the thing that is experienced and the self that
experiences, between the thing that is seen and the eye that
sees, between the thing that is felt and the body that feels. It is
both Picturesque and Picturesque-in-Reverse : the mountains

are enjoyed for the sake of the view, and the view is enjoyed for the sake of the mountains.

So it was yesterday afternoon. I passed down from Broad Crag, skirted the Precipices, and found myself cut off from a most sublime Crag-summit, that seemed to rival Sca' Fell Man in height, and to outdo it in fierceness. . . . The first place I came to, that was not direct Rock, I slipped down, and went on for a while with tolerable ease—but now I came (it was midway down) to a smooth perpendicular Rock about 7 feet high—this was nothing—I put my hands on the Ledge, and dropped down. In a few yards came just such another. I *dropped* that too. And yet another, seemed not higher—I would not stand for a trifle, so I dropped that too —but the stretching of the muscle of my hands and arms, and the jolt of the Fall on my Feet, put my whole Limbs in a *Tremble*, and I paused, and looking down, saw that I had little else to encounter but a succession of these little Preci- pices—it was in truth a Path that in a very hard Rain is, no doubt, the channel of a most splendid Waterfall. So I began to suspect that I ought not to go on; but then unfor- tunately, though I could with ease drop down a smooth Rock of 7 feet high, I could not *climb* it, so go on I must; and on I went. The next 3 drops were not half a Foot, at least not a foot, more than my own height, but every Drop increased the Palsy of my Limbs. I shook all over, Heaven knows without the least influence of Fear. . . . My limbs were all in a tremble. I lay upon my Back to rest myself, and was beginning according to my Custom to laugh at myself for a Madman, when the sight of the Crags above me on each side, and the impetuous Clouds just over them, posting so luridly and so rapidly to northward, overawed me. I lay in a state of almost prophetic Trance and Delight and blessed God aloud for the powers of Reason and the Will, which remaining no Danger can overpower us. O God, I exclaimed aloud, how calm, how blessed am I now. I know not how to proceed, how to return, but I am calm and fear- less and confident. If this Reality were a Dream, if I were asleep, what agonies had I suffered! what screams! When the Reason and the Will are away, what remain to us but Darkness and Dimness and a bewildering Shame, and Pain that is utterly Lord over us, or fantastic Pleasure that draws the Soul along swimming through the air in many shapes, even as a Flight of Starlings in a Wind.

At this point, however, he roused himself, saw that the storm was gathering, and looked round till he found a "Rent" or chimney in the cliff wide enough to allow him to climb down without getting wedged:

> So I began to descend, when I felt an odd sensation across my whole Breast—not pain nor itching—and putting my hand on it I found it all bumpy—and on looking saw the whole of my Breast from my Neck—to my Navel, exactly all that my Kamell-hair Breast-shield covers, filled with great red heat-bumps, so thick that no hair could lie between them.

Neither the difficulties nor the heat-bumps lasted much longer, and very soon he was following the course of the beck into Eskdale. By the time the storm broke he had reached the shelter of some large boulders and was ready once more to envisage further adventure. He slept that night in Eskdale and then made his way by Devoke Water to Ulpha in Dunnerdale, and so onward by Broughton, Torver, Coniston, and Charles Lloyd's at Brathay, reaching Keswick on Monday 9 August.

And this is the man who feared that he had lost the "shaping spirit of Imagination".

John Wilson, on the other hand, had no fears of losing anything. If he had not a tenth, not a hundredth, of Coleridge's imagination, he had ten times his physical strength. He came ripping and roaring into the Lakes like two men, like two different men; not so much two-faced as reversible, like one of those comic faces which one way up is a wide-browed old man and the other way is a wide-jawed old woman. The way his family saw him, he was a young poet, with blue eyes, £50,000 and a leaning towards platitude and piety—one not so much married to his muse as engaged to her. This was the man whom Crabb Robinson called "the female Wordsworth"; the man who walked the lonnings praying audibly for miles on end; the man who moped about churchyards, sentimentally eyeing a young girl, in the last stages of consumption, looking on the spot where she was to be buried. Years later, when the wealthy poet had turned into a comparatively hard-up journalist, this was the man who could describe Windermere and Grasmere in a mixture of half-chewed, half-digested sentiment, archness, gusto and genuine enjoyment.

Such was "Mr Wilson of Elleray", as Wordsworth called him when he introduced him to De Quincey. But turn him the other way up, and John Wilson changed into Christopher North, the man who leaped across the Cherwell, who followed cockfights and boxed with cobblers and planned to explore central Africa with Mungo Park; the man who, according to rumour, had run to sea, had lived among gipsies, and had been a strolling-player, a barn-stormer, up and down the villages and small towns of England.

If, as some say, Christopher North was Wilson as he wanted to be, then Wilson must have been North as he really was. Yet, in fact, the one was a pose as much as the other. The innocuous poet of *The Isle of Palms* no doubt felt sincere enough, but he grew into one of the most unscrupulous journalists of the day—one who was at least partly responsible for the atrocious *Blackwood's Magazine* attack on Keats; one who could offer to review Coleridge favourably in one magazine and then go and blackguard him in another; one who could attack Wordsworth under an assumed name and defend him under his own. It is a portrait very different from that of the genial literary sportsman who, according to Canon Rawnsley, still remained in the memories of the Westmorland people until the end of the nineteenth century.

Yet perhaps Rawnsley was not altogether wrong. In spite of the pink poems, the sentimentality, the religiosity, the Lakes brought out all that was truest in Wilson's character. "Christopher" was only one limb of this character, but here, among the mountains, that limb could grow into a giant. "Christopher" was essentially physical in his nature, not intellectual, and his prose has more stamina than style, yet he often reveals flashes of insight, or, more truly, of *out*-sight, that surprise and captivate. The manner is atrocious—a swill of rhetoric, facetiousness, affectations, invocations, and self-conscious croakings in the vernacular—yet the very enthusiasm makes it bearable,

at least for a page or two. He can coax and wheedle as flag-
rantly as a seller of vacuum cleaners:

> Windermere! Why, at this blessed moment we behold the
> beauty of all its intermingling isles. There they are—all
> gazing down on their own reflected loveliness in the magic
> mirror of the air-like water, just as many a holy time we have
> seen them all agaze, when, with suspended oar and sus-
> pended breath—no sound but a ripple on the Naiad's bow,
> and a beating at our own heart—motionless in our own
> motionless bark—we seemed to float midway down that
> beautiful abyss between the heaven above and the heaven
> below. . . .

Or he could be as hearty as a commercial traveller with a
snappy line:

> So . . . let us descend to the White Lion—and enquire
> about Billy Balmer. Honest Billy has arrived from Waterford
> —seems tolerably steady—Mr. Ullock's boats may be trusted
> —so let us take a voyage of discovery on the lake. Let those
> who have reason to think that they have been born to die a
> different death from drowning, hoist a sail. We today shall
> feather an oar. Billy takes the stroke—Mr. William Garnet's
> at the helm—and "row, vassals, row, for the pride of the
> Lowlands" is the choral song that accompanies the Naiad
> out of the bay, and round the north end of the Isle called
> Beautiful.

There is going to be a lot more about that "Isle called Beautiful" (Belle Isle, of course) in the next few paragraphs, yet,
among all the gush and giggles, Wilson has an eye to stare over
the boat's side into "that downward world of hanging dreams".
He seems to respond not only to the sunlight, when "every breezy
hour has its own regatta", but also to the deep, green stillness of
the summer evenings, when the fells seem only the floor of a
strange, overhead sea, and the rocks are draped with dark,
green, underwater weed, and currents of mist move about like
shoals of fish or driftings of spawn. It is a stillness which belongs
to the lakes of Westmorland rather than those of Cumberland,
though sometimes it floats down the valleys to the lower
meadows, or even as far as the mining towns on the coast,

where the furnaces could once be heard purring and churring in the drowned calm.

For Wilson, in his own phrase, was one whose heart leaped in the joy of the senses. He first came to the Lakes in 1807, having bought a cottage and some ground at Elleray, above Windermere. Here, for eight years he made his home—so far as he made a home anywhere—and even after 1815, when he moved to his mother's house in Edinburgh, he continued to visit Windermere as often as he could. And it was here, in this house and among these hills, that the fictitious character of "Christopher North" was born into real life—though the name was not invented till 1819, and, for a time, was common property among the *Blackwood's* contributors.

We can see, from De Quincey's memories, how magnificently Wilson carried his part: a tall man, immensely long in the leg, strong and lish, with hair as yellow as corn and a face as red as a poppy, a fine, full, almost feminine mouth, and eyes (De Quincey always noticed the eyes), "eyes not good, having no apparent depth, but seeming mere surfaces". This, surely, is the man of Raeburn's famous painting in the Edinburgh National Portrait Gallery—a young "Christopher", long of thigh and flat of belly, still elegant in his abandon, with leather leggings around his calves, and a glossy brown horse beside him and the brackeny brown trees behind him, and all of it rich, wholesome, and very nearly edible. Move along the walls in the same gallery and you will find "Christopher" again, a few years older, painted in his sporting jacket by Thomas Duncan.[1] By now the pose is wearing thin and the girth growing fat; jacket and hair and whiskers are dishevelled in the wind, the hat is thrown contemptuously into the bushes, and the gun is planted butt downwards in the fern. There is a terrifying chasm on the left, trees and clouds are whirled round like dust in the sky, and every sinew is stiffened in a defiant determination to live out the dream to the last breath.

In 1807, however, Wilson was very far from his last breath. He was rich, free of obligations, fantastically healthy and energetic, and charged with an enormous voltage of self-esteem. He

---

[1] This is the portrait which is usually reproduced as a frontispiece to *The Recreations of Christopher North*.

soon made himself famous and popular, for he took to the dale
sports like a dalesman born. At Oxford, cock-fighting and
jumping had been among his favourite pastimes, and now he
was able to add to these the art of wrestling in the Cumberland
and Westmorland style—a style handed down, very probably,
from the time of the Vikings. In the eighteenth century, the
most celebrated wrestling meetings were held in the east of the
district, at Melmerby and Langwathby, the latter every New
Year's Day. Then, about the beginning of the nineteenth century, the Carlisle ring became important together with Egremont and Arlecdon at the edge of the collieries of the west. But
Wilson drew the sport back to the dales, organized a ring at
Ambleside, presented a champion's belt, and himself took part
in many matches in which he was "a varra bad un to lick". He
had the great advantage of an unusual length of leg, for in
this sport mere strength counts less than agility and a sense of
balance, and above all the knack of being able to judge one's
opponent's intentions from the movements of his muscles. This
is a sport where the competitors cannot rely on their eyes, for
they never get a glimpse of each other once they have taken
their stance. Instead, they stand close together, embracing like
dancers, each with his chin on the other's shoulder, so that only
the tactile experience of skin and muscle and bone can organize
a defence or dictate an attack. It is a good-natured sport, a
sport for the individualist, a sport, too, for the participant
rather than for the spectator, and as such it made a direct
appeal to Christopher, who was always ready to have a "laal
furtle". His example not only encouraged the game among the
dalesmen but aroused interest among the local gentry, so that,
indirectly, he may be regarded as the founder of Grasmere
Sports.

He was almost as much at home on, in, or under water, as
on land. In his early days, while he still had almost unlimited
means, he established himself as "Admiral of the Lakes", and
engaged shipwrights from Whitehaven to build a large fleet of
vessels at Bowness. Even after he had lost most of his fortune
and was living in Edinburgh, he still maintained the fleet, and
in 1825, with the somewhat embarrassed co-operation of
Wordsworth, he was able to welcome Scott and Canning to the

Lakes with brass bands and a splendid regatta—after which he promptly published an anonymous article in *Blackwood's* calling Scott "a tame and feeble writer" and saying of Wordsworth that his pride was "like that of a straw-crowned King of Bedlam".

At another time his water games were more boisterous and less ceremonious. Edwin Waugh has preserved the story of his visit to Will Ritson of Wasdale, as told by Ritson's grandson.

> "'T' furst time 'at Professor Wilson cam to Was'dle Head", said Ritson, "he hed a tent set up in a field, an' he gat it weel stock'd wi' bread, an' beef, an' cheese, an' rum, an' ale, an' sic like. Then he gedder't up my granfadder, an' Thomas Tyson, an' Isaac Fletcher, an' Joseph Stable, an' 'aad Robert Grave, an' some mair, an' theer was gay deed amang 'em. Then, nowt wad sarra, but he mun hev a bwoat, an' they mun a' hev a sail. Well, when they gat into t'bwoat, he tell'd 'em to be particklar careful, for he was liable to git giddy in t'head, an' if yan of his giddy fits sud chance to cum on, he mud happen tummle in t'water. Well, it pleased 'em all gaily weel, an' they said they'd take varra girt care on him. Then he leaned back an' called oot that they mun pull quicker. So they did, an' what does Wilson du then, but topples ower eb'm ov his back i' t'watter wid a splash. Then theer was a girt cry—'Eh, Mr. Wilson's i' t'watter!' an' yan click't an' anudder click't, but nean o' them cud git hod on him, an' there was sic a scrow as nivver. At last, yan o' them gat him round t'neck as he popped at t'teal o' t'bwoat, an' Wilson taad him to keep a gud hod, fur he mud happen to slip him agèan. But what, it was nowt but yan of his bits o' pranks; he was smirkin' an' laughin' all t'time."[1]

It is true that the man who lay hidden behind the jovial robot called Christopher was a very different person—nervous, self-conscious, uncertain of himself, morbidly sensitive to criticism, pathetically afraid of being found out in his libellous anonymities. But this person need not concern us now. Instead, let us recognize in Christopher the first man to respond, with the whole of his bodily being, to the challenge of the Lakes. To him what the Lakes offered above all else was the physical stimulus of air, sunlight, space, and water. The gush and

[1] Edwin Waugh. *Rambles in the Lake Country* (Manchester, 1882).

growth of bracken and grass, the bubble and bounce of becks, the whirl and wuthering of the wind—all this made a clean challenge to lung and muscle. A response similar in kind though much less in intensity had been made once before by Captain Budworth, but his was only the response of a one-armed, near-middle-aged, retired sailor, sewn up tight in his eighteenth-century clothes. Christopher North anticipated the freedom of the present-day hiker. He tells how he had seen beauty bathing herself in the pool below Skelwith Force in Langdale, and "running up and down the braes to dry herself in the sunshine, as naked as the day on which Diana first dawned in heaven". To-day he might still come across a similar sight beside some tarn in the hills, though hardly at so populous a place as Skelwith.

To many people, and especially to the young, the Lakes appeal most of all as a gigantic gymnasium, a place to soak the soot from the lungs and the grime from the pores, a place to sweat out and purge away the scum and waste that comes from living in cities. Of such John Wilson is the pioneer. His pastimes, admittedly, were not quite the same as ours: wrestling, jumping, swimming, shooting, riding, chasing bulls through the meadows in the hours just before dawn—"a six-teen stoner who has tried it without gloves with the game chicken, and got none the worse, a cocker, a racer, a sixbottler, a twenty-four-tumblerer, an out and outer, a true, upright, knocking-down, poetical, prosaic, moral, professional, hard-drinking, fierce-eating, good-looking, honourable, straightfor-ward Tory", said one[1] of his own clan. In his *Letters from the Lakes* (which he wrote in imitation of *Don Espriella* under the character of a foreign visitor), he gives an account of an excel-lent two days' tour which included all the then little-known western dales. But for the most part his pleasures were more dashing, releasing the pressure of those spirits which as a young man hurled his body across streams, and, as an old man, made him weep bucketfuls at the sound of his own rhetoric. For Wilson was no clerk, or mechanic or factory hand, no inhabi-tant of working-class street or suburb, no product of a century and a half of industrial urbanization. He came to the Lakes

---

[1] William Maginn. See *Christopher North*, by Elsie Swann (Oliver and Boyd, Edinburgh, 1934).

superb in physique, insatiable in appetite, and unlimited in funds, and if his gusto was in part an impersonation, a loud laugh to cover a timid heart, it was also immensely and endearingly uninhibited.

The literary society of the Lakes was by no means confined to the new poets. Most of the gentry, in fact, had little sympathy with them, and De Quincey tells amusingly of two Scottish ladies settled in Clappersgate, near Ambleside, for whom the ban of *The Edinburgh Review* was so absolute that they would never so much as mention the names of Wordsworth and his colleagues. The sort of poetry they admired was very different from Wordsworth's. Richard Cumberland's much-quoted *Ode to the Sun*[1] might satisfy their demands, or, perhaps, they might venture to admire the more advanced style of William Cockin, the editor of the later edition of *West's Guide*, whose *Rural Sabbath* was based on the example of that revolutionary figure, William Cowper:

> And now the evening visitings recur
> Of friendly intercourse, and social chat,
> Enliven'd with the elegant regale
> Of much-loved temperate tea.

One poet, at least, the Rev. Charles Farrish, attended the same school as Wordsworth, and maybe some may hear a croak of a caricature in his *Minstrels of Winandermere*:

> They call the mountain Saterhow,
> The grass is slippery to the feet;
> There seldom cows are heard to low,
> But the sheep shake their bells and bleat.

One member of the Lake society, however, deserves more serious mention, for she herself was a picturesque figure. Elizabeth Smith remains in the history of the Lakes as a shadowy form such as might belong to one of the gentler pastoral fantasies of William Gilpin. It is a form so vague, so sketchily defined, as to seem almost transparent, a reflection in a green lake, a shadow beneath the trees, a ghost even while she was still alive. We see her almost entirely through the eyes of

[1] See Appendix B.

HARD KNOTT
PASS

STOCKGILL FORCE by T. H. Fielding

friends, for of the fragments she left behind, the translations reveal nothing of herself, and the letters seem to have received the treatment one might have expected from an editor whose name was Bowdler. She was born at Burnhall in Durham County in 1776 and lived in various parts of England and Ireland before coming to the Lakes in 1800. Captain Smith, her father, had been involved in a business failure, and now, with the help of Thomas Wilkinson, he took a cottage in Patterdale, on the banks of Ullswater, not far from the spot where Thomas Clarkson, the Abolitionist, was living in retirement, and then, a year or two later, moved to a house on the north-eastern shore of Coniston Lake. It is a singularly beautiful spot and one which completely satisfies the demands of the Picturesque. The meadows are as elegant as any park, gentle, green and dewy, the rich wet grass trimmed with the darker green of lady's mantle and the wild orchids; beneath it, the lake, a still darker green except when the sun is tipped on it or the wind whisks up the surface; and round the bay in receding arcs, the stony village, the farms, the mountain pastures, blurred and softened in the mists from the lake and the smoke from the cottages; and behind it all, correct as a model composition, the great balcony of the Coniston fells—Old Man, Wetherlam, Yewdale Crags, Tom Heights, and, farther away, glimpses of Langdale Pikes and Helvellyn. Here, for three or four years, Miss Smith lived the life of a romantic young lady after a pattern which was already beginning to grow old-fashioned. She climbed the hills with Wilkinson, made sketches with William Green, read Mrs Radcliffe, surrendered herself with immense enthusiasm to the hypnotism of Ossian. Her only formal education had been from a governess, a girl of about her own age, qualified to teach no more than French, yet she showed quite a remarkable talent for languages. As well as French, she taught herself Italian, Spanish, German, Latin, Greek and Hebrew, and acquired some knowledge of Arabic and Persian and a smattering of Welsh and Erse. She made a good many translations, especially from German and Hebrew, yet, with all her eager bookishness, she never seems to have felt the least curiosity about Wordsworth, or anything he had written, even though both Wilkinson and Green were friends of his.

It was not her learning, however, but her early death which aroused the interest of the literary Lakers, and especially of De Quincey. Slight, shadowy as her figure had always been, it now grew even less substantial. She seems slowly to have merged into her own element as a patch of stained water is gradually absorbed into the general colour and texture of the whole pond. She herself, in conversation with an old servant of the family, described the beginning of the metamorphosis:

> One very hot evening in July, I took a book, and walked about two miles from home, where I seated myself on a stone beside the Lake. Being much engaged by a poem I was reading, I did not perceive that the sun was gone down, and was succeeded by a very heavy dew; till in a moment I felt struck on the chest as if with a sharp knife. I returned home, but said nothing of the pain. The next day, being also very hot, and every one busy in the hay-field, I thought I would take a rake, and work very hard, to produce perspiration, in the hope that it might remove the pain, but it did not.

It was consumption, of course, and though the doctors of that age could do nothing to cure her, at least they let her decline in peace. After trying the spurious remedies of Bath and Matlock, she was allowed to return to Coniston, where she spent most of the day in a tent on the lawn—from which the house built near by is called Tent Lodge to this day. She died in August 1806, aged twenty-nine, fading out, melting away, without resentment, without bitterness, as quietly, as sweetly as the evaporation of early morning rain. It was—and I say this not unaware of the poignancy of her story—the almost perfect picturesque death: the gentle progression from the lesser fantasy to the greater, from the known to the unknown, the unnoticed going down of the sun, the book of poetry, the mountains, the shadows, the darkness. And eight miles away, unrecognized, unsought-for, unread, was living the greatest poet of her age . . . of all the men from the beginning of time, says De Quincey, the one whom he most fervently desired to see.

For, to De Quincey, when he first came to Westmorland, the mountains, the dales, the meadows and meres meant nothing but Wordsworth. Southey, Coleridge, John Wilson, each

had his own independent reason for coming, but with De
Quincey it was Wordsworth first and Wordsworth all the time.
He wrote to the poet impetuously in 1803 when he was seventeen, describing himself as "ready (I speak from the heart) to
sacrifice even his life". Wordsworth replied cautiously, no more
than a vague invitation to Grasmere which De Quincey twice
tried to accept in the next year or so. Once he turned back at
Coniston, and once he got as far as Hammerscar, where he
could look into Grasmere and across to the lake with "its
solemn ark-like island" and the woods on the far shore. Each
time his courage failed him, but in 1807 another opportunity
arose. Coleridge, who was then staying at Bristol, had been
engaged to give a series of lectures in London, and was therefore unable to travel to Keswick as had been planned. This left
Mrs Coleridge and the three children without an escort for the
journey, and De Quincey, hearing of their predicament, offered
to accompany them in a post-chaise. The journey, with a stay
at Liverpool, took ten or twelve days, and the party reached
Grasmere on a late winter afternoon in December.

De Quincey's description of that first meeting with Wordsworth belongs among the classics of English prose. In fact, his
portrait is one of the few that we have in which the poet seems
to move. There is an immense amount of information about
Wordsworth, masses of correspondence, diaries, memoirs, and
innumerable accounts of tea with the old man of Rydal. But
the features are set in that familiar, stiff expression; the figure
is rigid as a daguerreotype. There is never a smile, never a
gesture; scarcely an anecdote that is revealing, scarcely a remark that is memorable. Rarely, outside his own poems and
his sister's letters, do we get a glimpse of the living man who
inspired (one might almost say "exacted") such devotion and
loyalty for so many years. Not that De Quincey's portrait
reveals a lovable personality. He wrote with understandable
resentment at the lack of response to his proffered discipleship.
For Wordsworth is one of the supreme examples of the egoist
in poetry. He could not be bothered with disciples; he could
not be bothered with admirers, except when he wanted criticism or encouragement. He knew that he had to drive all his
faculties, all his powers of experience, for the one purpose. The

poetry justified the egoism. And afterwards, when there was no more poetry to speak of, the egoism continued as a habit.

But the personality in De Quincey's portrait, if it is not lovable, is certainly alive. Wordsworth, coming quickly through the gate of Dove Cottage, "a tallish man", holding out his hand; Wordsworth, dragging his delicate visitor round Grasmere and Rydal, six miles in the pouring rain of midwinter; Wordsworth, hacking his way through his friend's books with a buttery table-knife—these are sketches on which the ink is not yet dry. From De Quincey we can gauge the enormous power of the poet's personality, that sense of adventure, of new beginnings, new potentialities, which, to his contemporaries, seemed to give his work the force not just of prophecy but of revelation. We know that this is so, of course. We read in the text-books that Wordsworth revitalized poetic diction and opened new spheres of experience to the poet. But a true appreciation of this is blocked off by the dead weight of the respectability of Wordsworthianism—the Sunday School recitations, the picture postcards of Dove Cottage, the dreary centenary processions of daffodil-carrying children. Yet here, in this meeting of 1807, the urgency and excitement of Wordsworth's early poems still blow about the heads of his listeners like a mountain wind. Some of us, living today, will remember having had much the same feeling when we discovered the poetry of T. S. Eliot.

De Quincey's first visit to the Lakes lasted only a few days, but the next year he was up again for a long stay with the Wordsworths, who had now moved into Allan Bank. Here he became a great favourite with Dorothy and the children, especially Kate, the baby, who was to die before she reached the age of four. Later, he took over from Wordsworth the tenancy of the empty Dove Cottage, and, with the help of Dorothy, was able to move in towards the end of 1809. For the next year or two he spent most of his time at Grasmere, but in 1813, when he was desperately short of money, he joined Wilson in Edinburgh, where he soon made his mark in the brilliant literary society of the New Town. It was the time when the citizens were building the Athenic stage scenery on Calton Hill; when Raeburn was hatching out his portraits of

advocate or laird with the indiscriminate industry of a hen that
will sit on anything from a duck-egg to a marble; when the
nobility were leaving the Royal Mile for the promenade of
Queen Street, looking down the empty slope where soon Wilson
was to build his new house in what is now Gloucester Place.

Edinburgh exhausted De Quincey, and every now and then
he would retreat to Grasmere, ill with overwork and over-
excitement, his blood half-sodden with opium. The Wordsworths, with the pathetic example of Coleridge fresh in their
minds, had little sympathy with drug-taking, and De Quincey
felt a coldness towards him. His housekeeper at Dove Cottage,
old Mary Dawson, had annoyed them by refusing to let them
use the house while De Quincey was away, and now there was
to be a more serious obstacle to the friendship. De Quincey
had been spending much time with Margaret Simpson, the
eighteen-year-old daughter of a farmer of the Nab near Rydal.
In November 1816 she bore a child to him; in February 1817
they were married. Margaret was a girl of no education, but of
much sound and shrewd common sense, and there is no doubt
whatever that she made a splendid wife for De Quincey, and
that without her aid he would never have fought his way to the
comparative equilibrium of his later years. But the Wordsworths were shocked. To all intents and purposes they cut Mrs
De Quincey. The poet, it is true, never allowed himself to
gossip about his lost disciple, but he did nothing to restrain
or reprove the censure of the women of his household. It is,
one feels, a distressingly self-righteous attitude for one with
Wordsworth's personal history.

The effect of this estrangement on De Quincey is particularly
relevant for our story. It meant, first of all, that he turned
much more to the dale-folk for friendship and sympathy. In
many ways he was as helpless among them as a fledgling
sparrow that flies down through the kitchen window and can't
fly out again, yet they were not without understanding, and
were ready to give him the welcome and comfort which Wordsworth could not give. He must have looked an oddity to them,
with his tiny body, and his strange yet beautiful face, which
made him seem childish in boyhood, and boyish in manhood—
"One of the smallest man figures I ever saw," said Carlyle,

"shaped like a pair of tongs; and hardly above 5 feet in all."
His habits, too, were odd—often he would stay in bed all day
with the blinds drawn, and then turn out at night for long
walks on the dark tracks among the fells. In his room books
were piled all over the place, nothing could ever be found, and
his papers, his clothes, and even his hair were continually getting on fire. Of all the eccentrics who were soon to colonize
the Lakes, few can have lived so strange a life as did De
Quincey, yet, in spite of this, he got to know the dalesmen as
people, as *persons*, better than ever Wordsworth did. To the
latter they were all definite articles: The Dalesman, the Statesman, The Wanderer, The Solitary, The Pastor. To De
Quincey, they were William Parke, Barbara Lewthwaite, John
and Margaret Simpson. Wordsworth never knew his neighbours though in temperament and heritage he belonged essentially among them. De Quincey did not belong among them,
yet, in his own way, he knew them.

This knowledge, this understanding, can be seen in his
account of the tragedy of George and Sarah Green (*Early
Memories of Grasmere*) where he tells in prose a story which
may be compared with one of Wordsworth's pastorals, and,
indeed, it was from Dorothy Wordsworth that he got most of
the particulars. The Greens worked a poor scrap of a holding
in Easedale, and one night in March, on their way back from
a sale at Langdale, they were caught in a snowstorm, and
never reached home. Their five younger children were in the
care of the eldest, then about nine, who gave them supper and
sent them to bed. For two or three days they waited, feeding
the cow with hay from the loft, and boiling potatoes and a little
porridge for themselves, and then, as the storm began to sub-
side, the elder girl struggled through to a neighbour and asked
for the loan of a cloak in which to go to look for her father
and mother. In this way the news reached the rest of the dale,
and within an hour at the most a great search was begun and
eventually the couple were found—the man at the foot of a
crag over which he had fallen, the woman, dead of exposure,
at the top.[1] Wordsworth was away at the time, but when he

[1] This is De Quincey's account of the position of the bodies. Dorothy
Wordsworth says: ... "She was near a wall—and he lying a little above
her."

returned he set to work immediately to organize a relief fund
for the orphans. He himself drafted a short account to send to
personal friends, and Dorothy wrote a longer narrative which
was circulated in high society. The Queen and three of her
daughters subscribed to the fund; Scott sent "two Scotch Notes
of one Pound each"; Samuel Rogers whipped up £31 8s
among himself and his friends. Altogether about £500 was
raised, and the children were adopted or taken on as servants
by various families of the district—the Wordsworths themselves
accepting responsibility for Sally, for which they had reason,
eventually, to be sorry, for one day, when she was supposed to be
nursing little Kate, she put her down on the floor while she
made some porridge, and the child ate great handfuls of raw
carrot which she found lying about, and so brought on the violent sickness which was probably the main cause of her death.

De Quincey tells the story of the Greens with tenderness and
with real knowledge of the dales, of the dale-folk and of the
life they lived. Yet there is an odd division between the writer
and his subject. It is not detachment, for De Quincey was far
too compassionate to be detached : it is more that the *at*tach-
ment is too conscious, too much a matter of choice; that it has
a faint hint of the sentimental, and a still fainter hint of condescending. "That night," says De Quincey, "in little peaceful
Easedale, six children sat by a peat fire, expecting the return of
their parents upon whom they depended for their daily bread"
—and at once we realize that this is a very different place from
the Greenhead Ghyll of *Michael*, only a mile or two on the
other side of Grasmere dale. The picture is accurate, but there
is a faint glow from the peat fire. If we think rationally for a
moment we will realize that, after all, it is not very unusual for
children of nine and under to be dependent on their parents.
But De Quincey does not want us to think rationally. He wants,
like Thomson, to colour his landscape with the emotions, to
heighten his figures with sentiment. Grasmere to him was not
just the real place of houses and rocks and people; it was the
unattainable Eden, the land of the primitive, of the Noble
Savage. In spite of all the years he spent there, it was never so
much a home as a refuge. Among his *Constituents of Human
Happiness*, drawn up in 1805 partly at Coniston and partly at

Everton, he includes: "A fixed, and not merely temporary, residence in some spot of eminent beauty." And later, when he spent most of his time in Edinburgh, it was to the Lakes that he returned again and again as to a retreat, almost as to a sanatorium. He never saw Grasmere as the centre of his world. That centre was always the capital, London or Edinburgh, and he was fascinated by the power of the centre, by the control of the pattern, the shaping and ordering of the whole. He was fascinated by an organization like that of the mail-coaches, by the thought of thousands of miles of roads converging on one city. However far he might be from London, he was conscious of its magnetic pull, drawing to itself the wealth, the trade, the ambitions of every part of the island:

> ... a suction so powerful, felt along radii so vast, and a consciousness, at the same time, that upon other radii still more vast, both by land and by sea, the same suction is operating, night and day, summer and winter, and hurrying for ever into one centre the infinite means needed for her infinite purposes, and the endless tributes to the skill or to the luxury of her endless population, crowds the imagination with a pomp to which there is nothing corresponding upon this planet, either amongst the things that have been or the things that are.[1]

Grasmere may have provided his dream of peace, but London provided his dream of power.

De Quincey, in fact, for all his greater knowledge of the district and the people, was in the direct line of succession from the Picturesque. It is true that he could laugh at those who rushed through the Lake District "as if their chief purpose in coming were to rush back again like the shifting of a monsoon". It is true that he had no patience whatever with the stunts that the fashion gave rise to, such as that of climbing Skiddaw to see a sunrise that would have looked much more effective from below. It is true, too, that when he surrendered himself now and again to the stock responses of the cult, he did so with a flicker of irony on his face, doing as the Romans did in order to savour more subtly the experience of not being a Roman:

[1] De Quincey. *Autobiography.*

All I remember is—that through those most romantic woods and rocks of Stybarren—through those most romantic of parks then belonging to the Duke of Norfolk, viz. Gobarrow Park—we saw alternately for four miles, the most grotesque and the most awful spectacles—

> Abbey windows
> And Moorish temples of the Hindoos,

all fantastic, all as unreal and shadowy as the moonlight which created them.[1]

He wrote that passage, with Mrs Radcliffe as his model, of the descent from Kirkstone Pass. Of the top of that pass, of the "Kirk Stone" itself, with no model at all but the motets and madrigals of the seventeenth-century divines, he wrote one of his loveliest fantasias of contrapuntal prose:

> The church [i.e. the stone]—which is but a phantom of man's handiwork—might, however, really be mistaken for such, were it not that the rude and almost inaccessible state of the adjacent ground proclaims the truth. As to size, *that* is remarkably difficult to estimate upon wild heaths or mountain solitudes, where there are no leadings through gradations of distance, nor any artificial standards, from which height or breadth can be properly deduced. This mimic church, however, has a peculiarly fine effect in this wild situation, which leaves so far below the tumults of this world; the phantom church, by suggesting the phantom and evanescent image of a congregation, where never congregation met; of the pealing organ, where never sound was heard except of wild natural notes, or else of the wind rushing through these mighty gates of everlasting rock—in this way, the fanciful image that accompanies the traveller on his road, for half a mile or more, serves to bring out the antagonist feeling of intense and awful solitude, which is the natural and presiding sentiment—the *religio loci*—that broods for ever over the romantic pass.

The style, there, is unmistakably De Quincey's; the tone is oddly like that of Wordsworth. There is a deeply-felt, sensuous, almost animal, emotion analysed stubbornly and persistently down to the precise impressions which have given rise to it;

[1] De Quincey: *Recollections of the Lake Poets.*

there is the deliberate measurement of a non-human world by an essentially humanist perspective; there is the characteristic and familiar image of brooding. Here, surely, are the words of one who has moved a long way beyond the æstheticism of Gilpin, the sensationalism of Hutchinson, the fancy-dress fantasy of Mrs Radcliffe. And that, indeed, is true. De Quincey had left behind the pretences and self-deceptions of the early travellers. He does not distort what he sees. He does not confuse the external with the internal. He does not confuse them—but he chooses the latter. It is hardly an exaggeration to say that the Lakes were more important to him in his dreams than in his waking life.

For dreaming was, to De Quincey, a creative activity. It was "... the one great tube through which man communicates with the shadowy. And the dreaming organ, in connexion with the heart, the eye, and the ear, composes the magnificent apparatus which forces the infinite into the chambers of a human brain, and throws dark reflections from eternities below all life upon the mirror of that mysterious camera obscura—the sleeping brain."[1]

The connoisseurs of the Picturesque played tip and run with their senses. They used the external world to tickle their imagination and then pretended that their imaginings were objective truth. They mixed observation and invention, real and pretended, there and not there, till, like a clown in a hall of mirrors, they could not tell themselves from their own reflections. De Quincey scarcely bothered at all with the external world. It was there, of course, but its importance was to provide the imagery which was to be given shape and significance in his dreams. We can see the process at work in the series of three essays with the title of *The English Mail-Coach*. There is first of all the incident—the collision of the mail-coach and a small gig carrying a young man and a girl. The story is told factually, it would seem, yet with a curious heightening of perception. Even as he is passing through the experience De Quincey transmutes it into a dream, playing the double part of actor and audience. The mail hurtles along the dark roads between Lancaster and Preston, the driver is asleep, the horses run on with a

[1] De Quincey: *Suspiria de Profundis*.

blind momentum. It is nearly dawn but the moon is still up, and far away, faintly through the mist that covers the woods and the mosses, comes the sound of another carriage approaching on the same road. Every sensation, every vibration of that drive through the night is noted, drawn out, lingered over, and given the inexplicable excitement of a dream. It is as if above all the stillness, above the silence of the fields and the ominous noise of wheel and hoof—as if above it all there were a thin persistent sound, as of a piccolo trilling, very high up, almost too high for the ear to recognize it, yet unmistakable and inescapable and immensely frightening. By the end of the story the dream is already beginning to reshape the facts—since it is very hard to believe that the woman passenger really was killed in the accident, and not another word said or an inquiry made. And then, in the magnificent *Dream-Fugue* which follows, we see the whole of the material transformed by the art and genius of the dreamer.

There were times when De Quincey seemed to bring his dreaming consciousness into his waking life, making them one not by confusion of substance but by unity of person. In those years at Dove Cottage, for instance, the world of sleep and the world of wake were very close together. There was that strange Malay who knocked on the door, entered and lay on the floor, swallowed a large stick of opium, and went away without having said a word that anyone could understand. That such a figure got into De Quincey's dreams is not surprising. What puzzles us is how he ever got into Grasmere.

And there is that other incident, less grotesque, less incredible, which nevertheless has all that sense of batty significance, of mysterious implication, which is often attached in dreams to the most trivial happenings. De Quincey was walking from Grasmere to Keswick, at nine o'clock of a very cold, moonlit March night, and there, in an orchard by the roadside, he saw an old Cumberland farmer, a large mountain of a man, sitting in his shirt-sleeves, "moon-ing" himself in the bitter frost. The story is quite simple and quite daft, but as De Quincey tells it, that queer figure, ghostly white under his apple trees, takes on an unearthly glimmer, takes on, even, an unearthly beauty, which reminds me (preposterous as the comparison may seem)

of Wordsworth's white doe moving between the graves of
Bolton Abbey.

The great function of the Picturesque was to teach men to
use their eyes and to use their imagination, but they muddled
that task by confusing what they saw with what they imagined.
They used imagination, in fact, not to create but to distort;
they used it to tamper with the material world, the world of
the eyes, to trick it out and trinket it up with flashy, worthless
spangles and crackers. De Quincey returned to the true purpose
of the Picturesque, using his eyes to feed his dreams, creating
a world of the imagination which followed its own logic and its
own laws, free of the necessity of material causes, yet never
posing as a substitute for the material world. In the next chapter we shall see how Wordsworth worked in the opposite way,
using his imagination to feed his eyes, and concentrating all his
insight, all his wisdom, on the solid material world of the senses,
the world of rocks and stones and trees. Both were true to their
vision; neither tried to deceive himself or his readers. But, for
the moment, let us ignore Wordsworth's way and watch that
of De Quincey, as one of his hallucinations opens like a strange
flower in whose calyx are unfolded still stranger flowers that
float upwards and away, drawing their sustenance from the air
like the trailing tree-orchids of equatorial forests. It is a dream
where the knots and tangles of the past seem to be unloosed;
where, in language which continually suggests the *New Testa-
ment*, a penitent Magdalene is forgiven, redeemed and trans-
figured. It is a dream which starts from a familiar spot, the door
of Dove Cottage and the garden and graveyard of Grasmere
village. It starts with a loss—little Kate Wordsworth is dead.
But then it moves into the landscape of fantasy, and the loss
is healed, longings of many years are fulfilled, and the girl of
the streets whom he loved as a boy, the girl who was all lost
loves and all lost children, even his lost mother too—this girl
comes back to him, the exploring mind returns to its own
beginnings, the mountains of memory and the domes of dreams
all give way to a precise view of a London street. The mind,
stretching out to an enormous periphery, finds itself suddenly
and unexpectedly at its own centre; the imagination, creating
mysterious and limitless landscapes, finds that at the heart of

it all is the single, small, concrete, factual experience. The bubble reaches its greatest expansion at the very moment when it bursts. It is the *Reverie of Poor Susan* in reverse; it is the myth of romantic escape turned back on itself. It is the most wonderful and enchanting flowering of the Picturesque in the Lakes, and it is the cutting down of the flower; it is the drinking of the toast and the breaking of the glass:

I thought that it was a Sunday morning in May; that it was Easter Sunday, and as yet very early in the morning. I was standing, as it seemed to me, at the door of my own cottage. Right before me lay the very scene which could really be commanded from that situation, but exalted, as was usual, and solemnised by the power of dreams. There were the same mountains, and the same lovely valley at their feet; but the mountains were raised to more than Alpine height, and there was interspace far larger between them of savannahs and forest lawns; the hedges were rich with white roses; and no living creature was to be seen, excepting that in the green churchyard there were cattle tranquilly reposing upon the verdant graves, and particularly round about the grave of a child whom I had tenderly loved, just as I had really beheld them, a little before sunrise, in the same summer, when that child died. I gazed upon the well-known scene, and I said aloud (as I thought) to myself, "It yet wants much of sunrise; and it is Easter Sunday; and that is the day on which they celebrate the first-fruits of Resurrection. I will walk abroad; old griefs shall be forgotten to-day: for the air is cool and still, and the hills are high, and stretch away to heaven; and the churchyard is as verdant as the forest lawns, and the forest glades are as quiet as the churchyard; and, with the dew, I can wash the fever from my forehead; and then I shall be unhappy no longer." I turned, as if to open my garden gate, and immediately I saw upon the left a scene far different; but which yet the power of dreams had reconciled into harmony with the other. The scene was an oriental one; and there also it was Easter Sunday, and very early in the morning. And at a vast distance were visible, as a stain upon the horizon, the domes and cupulas of a great city—an image or faint abstraction, caught perhaps in childhood from some picture of Jerusalem. And not a bow-shot from me, upon a stone, and shaded by

Judean palms, there sat a woman; and I looked, and it was
—Ann! She fixed her eyes upon me earnestly; and I said to
her at length, "So, then, I have found you at last." I waited;
but she answered me not a word. Her face was the same as
when I saw it last, and yet, how different! Seventeen years
ago, when the lamp-light of mighty London fell upon her
face, as for the last time I kissed her lips (lips, Ann, that to
me were not polluted!) her eyes were streaming with tears!
The tears were now wiped away; She seemed more beautiful
than she was at that time, but in all other points the same,
and not older. Her looks were tranquil, but with unusual
solemnity of expression; and I now gazed upon her with
some awe, but suddenly her countenance grew dim, and,
turning to the mountains, I perceived vapours rolling between us; in a moment all had vanished; thick darkness
came on; and in the twinkling of an eye I was far away
from mountains, and by lamp-light in Oxford Street, walking again with Ann—just as we had walked, seventeen years
before, when we were both children.[1]

[1] De Quincey: *Confessions of an English Opium-Eater.*

CHAPTER TEN

THE WORDSWORTHS

WITH DE QUINCEY the Picturesque evaporated into a dream; with William Wordsworth it solidified into a fact. Obviously that does not mean that he was lacking in vision, but rather that the vision shone through the fact, illuminating but never distorting. It is not the vision, however, with which we are concerned at the moment, nor with Wordsworth's teaching about man and the world, his religion of nature. We are concerned less with what he understood than with what he *saw*, and with the part he played in the history of picturesque travel. We are concerned less with the poet than with the author of the celebrated *Guide to the Lakes*, and we must try to put ourselves in the place of the clergyman who praised the *Guide* in Wordsworth's presence, and then went on to ask if he had ever written anything else.

The first thing to remember is that Wordsworth was a native of the district, an out-and-out Northerner of largely Scandinavian stock. His father's family came from Penistone in Yorkshire, and his mother, Anne Cookson, was the daughter of a mercer in Penrith, himself of Yorkshire descent, who had married one of the Crackenthorpes of Newbiggin Hall. Now the Crackenthorpes were true Cumbrians, almost certainly derived from the Vikings who colonized the dales in the eighth and ninth centuries:

> Christopher Crackenthorpe men did me call,
> Who in my time did build this hall,
> And framed it as you may see
> In one thousand, one hundred, thirty and three.

(The words were carved on a wall at Newbiggin Hall by someone who faintly anticipated Wordsworth's genius.)

But the poet was not himself a man of the dales. He was

born at Cockermouth, which stands where the River Cocker flows into the Derwent, in the broad country that looks west to the sea, north to Carlisle, and south to the fells of Crummock and Buttermere. In Wordsworth's time it was a busy market town, with streets and warehouses packed tight in the angle between the two rivers, and a thousand or so inhabitants crowded into narrow courts and alleys. John Wordsworth, as law agent to the rapacious Sir John Lowther, lived in a large modern house inset a few yards from the High Street. At the back was a walled garden, leading to a paved terrace about twice the length of a cricket-pitch, from which you could drop a conker into the river. Here, in this almost urban landscape, among the limestone walls, the blossoming trees, and the riverside gardens, Wordsworth felt his first, breathtaking animal response to nature:

> Oh many a time have I, a five years' child,
> In a small mill-race severed from his [the Derwent's]
>   stream,
> Made one long bathing of a summer's day;
> Basked in the sun, and plunged and basked again,
> Alternate, all a summer's day, or scoured
> The sandy fields, leaping through flowery groves
> Of yellow ragwort; or when rock and hill,
> The woods, and distant Skiddaw's lofty heights,
> Were bronzed with deepest radiance, stood alone
> Beneath the sky, as if I had been born
> On Indian plains, and from my mother's hut
> Had run abroad in wantonness, to sport,
> A naked savage, in the thunder shower.

The limestone walls clearly showed that this was not the dale country. Their trimness, their astonishing whiteness shining from the deep green grass could not be found where Skiddaw was no longer distant. Moreover, they pointed west, to the ore-bearing limestone which ran through Cleator Moor and Egremont almost to the sea, so that not very far from Cockermouth were iron-mines and collieries and the industrial coast of Whitehaven and Workington. Thus Wordsworth's life from the beginning was closely associated with industry and the sea. His father managed the royalties which were making

the foundation of the great wealth of the Lords Lonsdale; one
of his sons married a daughter of the coal-owning Curwens
of Workington and became vicar of Moresby. His uncle was
an excise officer at the port of Whitehaven, and it was on a
visit to him, at a spot quite near to Moresby, that Dorothy
Wordsworth first saw the sea and burst into tears. Fletcher
Christian, the leader of the mutiny on the *Bounty*, was a pupil
at Cockermouth Grammar School round about the time when
Wordsworth was there, and Paul Jones raided Whitehaven
harbour when the poet was eight years old. Yet the sea meant
little to him—if he thought of it at all in later years, it was only
as the force which had drowned his brother. Dorothy alone of
the two responded to its beauty, and mystery, and mutability
—glad to catch a glimpse of it from Helvellyn; excited to see
it at Dover, breaking against the pier "with greenish fiery
light", or at Alfoxden, ". . . obscured by vapour . . . that . . .
afterwards slid in one mighty mass along the sea-shore; the
islands and one point of land clear beyond it".[1]

When Dorothy was six, she and her brother moved some
twenty-five miles farther inland to Penrith. Here, the very
houses took a different colour; neither the blue slate of the dales,
nor the white limestone of Cockermouth, but the red sandstone of the Cumberland Plain and the lower Eden Valley.
Here they were on the edge of the old Forest of Inglewood,
the land of Adam Bell, Clym of the Clough, and William of
Cloudesley. Here, too, they were within the range of the old
Border raids—not the continual beggar-my-neighbour of the
Debatable Lands, but the large-scale forays of the time of
Robert Bruce. The castle stood almost in the centre of the
town, a few miles off were the magnificent ruins of Brougham,
and close by, on the hill above what is now the cemetery,
was the warning beacon. There were also dangers less ancient,
dangers still living in the memories of the townspeople—Bonnie
Prince Charlie's highlanders coming south and Butcher Cumberland chasing him north again. Soldiers, moss-troopers,
outlaws, hunters, Jacobites—it was a land of brag and ballads,

---

[1] Dorothy Wordsworth: *Alfoxden Journal*. All quotations from the
Journals and Tours of Dorothy Wordsworth are taken from William
Knight's edition (Macmillan & Co. (one vol), 1924).

of luck and legend, cave and castle, a land as romantic as Ossian, as picturesque as Pope's grotto, as brimful of popular poetry as the authentic skull of a monk.

On all this material Wordsworth had an undoubted copyright, yet he chose largely to ignore it. Scott, who at Edinburgh was born no nearer the Border than was Wordsworth at Cockermouth, seized on the ballads as his heritage and pegged out a prospector's claim even as far south as the Solway and St Bees. But when Wordsworth uses a ballad theme he is interested less in what he finds than in what he puts there himself. The *Song at the Feast of Brougham Castle* is by no means just a song of triumph; the Lord Clifford's exile among the shepherds of Threlkeld matters far more than his restoration to the pride and honour of nobility:

> Love had he found in huts where poor men lie;
> His daily teachers had been woods and rills,
> The silence that is in the starry sky,
> The sleep that is among the lonely hills.

The sea he rejected, together with the evocative horrors of the coal-mines, and the romance of trade. He had no deep interest in history or in folk-lore, in ruins or monuments or the preoccupations of the antiquary, while regattas and museums and the tricks of the tourist could be tolerated merely as toys. He rejected, in fact, all the stock paraphernalia of the picturesque; rejected its sham ecstasies, its titillation of the senses, its self-abuse of the fancy. To use nature as a stimulus for a razzle of the spirit, a subjective self-indulgence, seemed to Wordsworth not just deceptive, not just silly, but sacrilegious.

Nevertheless, he admits that for a time he was tainted with the "strong infection of the age", and because of this had partly lost his youthful awareness of the "impassioned life" of Nature:

> ... Nor this through stroke
> Of human suffering ...
> But through presumption; even in pleasure pleased
> Unworthily, disliking here, and there
> Liking; by rules of mimic art transferred
> To things above all art.

It was, he defends himself, never much his habit, yet for a while—presumably round about his years at Cambridge—he allowed his natural, spontaneous perception to be blurred by the fashion:

> ... giving way
> To a comparison of scene with scene,
> Bent overmuch on superficial things,
> Pampering myself with meagre novelties
> Of colour and proportion; to the moods
> Of time and season, to the moral power,
> The affections and the spirit of the place,
> Less sensible.[1]

Against this he places Dorothy's response, less intellectual, more sensuously direct:

> ... from Appetites like these
> She, gentle Visitant, as well she might
> Was wholly free, for less did critic rules
> Or barren intermeddling subtleties
> Perplex her mind: ...
> She welcomed what was given, and craved no
>   more.
> Whatever scene was present to her eyes,
> That was the best.[2]

Yet he learned a good deal from the Picturesque, especially from Gray and Gilpin, both of whom he had read carefully, as well as Payne and Knight. He learned, for instance, to analyse a landscape and by doing so to store it in his mind; he learned to notice the varying effects of light on the contours of a valley, and to balance scene against scene as a composer balances movement against movement in a sonata. Speaking then, of the "wheel" shape of the dales:

> ... in the several ridges that enclose these vales, and divide
> them from each other, I mean in the forms and surfaces,
> first of the swelling grounds, next of the hills and rocks, and
> lastly of the mountains [there is] an ascent of almost regular
> gradation, from elegance and richness, to their highest point
> of grandeur and sublimity. It follows therefore from this,

[1] *Prelude* (1805), Book XII.
[2] *Ibid.* I have quoted from the 1805 version of the poem to show how soon Wordsworth had organized his opinions on this point.

first, that these rocks, hills, and mountains must present themselves to view in stages rising above each other, the mountains clustering together towards the central point; and next, that an observer familiar with the several vales, must, from their varying position in relation to the sun, have had before his eyes every possible embellishment of beauty, dignity, and splendour, which light and shadow can bestow upon objects so diversified.

But he realized that this æsthetic approach was only one of the many ways in which to come to the reality of nature. The canons of Gilpin were useful for training the eyes and the sensibility, but their limitations must be recognized, they must not be imposed outside the art to which they were appropriate. "I should be sorry," he says, comparing the scenery of the Lakes with that of the Alps, "I should be sorry to contemplate either country in reference to that art, further than as its fitness or unfitness for the pencil renders it more or less pleasing to the eye of the spectator *who has learned to observe and feel, chiefly from Nature herself.*"[1]

His æsthetics, in fact, were derived from nature. He observed the natural world and drew from it a code, and though he may seem, often, to use the language of the Picturesque, it is really the *naturalness* of art which is his basic criterion. Indeed, his language draws its meaning from nature, not from art. Even such key words as "sublime" and "beautiful" take their associations not from æsthetics but from such natural processes as glacial action, the buckling and folding of geological strata, and the erosion and weathering of air and water:

... The opposite sides of a profound vale may ascend as exact counterparts, or in mutual reflection, like the billows of a troubled sea; and the impression be, from its very simplicity, more awful and sublime. Sublimity is the result of Nature's first great dealings with the superficies of the earth; but the general tendency of her subsequent operations is towards the production of beauty; by a multiplicity of symmetrical parts uniting in a consistent whole.

All Wordsworth's criticisms of building, planting, "improvement", and so on, though they may be expressed in terms of

[1] *Guide to the Lakes.* (Italics mine.)

landscape painting, are in fact criticisms of an offence not against art but against nature. The thing looks wrong because it *is* wrong (in a biological, ecological, even a moral sense); because it is alien to and out of harmony with its surroundings. His well-known (and, to my mind, mistaken) objection to white buildings in the Lake country is a good example of this. He complains about them in language which comes direct from Gilpin: "Five or six white houses, scattered over a valley, by their obtrusiveness, dot the surface, and divide it into triangles, or other mathematical figures, haunting the eye, and disturbing that repose which might otherwise be perfect." But the real objection was not nearly so academic—it was that in nature "pure white is scarcely ever found but in small objects, such as flowers; or in those which are transitory, as the clouds, foam of rivers, and snow". If, one feels, one of the volcanic rocks had been found pure white, like a spar, Wordsworth would instantly have modified his argument. In any case, his general rule for all buildings, laying out of grounds and other alterations was simple—"work, where you can, in the spirit of Nature, with an invisible hand of art".

At the time of his greatest creative power, Wordsworth gave little thought to landscape, in the ordinary sense of the word. *The Excursion* had its long elaborate panoramas, but before this, in his best poetry, detailed landscape is rare. His work resembles the sketches of a master rather than a completed canvas. The multiplication of detail took too much time, it blunted the vision, and he rarely resorted to it except in the later years when there was no vision to blunt. As in Milton's *L'Allegro*, we are often left with the impression that we have been shown a landscape when in fact we have built our own landscape out of the one significant feature which has been offered to us:

> What's Yarrow but a river bare
> That glides the dark hills under?

Often, when we are given a succession of such features, the effect is stereoscopic. For Wordsworth rarely paints on a flat, static, surface; his pictures move and grow, develop and flower. Even in a comparatively casual poem like *Fidelity* he can con-

vey an impression of multi-sensual, multi-seasonal complexity
which catches at your lungs like a mouthful of cold air:

> There sometimes doth a leaping fish
> Send through the tarn a lonely cheer;
> The crags repeat the raven's croak,
> In symphony austere;
> Thither the rainbow comes—the cloud—
> And mists that spread the flying shroud;
> And sunbeams; and the sounding blast,
> That, if it could, would hurry past;
> But that enormous barrier holds it fast.

That is just plain description, but at his greatest, Wordsworth, like Blake, was gifted with double vision. With Blake,
the one vision subdued the other: the eternal shone through
and superseded the temporal. With Wordsworth, temporal and
eternal existed simultaneously, and both had the same shape.
The object becomes the image, it is lifted to a higher power of
significance—the fells looming above the boat on Ullswater,
the owls beside Esthwaite, the "tumultuous brook of Greenhead Ghyll". Yet always the image remains true to the same
laws which governed it as an object: the new significance does
not distort the old. Often, indeed, object and image, material
fact and symbolic meaning, reflect backwards and forwards,
each illuminating the other. There is a wonderful example of
this two-way traffic of allegory in *Resolution and Independence*. It is early morning, and the poet, in a mood of despon-
dency, comes across an old man gathering leeches on the moor
beside a pool "bare to the eye of heaven". He describes the
man in a series of similes, which open each into the other, like
a system of valleys among the hills:

> As a huge stone is sometimes seen to lie
> Couched on the bald top of an eminence;
> Wonder to all who do the same espy,
> By what means it could thither come, and whence;
> So that it seems a thing endued with sense;
> Like a sea-beast crawled forth, that on a shelf
> Of rock or sand reposeth, there to sun itself;
> Such seemed this man.

It is a magnificent image, conveying the loneliness, the poverty and ruggedness, even the grandeur, of the old man, and almost equating him with the landscape, making him part of the background against which he is seen. And at the same time, it is a most superb evocation of the rocks themselves, while the shapes of the sea-beasts seem to hint at the theory of the Ice Age and the geological origin of the erratic boulders.

For such understanding, such interpretation, "observation" is too small a word. The poet was observing, certainly, and observing with all his senses at once, observing—if the term may be so used—with his breathing, with the nerves of his skin, and with the beat of his blood. The senses seem to *convey* information as much as to receive it—the poet identifies himself with the object, shares its experience and even allows it to share *his*. Yet this reciprocity of understanding rarely happens with a landscape, a view, but nearly always with some fragment of nature. Often quite a tiny fragment, which can be seen whole, can be swallowed, as it were, at one gulp. There is the ash, at Aira Force, that

> ... in seeming silence makes
> A soft eye-music of slow-waving boughs.

There is the grass in *The Idiot Boy*, so quiet the night, "you almost hear it growing". There is, most exquisite of all, *The Green Linnet*:

> Amid yon tuft of hazel trees,
> That twinkle to the gusty breeze,
> Behold him perched in ecstasies,
>   Yet seeming still to hover;
> There! where the flutter of his wings
> Upon his back and body flings
> Shadows and sunny glimmerings,
>   That cover him all over.

That poem, so unmistakably Wordsworthian, does not, however, belong exclusively to William. It belongs also to Dorothy. Whether or not it was suggested by the note[1] in her journal for

[1] "The little birds busy making love, and pecking the blossoms and bits of moss off the trees. They flutter about and about, and thrid the trees as I lie under them." Grasmere Journal: 5 June 1800. *The Journals of Dorothy Wordsworth*, ed. by E. de Selincourt (2 vols, Macmillan, 1941).

the 4th of June 1800, there can be no doubt whatever that this kind of response, so tremulously sensitive, was enjoyed as much by her as by her brother or by Coleridge. In a way the faculty was hers more truly than theirs. She could not translate the delights into symbols, she drew no philosophical or moral principles from them, but she gave herself to them with a gladness and wholeness of surrender which neither of the poets could excel. For a while, at Alfoxden, there was a triple response, shared by them all, but it was Dorothy alone who retained her quivering sensitivity until middle age, and paid for it by the stony insensibility of her last years. The occasional correspondences between passages in Dorothy's journal and the poems of both William and Coleridge are well known. There is, for instance, an entry which seems to have evoked the image of the White Doe in the graveyard of Bolton Abbey; and there is the better-known example of the daffodils in Gowbarrow Park. There are entries, too, which anticipate lines in the first part of *Christabel*: the late spring, the night "chilly but not dark", the mastiff howling to the moon, and the one dead leaf dancing round and round at the top of the withered bough. At least once she came much nearer to poetry in her simple record than did her brother in the verses[1] he wrote at the same time. It was a Good Friday morning beside Brother's Water:

> There was the gentle flowing of the stream, the glittering, lively lake, green fields without a living creature to be seen on them, behind us, a flat pasture with forty-two cattle feeding; to our left, the road leading to the hamlet. No smoke there, the sun shone on the bare roofs. The people were at work ploughing, harrowing, and sowing . . . a dog barking now and then, cocks crowing, birds twittering, the snow in patches at the top of the highest hills, yellow palms, purple and green twigs on the birches, ashes with their glittering spikes quite bare.[2]

It is not necessary to infer from this that the two poets deliberately copied from Dorothy's journal. It would be truer to say that both journal and poems celebrate many experiences

[1] *Written in March*: "The cock is crowing . . . etc."
[2] Grasmere Journal: 16 April 1802.

which were almost communal, experiences not so much shared
as jointly created. Dorothy, perhaps, having better eyesight
that her brother, was first to notice; Coleridge, if he were
there, found the image; Wordsworth found the words. In the
Excursion on the Banks of Ullswater, written in 1805 and re-
hashed by Wordsworth in his *Guide*, she describes the larger of
the Rydal islands reflected in the water: "... as I remember
once in particular to have seen it with dear Coleridge, when
either he or William observed that the rocky shore, spotted and
streaked with purplish brown heath, and its image in the water
were together like an immense caterpillar, such as, when we
were children, we used to call *Woolly Boys*, from their hairy
coats."

The fancy, one feels certain, was Coleridge's, and was lovingly remembered and recorded by Dorothy to be given to the
world eventually in William's more precise but less spontaneous
language.[1]

For among all the immeasurable mileage of Lake District
prose, Dorothy Wordsworth's Grasmere journals are supreme.
Of course, she did not think she was writing prose at all. She
had her own delicate felicities—speaking, long before Keats,
of "that noiseless noise which lives in the summer air"—but
she did not try to gather and shape her phrases into full periods.
When she did try—as, for instance, in the draft which she
prepared for possible publication of her *Recollections of a Tour
made in Scotland*— she was altogether more stodgy, more conventional both in phrase and in point of view. But here, in the
journals, her hands have the quick, living, nervous movements
of an artist sketching from life. The movements are not a
definition of the image, a line drawn round the thought—they
are part of the physical act of seeing. They are not observation
but experience. Here is the Lake district as it looked, as it felt,
to one exquisitely gifted person one hundred and fifty years
ago.

---

[1] "We noticed, as we passed, that the line of the grey rocky shore of that
island, shaggy with variegated bushes and shrubs, and spotted and striped
with purplish brown heath, indistinguishably blending with its image reflected in the still water, produced a curious resemblance, both in form
and colour, to a richly-coated caterpillar, as it might appear through a
magnifying glass of extraordinary power."

The whole record is infinitely more real, more tangible, because it was not intended to be a record at all. Dorothy made no attempt at systematic description. In all her Grasmere journals there is scarcely a single "view"—she left such things to her brother, and was probably quite content to believe that his *Guide* was an accomplishment far beyond her own powers. Again, though she has no intention of depicting the social life of the dales, her studies of the people are more convincing, more fundamentally true, than those left by any of her contemporaries. Even William's superb portraits—Michael, the old leech-gatherer, the widow of the first book of *The Excursion*—are invested with a nobility that came more from the poet's mind than from the subject. But in Dorothy's eyes they were all completely alive and completely themselves. She was interested in everybody she met, and she had a way of gaining the confidence, of worming out the secrets, of the most diverse characters—from an old sailor on tramp to a painfully self-conscious genius like De Quincey. Her sympathy went out immediately to all the many beggars who passed through Grasmere, and she had enough of her family's shrewdness to be able to spot a malingerer at sight, though even then she was usually too kind-hearted to refuse him. She did not hold herself back; did not moralize or sentimentalize about people, even the poorest. Once, on Dunmail Raise, she met a Cockermouth woman with a little girl—a woman of about thirty, who must have been a child in the town when she, too, was a child. She saw herself immediately in that woman's place, was greatly moved and gave her a shilling, which, from her own tiny income, was a good deal. Children always captivated her —she seems to have had a vocation for aunt-hood as some women have for the convent. She could remain disturbed for hours after having heard a child crying, and when she passed through Glasgow on her tour of Scotland she got down from her cart to give a ride to four schoolboys who were trying to jump up behind—she "would have walked two miles willingly," she said, "to have had the pleasure of seeing them so happy". She was friends, too, with all the Grasmere children, and delighted in the sight of "old Fleming of Rydal, leading his little Dutchman-like grand-child along the slippery road," the same pace natural to both the man and the child, ". . . the grandfather cautious, yet looking proud of his charge". Unlike most Good Samaritans, who find it easier to have compassion on the man found by the roadside than on the man who lives next door, she had the same sympathy, the same understanding for all her neighbours—Peggy Ashburner, to whom she sent some goose and who immediately sent honey in return; or the postman who went about half-double, with his box of letters strapped on his back. Even a Miss Hudson of Workington was tenderly remembered because she used to scatter flower-seeds in the fields round about the colliery towns so that she could take her mother to watch them grow.

In these journals we feel the integrity, the immediacy of those first years at Grasmere—not only the birds, the birches, and the breezes of summer, but the cold beds, the scrappy meals, the long journeys over the Raise to Keswick, battling against the hail, or crawling on all fours to keep on the road in the dark. On Dorothy, more than on anyone else, that time made great demands. There was the washing and baking, the endless copying of William's poems, unexpected visitors arriving any day and at any time of the day. There were the long walks on the fells, the innumerable shorter journeys to Ambleside and the farms for letters or for food. And all the while she was struggling between two loves, and understanding the nature of neither. For William, straining himself ill with his poetry, she ached with a tenderness which was half-maternal, half-incestuous. When he sat late in the garden she would throw a cloak to him through the window, and afterwards take his bread and milk to bed, and when he was away she would cherish even a half-eaten crab apple that he had left behind. Her love for Coleridge, on the other hand, though it was more normal, was more secret because of his marriage. She hardly acknowledged it even to herself, and certainly hid it from her brother who seems to have suspected nothing, though he resented Coleridge's attentions to his sister-in-law, Sarah Hutchinson.

All the time, too, she was feeling the full, sensual shock of the world around her, standing naked in a great downpour of impressions, feeling the impact with every nerve, soaking in the ecstasy at every pore. Not even her love could distract her —in fact, it made her more sensitive. She did not know what she was loving—Coleridge, William, the birds and the grass became all one in her longing and sometimes loneliness. She touched even the wind with the hands of a lover:

> ... Afterwards William lay, and I lay, in the trench under the fence—he with his eyes shut, and listening to the waterfalls and the birds. There was no one waterfall above another—it was a sound of waters in the air—the voice of the air. William heard me breathing, and rustling now and then, but we both lay still, and unseen by one another. . . . The lake was still; there was a boat out. Silver How reflected with delicate purple and yellowish hues, as I have seen spar; lambs on the island, and running races together by the half-dozen in the round field near us. . . . As I lay down on the grass, I observed the glittering silver line on the ridge of the backs of the sheep, owing to their situation respecting the sun, which made them look beautiful, but with something of strangeness, like animals of another kind, as if belonging to a more splendid world.[1]

There is so much in that passage which is typical of Dorothy Wordsworth. First of all, the intense personal feeling, the projection of an inner emotion into the world around her without ever distorting that world. The objects are seen like pebbles, as if through clear water, and the water does not alter the fact of the pebbles. And when she liked she could conjure up her images with astonishing economy—"The lake was still; there was a boat out." No one, indeed, in the whole of English literature has such a gift of evoking the natural world, of bringing it before our eyes, merely by naming it. The journal is full of examples: "A beautiful evening. The crescent moon hanging above Helm Crag"; "A very wild moonlight night. Glow-worms everywhere"; "Catkins are coming out; palm trees budding"; "The ground thinly covered with snow. The road, black, rocks bluish."

Then, when she wishes to fill in a detail, not John Clare, not Crabbe, not even her own brother, can catch the likeness more vividly or more swiftly. But she was no naturalist. She

[1] *Grasmere Journal*: 29 April, 1802.

was not able to distinguish between the song of the thrush and that of the blackbird, she confused the yew with the juniper, hart's tongue with adder's tongue, and she scarcely knew more than a score or two of wild flowers by their names. Yet she has that quick, confident eyesight by which a botanist can recognize a flower ten yards away at a mere glance, a glimpse of cut or colour, just as one recognizes an acquaintance in the dusk by a gesture or the shape of a shadow. Plants and flowers existed for her not in a blur of prettiness; they were all clear and bright and individual, the crisp of a petal, the curl of a leaf, each a personality to be admired, a friend to be greeted. There was ivy, "twisting round the oaks like bristled serpents"; there was the single bud of the honeysuckle, close to the wall and away from the wind, "as snug as a bird's nest"; there were the oak trees, "putting forth yellow knots of leaves", and the pilewort, or as we would call it, the lesser celandine, spreading on the grass "a thousand shining stars". There were the effects of weather and atmosphere which she noted and recorded as carefully as a young mother recording the weight of her child: "Nab Scar was just topped by a cloud which, cutting it off as high as it could be cut off, made the mountain look uncommonly lofty." Or the harsher more spectacular effects of winter: "The snow hid all the grass, and all signs of vegetation, and the rocks showed themselves boldly everywhere, and seemed more stony than rock or stone." And again, with a queer wincing tenderness, a longing as if to warm the world at her breast: "We stopped to look at the stone seat at the top of the hill. There was a white cushion [i.e. of snow. N.N.] upon it, round at the edge like a cushion, and the rock behind looked soft as velvet, of a vivid green, and so tempting! . . . A young foxglove, like a star, in the centre."

Then, in her walks with Coleridge, she had learnt—if she needed to learn—how to notice and appreciate the subtlest effects of light and colour. Grading, sifting, testing, tasting, she records more accurately, more delicately, than any water-colourist, the slightest, the most elusive variations in tone— from the winter wheat, "like a shade of green over the brown earth", to the island at Grasmere, lit by one beam in an other-wise clouded evening, that "arrayed the grass and trees in gem-like brightness". So, too, it was with the differing lights on her own lakes which perhaps she watched and understood better than anyone who has yet lived. Sometimes there were just "the gleams of sunshine, and the stirring trees, and gleaming boughs, cheerful lake, most delightful". At others "there was a curious yellow reflection in the water, as of corn-fields". Or there was "a soft grave purple on the waters"; and again, "a saffron light upon the upper end of the lake"; and finally, in an astonishing pair of epithets which makes one blink at its sudden truth, "the lake was of a bright slate colour".

Yet brilliant as these examples are, they do not reveal her response to nature at its most complete, most precious, most personal. For this response was not a matter of quickness of eye or deftness of phrase, not of observation or of knowledge, but of feeling, and of a feeling so unselfconscious, so un-egotistical, that it was an act of self-abandonment, an act, almost, of positive substitution of the natural world for the self, of object for subject.

I have already mentioned how, as a child, she had burst into tears at the first sight of the sea : this was typical of her throughout her life, until the pathetic senility of her later years. The beauty of the world did not just delight her; it *surprised* her. "The moon", she says, "was startling as it rose." And at another time, it shone on the lake like herrings and the stars flitted about like butterflies. These are not just the phrases of one who is pleased with a good image—they are the little spontaneous cries of one who is astonished, almost alarmed, at the newness and the wonder of the world.

To the wild, or half-wild, creatures of the fells and beck-sides she gave her heart almost as readily as she gave it to children. To lambs, and horses, and sheep-dogs, above all to the birds. In the early summer of 1802, she watched a pair of swallows building in the wall just above her bedroom window. They would cling to the bars, pressing their bellies against the glass and twittering, and when after ten days the nest cracked and fell into the grass, the birds themselves were not more distressed than Dorothy. Yet she was girl enough to be afraid of a cow, and would wait half an hour by a gate or a

path, trying to make up her mind to shoo it out of the way—
"The cow looked at me, and I looked at the cow, and whenever I stirred the cow gave over eating." Moreover, the flowers
and trees seemed to have this same life and personality as the
animals and the birds. There was a birch near Silver How,
which she often used to visit: "It was yielding to the gusty
wind with all its tender twigs. The sun shone upon it, and it
glanced in the wind like a flying sunshiny shower. It was a
tree in shape, with stems and branches, but it was like a Spirit
of water." It is not surprising that at another time she could
say that "the trees were more bright than earthly trees", for
not even William himself saw the world in a more heaven-fro
light. Traherne could have made himself happy beneath those
trees; Blake would have known their Christian names.

I have drawn my examples from the journal of Dorothy
Wordsworth, but it must be remembered that her vision was
shared also by William and Coleridge, each after his own character. "Vision" is perhaps a misleading term. There was nothing mystical about Dorothy's view of nature. It was a matter
not of revelation but of intuition and the senses, of physical
perception and sympathetic insight intensified and heightened,
but not changed, not different in kind from that of ordinary
people. Her view, therefore, is one which we can all share, but
only fitfully, only in momentary flashes. We can see the "gem-
like brightness", the "visionary gleam", more clearly in her
prose or in her brother's poetry than in the world itself. When
we look round not with their eyes but merely with our own,
the trees are just green again, the sky is just blue. The world
in which we live, compared with the world which they show
us, is one where the sun has gone behind a cloud.
    Indeed, this is precisely what the world was like for William
Wordsworth himself during the greater part of his life. The
senses, the nerves, could not respond for ever to the immense
demands made upon them. Dorothy lapsed into near-imbecility,
William—to whom the view had nearly been a vision—stiffened
his sinews and, almost deliberately, hardened his arteries. He
gained his soul but he lost the world.
    He lost, that is to say, the world that he had once known,

but he had not lost the world that we all know. "The light that never was on sea or land" was gone for ever; but the sea and the land were still there. In those difficult years when he began to realize that his vision and his creative powers both were ebbing, he turned to the external world with a new need, a new gratitude, almost a new passion. That world was no longer "an unsubstantial, faery place"; it was a world of "rocks and stones and trees". A world, in fact, of *things*. His mind attached itself to solid objects, as a creeper attaches itself to a stone wall. He began to observe and record their appearance with a new accuracy, photographic rather than imaginary.

"Their perpendicular sides", he says, speaking of the slopes of the fells, "are seamed by ravines . . . which, meeting in angular points, entrench and scar the surface with numerous figures like the letters W and Y." We know that this is true, and we are glad to have it pointed out, glad, at any rate, to be reminded of it; but it tells us nothing that we could not have discovered for ourselves. It is true to the letter and not to the life.

Yet it was the letter which saved him; saved him not as a poet but as a man. Saved him from years, perhaps, of disillusion, of disappointment, of spiritual impotence; saved him, perhaps, from the despair which threatened Coleridge and the stupor which overcame Dorothy. No doubt, in the popular view, despair, madness, or death would be a more appropriate end for a poet, but we have no right to make such a demand or to complain that Wordsworth chose otherwise. The strain of those fifteen or twenty years—the privations, the frustrations the self-dedication, the searchings, the strivings, the headaches, the sore eyes, the colossal effort of creation—left him exhausted, anxious, uncertain. He put out a hand to steady himself, and he grasped the solid world—a gate, a wall, a tree, a crag, a mountain. He had turned from the mystery to the fact.

There was a price to pay, of course. We see this partly in the narrowing of interests, the restriction of sympathy, the self-centredness, the conservatism, the petty tyranny of his old age. We see it also in his hatred of change, especially of change in his physical environment. He objected to the larch because it was a newcomer to the district; he disliked any alteration to a

THE RIVER DUDDON AT COCKLEY BECK

HONISTER CRAG
by T. Allom

building or a garden; and he strongly opposed the making of the Kendal and Windermere Railway.

Yet his new view of nature preserved his sanity and gave him consolation for the view that he had lost. He began to cherish the scenes around him with a new affection, not entirely free from the sentimental, but having, also, a kind of humility. Doves' feathers, rocks, bracken—he remembered the glory and he still saw the beauty, but what really mattered now is that feathers, rocks and bracken are what they are. Sometimes he found more than consolation. As he stood, leaning against the wall to steady himself, gripping the solid stones, he saw on the hills at least an afterglow of poetry. There was that evening of "extraordinary splendour" when he was thirty-eight:

> No sound is uttered,—but a deep
> And solemn harmony pervades
> The hollow vale from steep to steep,
> And penetrates the glades.
> Far-distant images draw nigh,
> Called forth by wondrous potency
> Of beamy radiance, that imbues
> Whate'er it strikes with gem-like hues!
> In vision exquisitely clear,
> Herds range along the mountain side;
> And glistening antlers are descried;
> And gilded flocks appear.

This was the mood of the *Guide*, or, to give it its first title, *A Description of the Scenery of the Lakes*. It was written in 1810, when Wordsworth was forty—a time when poetry had not yet entirely left him though its visits were intermittent, undependable, and rare. No longer could he take an everyday incident, a commonplace scene, and brood over it till it assumed a universal significance. He tried, many times, but, now, too often it was the significance which was commonplace while the description was inflated and grandiose.

In the *Guide* he did not try. Instead of describing particular scenes and searching for a meaning that he could not find, he was content to generalize. His generalizations, however, unlike those of the eighteenth-century poets, were not abstractions,

N

formal symbols, almost ideographs; they were the careful accumulation and organization of remembered particulars. He spoke first of all of the structure of the district: the valleys and ridges radiating from a centre. He spoke of the varying effects of light and of season, and of the differing surfaces and upholstery of fell and flank. He constructed lists of reminiscences, as Cowper did, remembering, for instance, the colour of the trees in winter—the oak, still with its russet leaves; the birch bare, "with its silver stem and puce-coloured leaves"; the dark green holly conspicuous in the woods now that the other trees no longer have leaves to conceal it. He begins to catalogue the visual memories of forty years; to tabulate and index, to make mental cross-references.

Occasionally, he will let his memory dawdle over some scene which never quite becomes any specific place for the reader, not because Wordsworth is confused in his thoughts, but because he deliberately suppresses the distinctive features as if rubbing out the signature. Yet the result is not at all like the identity-less portraits of Gilpin, much make-up and no face, for in every word there is the sign of passionate and prolonged observation:

> But it is in autumn that days of such affecting influence most frequently intervene;—the atmosphere seems refined, and the sky rendered more crystalline, as the vivifying heat of the year abates; the lights and shadows are more delicate; the colouring is richer and more finely harmonised; and, in this season of stillness, the ear being unoccupied, or only gently excited, the sense of vision becomes more susceptible of its appropriate enjoyments. . . . The happiest time is when the equinoxial gales are departed; but their fury may probably be called to mind by the sight of a few shattered boughs, whose leaves do not differ in colour from the faded foliage of the stately oaks from which these relics of the storm depend: all else speaks of tranquility;—not a breath of air, no restlessness of insects, and not a moving object perceptible,—except the clouds gliding in the depths of the lake, or the traveller passing along, an inverted image, whose motion seems governed by the quiet of a time, to which its archetype, the living person, is, perhaps, insensible:—or it may happen, that the figure of one of the larger birds, a

raven or a heron, is crossing silently among the reflected
clouds, while the voice of the real bird, from the element
aloft, gently awakens in the spectator the recollection of
appetites and instincts, pursuits and occupations, that de-
form and agitate the world,—yet have no power to prevent
Nature from putting on an aspect capable of satisfying the
most intense cravings for the tranquil, the lovely, and the
perfect, to which man, the noblest of her creatures, is subject.

Of all Wordsworth's prose, that is the passage which comes
nearest to his poetry. Yet how far it is from "There was a boy".
For already the poetry is only the glow after sunset, the once-
poet is beginning to feel safer with the world without than with
the vision within. And it is this very process, the shifting of focus
from the inside to the outside, from the imagination to the
material fact, which is revealed in the development of the
Guide during the last forty years of Wordsworth's life.

Its first appearance was quite fantastically inappropriate,
for it was written as an anonymous introduction to *Select
Views in Cumberland, Westmorland and Lancashire*, a book
of drawings by the Rev. Joseph Wilkinson. Now of all the
prints and engravings of the Lakes which appeared round
about this time, these of Wilkinson's seem to me incomparably
the worst. Many of the others were more fantastic, with mountains fuming like volcanoes, crags spearing the sky, and great
geysers of waterfalls spouting from every cleft and crack in
the rocks. Often, though they might be labelled "Derwentwater" or "Windermere", they had nothing about them which
could be identified, and were, in fact, largely ideal or invented
landscapes. This was not the case with Wilkinson's, which
were among the first to pay close attention to topographical
accuracy, often recording easily recognizable subjects—a
bridge, a house, a bend in a river. But they were stone dead.
The fantasies of the early artists nearly always have charm,
often spirit, and sometimes imagination. We know that they
are excited, even if it is hard to tell what they are excited about.
Wilkinson's, on the other hand, record a flat, dull, colourless,
lifeless scene—a scene in which the mountains hang as listless
as the backcloth at an amateur operatic production; in which
the trees look as if they had been cut out of paper and stuck

on; in which every lake has a boat or a sail, but the water is as stiff and sticky as a cold rice-pudding.

As might be expected, Wordsworth soon realized that the drawings were poor company for his *Description*, so he reprinted the latter in 1820, as an appendix to *The River Duddon and Other Poems*, and in 1822 as a separate volume: *A Description of the Scenery of the Lakes in the North of England, Third Edition*. This volume, which included a map and *Illustrative Remarks upon the Scenery of the Alps*, was reprinted several times, and then, in 1835, Wordsworth produced his final text, called *A Guide Through the District of the Lakes*.

The book was now frankly intended for the tourist. There were hints to him about the time of year in which he should visit the Lakes, together with a suggested itinerary and an account of two excursions, to Ullswater and to the top of Scafell, adapted, somewhat clumsily, from Dorothy's journal. To this the publisher had added a list of inns, distance between towns and so on. It is obvious that Wordsworth was now much more tolerant of the tourists, partly, no doubt, because they showed more interest in his poetry than did the local inhabitants. Partly, too, because, as he grew older, he had moved away from the people, the life of the dales and small towns, to the life of the gentry, of country-houses, of wealthy residents and fashionable visitors. He was rather like a man who, by mixing almost exclusively with foreign immigrants, begins to lose his native accent even in his own home.

The 1835 *Guide* was the final form of Wordsworth's own text, but the book went through yet another change, and a very significant one. In 1842, with the poet's permission, it was reissued by Hudson and Nicholson of Kendal. This version, which is often known as *Hudson's Guide*, was very popular and went through several editions, and can still be obtained at the second-hand bookshops of the district. The basis of the book is Wordsworth's original *Description*, printed in full, but the Notes for Tourists have now been expanded until they fill about half the whole. Wordsworth himself seems to have had some say in the compiling of these notes, and he also persuaded his friend Professor Sedgwick to contribute three letters on

geology, while another friend, the blind John Gough, supplied
lists of plants discovered in each area. In addition, the pub-
lishers added "Itineraries" and "Admeasurements of Distance", taken chiefly from Green's *Guide*, together with four
diagrams drawn by Mr Flintock of Keswick, designed to help
the visitor to recognize the mountains as seen from one or two
selected viewpoints.

As edition followed edition, still more notes were added, so
that the volume did not reach its full and final shape until after
Wordsworth's death. The fourth edition, for instance, of 1853,
contains two more geological letters from Professor Sedgwick,
together with lists of fossils and shells, and a chapter on the
derivation of local names.

It is easy enough to say that to some extent Wordsworth
was conforming to the interests and habits of the tourist, but
it is more important to notice that in his progress from general
description to factual data he was pointing the way for his
successors. The man who had once attacked the geologist with
heavy-handed irony in *The Excursion*, now helped to present
to the public the first scholarly study of the Lake rocks. The
Picturesque Traveller was already an anachronism, and the
future lay with the geologist, the botanist, the archæologist and
the anthropologist. The fells were solid again.

CHAPTER ELEVEN

MOUNTAINS AND MORALS

AFTER WORDSWORTH the true Picturesque was dead. Excited journals were no longer published: fanciful drawings were no longer engraved. The Lake books of the eighteenth century were written by strangers, but those of the nineteenth, by residents—men, often, who had given many years to the patient and unspectacular study of their district. There was Jonathan Otley, swill-maker and watch-repairer, born in 1766 near Loughrigg Tarn, whose studies led Professor Sedgwick to the Lake rocks. His *Guide*, first published in 1823, is the basis of all sound factual writing on the district. There was William Green, of Manchester, a surveyor, who gave up his profession and settled at Ambleside as an artist. His *Tourist's New Guide*, published in 1819, is the first of the Highways-and-Byways type of book, leading the reader up every dale and every pass with the certainty of a man who knows his way blindfold. Green's work as an artist was appallingly industrious and almost completely uninspired, yet he set a new standard in topographical literalness—a standard which has been maintained by most succeeding artists to the almost total loss of every other merit. The larger subjects obviously beat him—fells becoming mere outlines, flat and empty as a transfer pattern, but there is charm and what Keats might have called a "low surprise" in his lovingly conscientious studies of boulders, walls, bridges and odds and ends of rock.

The tourists of the mid-nineteenth century were quite happy with this literalness, but they were not satisfied by it. They needed something more. Times had changed and so had they. They belonged, now, to the middle classes rather than to the gentry; they came from the industrial towns rather than from the country estates and the university cities; they were business people rather than intellectuals. Above all they belonged to a busy, prosperous, self-satisfied generation, and they were not in any way in revolt against that generation. They no longer came as explorers searching for the wild, the primitive, the edge of civilization; but rather as good, honest, practical men, giving their families the benefit of their initiative and sobriety. Yet the plain hills were not enough. They needed the extra glow, the extra excitement which they had neither the imagination to discover for themselves nor the training to learn from art. And they found it in Wordsworth.

In dealing with Wordsworth so far I have taken care to avoid the heart of his vision: his religion of nature, his "mysticism", pantheistic or sacramental, whichever you will. It is a subject obviously beyond the scope of this book, which is concerned with a fashion, with popular fancies and foibles rather than with the more profound thought of the age. Yet Wordsworth's poetry now began to affect that fashion. For the agnostic, the earnest high-principled materialist of the Victorian age, it threw a glimmer of the transcendental over what was still rather a purposeless creed, an empty house rather than a new building. For the rest, it covered hill and dale, farm and inn, wagonette and picnic-basket, with the fat, yellow, comfortable warmth of religiosity. The Picturesque, which had once been æsthetic, was now moral.

The last taint of this attitude has probably disappeared from the cities, but it still lingers faintly in the small towns of the Lake border. How many boys, and, more specially, how many girls, have been prejudiced against the Lakes for life because they were preached to them as something they *ought* to enjoy, something which would do them more good than Blackpool or dancing or the cinema? There is a very important sense in which this is true, yet in classing the Lakes with Sunday School, in confusing the exhilaration of mountain climbing with the fervour of religious experience, it is clear that the open-air evangelical was deceiving himself just as much as the early romantics had done. An authoress like Mrs William Heys (the title is the one she herself has inscribed in the copy I hold in my hands: "R. Northmore Greville from the Authoress") went about determined in every nerve to see all things bright and beautiful. No woman of the 1790s produced her shudders and ecstasies more easily than Mrs Heys produced her principles and parables. There were sermons in every stone—and all of them sermons of the most acceptable, expectable, evangelical orthodoxy:

> I know a little church 'mid Cambrian[1] hills,
> A lowlier one methinks did never claim
> The solemn sanction of that honour'd name;
> No symphony, save that of mountain rills,
> The pauses in the psalm's rude chorus fills;
> Yet all our ritual asks is there, I ween,
> Font, pulpit, altar, and inclosure green,
> Where sleep the dead in loneliness that chills
> The inmost heart. But who can doubt, if there
> The bread of life, unmix'd with earthly leaven,
> Be wisely dealt; if those who do repair
> To that rude altar, seek to be forgiven
> Through Christ alone,—that lowly place of prayer
> Will prove "the house of God, the gate of heaven?"[2]

Now I do not wish to seem to ridicule the argument of these lines—with which, in fact, I thoroughly agree—when I say that they do not show the slightest sign of genuine religious feeling. Mrs Heys may have been unusually devout as a person, but as a poet—or would she have preferred poetess?—she was simply putting it on. Her sonnet was supposed to have been suggested by a view of Buttermere Chapel, but she had observed it so casually that she had not even noticed that there was no graveyard there at all. The chapel was nothing but an excuse—an excuse, however, for a picture very different from that which might have been drawn by Gilpin or Gray. The same "properties" are still there—the fells, the beck, the small, stone building—but the scene is so different that it might belong to another continent. Yet all Mrs Heys had done was to walk into another room, to look at the same scene through another window, through the Venetian blinds, the lace curtains, the velvet and tasselled ribbons of Victorian piety. It was a piety far removed from the broadminded, large-handed design of the eighteenth century, and from the bare, spontan-

---

[1] She means Cumbrian, of course.
[2] *Recollections of the Lakes and other Poems* by the Author of *The Moral of Flowers* (London, 1841).

eous faith of a Quaker like Thomas Wilkinson. It was smugger, smaller, prettier, pettier; it was the piety of the comfortable, the easy-going, the unworried. It was the piety which belonged with hassocks and lavender, which was placed on the piano and dusted every morning by the servants; the piety which wrapped up its ideas in mufflers of soft, warm, cosy words like "little" and "meek" and, softest and most favoured of all, "lowly".

The model for Mrs Heys's poem is, obviously, Wordsworth, the Wordsworth of *The Excursion* and the *Ecclesiastical Sonnets*, and if it sounds like a parody it must be admitted that the poet, in his later years, deserved to be so parodied. Yet as the century went on, Wordsworth was replaced, in the eyes of the tourists, by a man who had given still less excuse for the distortions of hagiology. Without expecting it, without wishing for it, perhaps without even realizing what was happening, John Ruskin became the new Sage of the Lakes, the Picturesque Figure, the Old Man of Coniston.

Ruskin belonged to a generation which had no need to discover the Lakes for itself. He grew up among people to whom mountain scenery was the most natural of joys—like water, food, sleep, grass and the seaside. His father was a wine-merchant who in summer would take with him his wife and son as he travelled by coach about the counties, calling at the great houses for orders. In this way, the boy made his first visit to Keswick when he was only five years old, so that the view from Friar's Crag became one of his earliest and most precious memories. Other visits followed quickly, and by the age of eleven he was ready to start on a long poem, the *Iteriad*, a jaunty mock-picturesque travelogue describing the scenes he was one day to know much better. But already he knew them astonishingly well. He was no poet, not even at twenty, so that it is not surprising that he was none at eleven; his lines have the hippety-hop of the horse-trap on a paved street, and his language is just what he had picked up from his reading. Yet already he has learned to see. Arthur Young, Anne Radcliffe, Adam Walker had puffed and blowed and staggered and swooned all over Skiddaw without one of them noticing nearly

as much as he did of the bare summit, the screes, or the long
crest of the ridge running off from the peak:

> How frowned the dark rocks which, bare, savage and wild,
> In heaps upon heaps were tremendously piled!
> And how vast the ravines which, so craggy and deep,
> Down dreadful descending divided the steep! . . . .
> Then turned we around to the maze of the mountains,
> All teeming and sparkling with thousand bright fountains:
> Where the brow of Helvellyn superior tow'r'd—
> Where the beetling Scafell so tremendously low'r'd—
> Tost confus'dly in clusters all barren and grim,
> While the clouds o'er their sky-braving battlements skim;
> Till, their scarce-discerned outlines all misty and grey,
> On the distant horizon they faded away.[1]

He returned twice, some years later, during undergraduate
vacations—searching for garnets with Wright, the mineralogist
of Keswick; studying the Westmorland cottages and sketching
the chimneys of Coniston Old Hall. In 1847, then aged twenty-
three, he was at the Salutation Inn at Ambleside, feeling so
despondent that from his boat on Windermere the water
appeared leaden and the hills low. The following year he was
back again, on his honeymoon, but in no better spirits, and
when next he returned, in 1867, he was in appearance and
outlook almost an old man; famous, worn-out, weary and
profoundly unhappy.

There have been many attempts to explain the tragedy of
Ruskin's life—the impotence of mind or body which lost him
his wife, and left him aching for love yet unable to take it;
which made him idolize girlhood and adolescence till he could
break his heart over a child and canonize her, after her death,
with the incense of madness. These we need not consider now.
Yet Ruskin was yet another of the sexually deprived or distorted who found consolation and comfort in the feminine
hollows and roundnesses of lakes and hills and the masculine
verticals of crags and trees. Few of his readers could understand this, yet, oddly enough, it was this very tragedy, this
weariness and despair, which caught the sympathy of the Lake
visitors. They, too, turned to the Lakes for comfort and rest,

[1] Ruskin: *Iteriad.*

no longer demanding the stimulus and excitement which had been the joy of the earlier travellers. The first great thrust of the Industrial Revolution had overstretched itself; the muscles were beginning to sag, the energy to fail. In the parlours, the drawing-rooms, the pews, all was still comfortable and secure; but in the back-alleys, the rotting cottages, the slave factories, there was the strain and anger of a society at one and the same time vigorous and stunted, opulent and starved. In spite of all the clangour of the railways, the grasp and grab of trade, the grandiloquence of empire, the flags, the dividends, the Harvest Festivals, the brass bands, the gold watches and Prince Albert himself, there was hidden somewhere in every Victorian a tired, rather frightened, rather lost little dog that wanted to crawl under the table and sleep. So the Lake tour became a rest-cure rather than an adventure, and the hills became a refuge rather than a discovery. And when, in 1871, Ruskin bought Brantwood without even coming north to look at the place, he was making the sort of gesture which many people of his time longed to make but could not.

There is, of course, little connection between the Lakes and the bulk of Ruskin's work. His immense studies of mountain forms were carried out in the Alps, not in Cumberland. Nevertheless, he is perhaps the culminating figure of the Picturesque, for in him are combined its three main phases—the æsthetic, the scientific, and the moral, as can be seen, quite adequately, from one or two of the few works in which he deals specifically with the Lakes.

First of all there is the lecture on *Yewdale and its Streamlets*[1] delivered to the members of the Literary and Scientific Institution of Kendal in 1877. Yewdale is a short valley, shallow and open, lying beneath the flanks of Coniston Old Man and Wetherlam, between the knobbly heights around Tarn Hows and the great bared teeth of the Yewdale Crags. In spite of the threat of these latter, it has little of the wildness and secrecy of the true dale, seeming more like a pastoral intake, a "ground", an outer meadowland of Coniston village slipped like a mat right up to the doorstep of the fells. Everywhere among the rocks there are huge clefts and hackings, gullies and ghylls,

[1] Printed in the volume called *Deucalion*.

down which the water spouts, yet the valley bottom is green
and lush as a bed of cress, the beck easy-coming, easy-going,
as if it had dawdled all the way down Tilberthwaite and never
heard of a waterfall. Only after rain, when every syke blows
like a whale, and the rocks are hung with slithers of water like
lace curtains against the black slate—only then the beck scrim-
mages among the boulders, barking the shins of the rowans
and hobnailing deeply into the bank at every curve and corner.

Ruskin approaches his subject scientifically. He speaks of
the volcanic rocks out of which the crags are formed, of the
way they stand above the lesser southern hills of Westmorland
and Furness as "the first rise of the great mountains of England
out of the lowlands of England". He speaks of the Ice Age,
the scooping-out of valley and lake-bed, of the erosion of wind
and weather, of the silting up of Coniston Lake and the forma-
tion of the delta almost opposite his own windows at Brantwood. Yet, in spite of all his knowledge, he is not really interested in the geological process. He doesn't want to know the
why and wherefore of landscape. He even doubts the erosive
powers which geologists attribute to running water, and makes
experiments with pie-crust to show that they do not really
understand the action of folding and compression. The truth is
that he himself did not want to understand, because he feared
that such understanding would destroy the wonder of creation
—and, indeed, since people continually confuse "How" with
"Why", this is just what has happened. "We cannot fathom the
mystery of a single flower," he says in *Modern Painters*, "nor
is it intended that we should; but that the pursuit of science
should constantly be stayed by the love of beauty, and accuracy
of knowledge, by tenderness of emotion."

He turned to geology, therefore, not to understand the way
the rocks had come into being, but rather to learn how to look
at them. He studied science as an artist studies anatomy in
order to draw the human figure more accurately. The whole
of the fourth volume of *Modern Painters* is an application of
science as an aid to vision, and though this method may have
been dangerous for the creative artist, it helped the ordinary
man to see the mountains in a clearer way than before. In *The
Seven Lamps of Architecture* Ruskin had defined the Pic-

turesque as "Parasitical Sublimity"—a sublimity which depended on the inessential characters of a scene. Thus, in the Picturesque, the shadows on a face become more important than the face; the featheriness of trees becomes more important than the trees; the broken shapes of rocks become more important than the rocks.

Yet in directing the eyes back once again to the subject rather than the picture, to the mountain rather than the scene, Ruskin failed, quite as much as Gilpin, to understand the essential nature of rock. He never succeeded, as Wordsworth sometimes did, in thinking of a rock as it might think of itself. He never succeeded, as Henry Moore often does, in feeling the shape of the rock as from the inside. He knew its outward shape and colour better than any man of his time; but he never penetrated beneath the shape and colour. Science to him was a branch of æsthetics.

From the very beginning he was attracted by the prettiness of minerals. They were among his favourite toys as a child, and we can still see them at the Ruskin Museum in Coniston— marbles, micas, barytes, quartz, coloured as curiously as a thrush's egg or a dying blackberry leaf, or grained like wood, or lined and shaded like a contour map; clusters of crystals, growing together, inorganically organic, like strange colonies of angular molluscs; stones with a tarnish of gilt like gingerbread or pocked and corroded and green as gorgonzola cheese; and large coarse-looking stones with the faintest hint or brushing of colour more delicate than any jewel; slabs of local slate, green or grey, grooved and ruled like the shaft of a Norse cross; carbonate of lime, like frozen dollops of tapioca; pincushions and barnacles and hedgehogs of crystals; lead, silver, gold; garnets from Scafell; copper from Coniston Old Man, veined with peacock blue, or dusted with green gold-leaf; hæmatite from the mines of Furness; great bubbles and blebs of kidney ore from Roanhead, and thin bilberry-coloured slivers and skewers of pencil ore. He arranged and labelled them; drew them; studied their intricacies of pattern and form; and finally he heaped them together and built them into the great, glowing mystery of mountains that Turner used to paint.

It was in this mystery, in the end, that he found his religion, not in the gentle orthodox piety which was attributed to him by the Coniston people. Yet, though the experience behind it was primarily æsthetic, it expressed itself, with characteristic Victorian practicability, in a moral point of view. At Brantwood, for instance, he watched a dome of cloud lying two hundred feet deep on the Old Man:

> Behind it, westward and seaward, all's clear; but when the wind out of that blue clearness comes over the ridge of the earth-cloud, at that moment and that line, its own moisture congeals into these white—I believe *ice*-clouds; threads, and meshes, and tresses, and tapestries, flying, failing, melting, reappearing; spinning, and unspinning themselves, coiling and uncoiling, winding and unwinding, faster than the eye or thought can follow: and through all their dazzling maze of frosty filaments shines a painted window in palpitation; its pulses of colour interwoven in motion, intermittent in fire—emerald and ruby and pale purple and violet melting into a blue that is not of the sky, but of the sun-beam; purer than the crystal, softer than the rainbow, and brighter than the snow.[1]

That is beyond argument the writing of a man who can see, yet it conveys no very clear visual impression. It conveys, instead, the dazzle, the glow, the exaltation—which is what Ruskin intended to convey. He taught people to see for the sake of seeing, and for the sake of feeling, and ultimately, for the sake of acting. The experience might be æsthetic, and the interpretation of the experience might be religious, but the purpose was always practical and moral. Here, for instance, is another kind of cloud seen from that same window above the lake:

> The most terrific and horrible thunderstorm, this morning, I ever remember. It waked me at six, or a little before —then rolling incessantly, like railway luggage trains, quite ghastly in its mockery of them—the air one loathsome mass of sultry and foul fog, like smoke; scarcely raining at all, but increasing to heavier rollings, with flashes quivering

[1] Ruskin: *The Storm-Cloud of the Nineteenth Century*—included in the volume called *Queen of the Air*.

vaguely through all the air, and at last terrific double
streams of reddish-violet fire, not forked or zig-zag, but
rippled rivulets—two at the same instant some twenty to
thirty degrees apart, and lasting on the eye at least half a
second, with grand artillery-peals following; not rattling
crashes, or irregular crackings, but delivered volleys. It lasted
an hour, then passed off, clearing a little, without rain to
speak of,—not a glimpse of blue,—and now, half-past seven,
seems settling down again into Manchester's devil's darkness.

There, you may think, is Hutchinson's thunderstorm, rolling
and echoing still. But God—or in this case, the devil—is not in
the thunder. It is that Manchester darkness with which Ruskin
is really concerned. After years of watching the weather, he
had arrived at the belief that the nineteenth century had produced a new meteorological phenomenon: "the plague-wind",
as he called it. It might blow from any quarter. It might be
wet or dry, bringing storm or almost static weather, but always
it was dark and bitter, blowing intermittently and malignantly.
It would make the poplars quiver with a ghostly feverish hiss,
blot out the sun or turn it grey with a thin persistence of
grubby cloud. All this, according to Ruskin, was due to the
pollution of the atmosphere by nineteenth-century industrialism. Taken literally, neither his observations nor his deductions
are very convincing. The prevailing direction of the plague-
wind, he says, is south-west, and south-west from Coniston lay
only the small iron-town of Millom with, a little farther round
to the south, the port of Barrow-in-Furness, then by no means
as big as it is today. The small scattered iron-ore mines of Low
Furness were scarcely any larger than they had been for nearly
a couple of hundred years, and the charcoal-burners had
already abandoned what was left of the woods. Between
Coniston and the mines were miles and miles of moorland and
fell, with bracken and birch to trap and filter any grain of
smoke which drifted past the Duddon or Kirkby Moors; and
beyond, south and west, were the Irish Sea, the bogs, Killarney,
the Western Isles, and half a hemisphere of the Atlantic. If
there was any spot in England with pure air to breathe then
surely that spot was Coniston. But Ruskin's wind, whatever
quasi-objective data he might bring out to support it, was a

spiritual rather than a climatic phenomenon. "Blanched Sun—", he says, "blighted grass,—blinded man"—the symbol is obvious, but there were not many who realized, as he did, that pollution was not confined to the mines of Durham and the factories of Lancashire, but was spreading, as it is still spreading, through the hearts and eyes and minds of a whole society. The gentry, the manufacturers, the professional people, blowing their noses on the stench and stew of the money-grubbing cities, rushed to the Lakes to forget it all, at least for a fortnight. Some of the wealthier among them bought or built houses and settled at Ambleside or Windermere. Ruskin, too, settled in the Lakes, but not before he had said, with eloquence as spectacular as a sunset, that the cure for the plague-wind was not a retreat to the mountains but a change in society.

The majority of the Lake visitors, however, took no more notice of this eloquence than of a match struck in the mid-day sunshine. Small home factories were set up at Keswick and elsewhere for linen weaving, metal working and wood carving, but, whatever may have been the intentions of the founders, the visitors looked on them merely as part of the art-and-crafty quaintness of holiday places. They seemed a survival rather than the growing edge of a new society. There was little here of that revolutionary spirit which had alarmed the leaders of *laissez faire*.

Gradually, with age, the old man grew green and mossy as a stone wall. Brantwood is about two miles by road from Coniston village, though less than a mile across the water. At the first glance, it seems to be on the wrong side of the lake, half-buttoned up in the woods beneath the low, rather shapeless Monk Coniston Moors;—but from it the fells are seen displayed like a piece of sculpture, a huge "reclining figure" with draped thighs and knees, in the hollow of whose lap lie the unseen tarns. And behind the house, in those same apparently shapeless moors, are all the hidden clefts and cupboards where an old man can potter about—two-gallon becks that cut their own two-foot canyons; rocks no bigger than a barn, that in their cleavage and folding, their weathering and wearing, in their terraces of niche and ledge, their hanging gardens of golden saxifrage and corydalis, offer a miniature model of the

GREAT LANGDALE WITH WETHERLAM

KESWICK LAKE
FROM BAR ROW
COMMON
by William Westall

Alps or the Appenines; beechwoods, bare of bracken or bil-
berry, where in autumn the fungi fume and smoulder and
glow in colours as rare, as strange and unexpected as any
mineral. There Ruskin went to earth. He made friends with
the farmers, and became a favourite, in a rather frightening,
austere way, with the village children. He helped to found a
savings bank for the workers at the quarries and the copper
mines. He became, as it were, a younger elder brother to the
two old ladies, the Misses Beever of The Thwaite (The "Garden
Enclosed") who, when he was away, could look right down the
lake from their house near Waterhead and keep a careful,
coddling eye on Brantwood. To the younger of the two ladies,
Miss Susie Beever, he wrote tenderly playful letters addressed
as to a girl of ten, for the obsession with adolescence grew
stronger in his old age. His dreams were visited by the ghost
of Rose de la Touche, now no longer grown up but a little girl
in her child's paradise of little saints. The village people became proud of him, first as a public figure and then, rather
touchingly, as one of themselves. On his advice, a favourite
maid is said to have named her two daughters Snowdrop and
Buttercup. His photograph was sold on postcards at the village
shops. And when at last he died, in 1900, not even so intelligent a man as Canon Rawnsley could stop himself from falling into a mush and mutter of sentimentalism, praising the
professor for everything except the courage and insight which
had made him a power in English letters.

That mutter, grown fainter and fainter during the last fifty
years, can still be heard in the Ruskin Museum if one stands
very still and listens very hard. There are many pictures of
course—studies of leaves and stones and fragments of sculpture; engravings of the illustrations to *Modern Painters*; engravings of Ruskin's local drawings, a sketch of Rydal, a view
of Coniston Old Hall from across the lake. But it is not the
pictures at which the present-day visitor looks—nor perhaps,
did the visitor of half a century ago. He looks, instead, at the
extraordinary bric-à-brac with which men try to preserve the
memory of genius—the master's umbrella and walking sticks;
his handbells, and the mallet he used on his geological expedi-
tions; his paintbox, with the colours still staining it like the

o

blood of a saint on the floor of a Byzantine church; his seal,
"TODAY" carved on the tip of a fist-sized chunk of chalcedony;
his tape-measure, bill-hook, Bible, certificate of matriculation;
a lock of his hair; and his funeral pall, designed and made at
the Ruskin Linen Industry, embroidered with wild roses and
"UNTO THIS LAST".

It is a strange jumble-sale of sentiment which today be-
wilders most of the visitors who pay at the turnstile. All true
understanding has long been forgotten; most of them have
only a vague feeling that he must have been one of the Lake
poets. Yet, when last I was there, two young village children,
having nowhere else to spend their pennies—for it was early
closing day at the village—came into the museum with which
obviously they were well acquainted. First of all they knocked
a vigorous, clashing, Bartok-like tune on the musical stones.
Then they went over to a case of minerals, and pointed to a
strange piece of quartz, golden, glittering and contorted as a
Chinese lizard.

"That's my favourite."
"Smashing, isn't it."

And from their direct and unperturbed response to natural
beauty—even though that response might be half-ironic with
the almost unconscious irony of childhood—I felt that here,
after all, were eyes that could see at least something of what
Ruskin had seen.

By the time Ruskin came to the Lakes the Victorian tourist
trade had already reached its height. Keswick and Ambleside
were well supplied with old and new hotels, and a completely
new town had arisen at Windermere—a town of boarding-
houses and shops, an inland watering-place with neither the
raffishness of Brighton nor the honest vulgarity of Blackpool.
Everywhere wealthy new residents were building their villas,
in a style derived, for the most part, from the Elizabethan,
but transformed by the dark green stone into something very
different from Compton Wynyates. The steep gable roofs, the
dark crag-like walls, the window-sills of grey limestone or
purple sandstone, would scarcely accept the discipline of architecture, and after a few years of weathering they seemed to

slump back again into rock like the artificial screes beside a quarry. The woodwork, often curled and scrolled, on porch and window and gable-end, seemed to try to bind the stone together, fencing and shelving it as with a dour, sour romanticism; while huge black rhododendrons unfolded shadows thicker and fatter than their own leaves. There might even be a motto on a stone sun-dial or a wrought-iron gate set in rolled-back walls. But the stone refused to play. It belonged to the chronology of the rock, and would not wear the fancy-dress of this century or that. It hunched itself against the rain and let the years grow over it like moss, and very soon it looked as old as the Old Man.

The age, however, was able to display itself more fully on the water, where, fortunately, it could leave no permanent mark. Steamers sailed to regular time-tables on Windermere, Ullswater and Derwentwater, and a steam gondola made trips on Coniston timed in connection with the trains. Windermere now held an annual regatta, a set of races for sailing-craft, less boisterous and less ingenious than Pocklington's frolics on Derwentwater. Maps, engravings, postcards, guide-books were available everywhere, the books often packed with advertisements. Visitors were reminded that *White and Sound Teeth* were indispensible to *Personal Attraction*, health and longevity by the proper mastication of food. Notepaper could be obtained headed with tiny prints of views of the Lakes—nearly a hundred views to choose from, or sold assorted in packets. For three and six you could buy a "scientific souvenir" of *Ferns From The Lakes*, with "specimens carefully mounted and enclosed in a tasteful cover". Somewhere a few of these must still remain—scaly spleenwort or rustybacks now rusty all over, and the feathery barren fronds of parsley fern now dry and brown as its own spore branches. The glass case was beginning to be lowered over the Lakes.

Yet there was one woman who was always ready to poke her umbrella through that glass, always ready to look shrewdly and unsentimentally at the real society of the Lakes—Harriet Martineau, who had already lived one life and fulfilled one career before she settled at Ambleside. She came, in fact, on her second wind.

She was born in 1802 at Norwich when that city was not so much the English Athens as the English Boston. She grew up in a society prim yet practical, puritanical yet liberal, which seemed to belong more to New England than to the old. It was a society which both stunted her and strengthened her. Her parents were well-meaning, but lacking in understanding; they gave her an excellent education, but starved her of affection. Her mother, by insisting that she drank a pint of milk every day, condemned her to years of indigestion and sour biliousness. She never had much sense of taste or smell, and by the time she was sixteen had become almost stone-deaf, so that of the five main windows that open on the external world only two were left to her.

All these circumstances of health and environment led Miss Martineau to draw back into her own thoughts like a spider into its hole. As with a spider, however, it was essentially a practical withdrawal. Neither Norwich nor the Martineau household encouraged the idler. Even religion—and Harriet was a passionately religious girl—was practical. It had no place for hell, little for heaven, but a great deal for morality. When Miss Martineau published her first essay, on "Female Writers of Practical Divinity" she was not in any way concerned with dogma, but only with the laws of right conduct. She looked on God, from childhood, as a schoolmaster giving instruction and correcting homework, and later, when she believed that she had learnt the rules, she was quite ready to manage her curriculum without Him. It was with this practical approach that she entered a three-fold competition for essays designed to convert the Catholics, the Jews and the Mohammedans, sending three anonymous entries, one for each section, and winning all of them. It was in the same way, after the death of her father had left the family comparatively hard-up, that she set about the job of earning her living by sewing, by the making of little bags and baskets, and by writing. And it was once again the practical rather than the imaginative side of her nature which brought her first success—the *Illustrations of Political Economy*, in which the principles of Adam Smith, Malthus and Ricardo were demonstrated in a series of moral tales for the masses.

Success, now that it had come, was spectacular. The King of France enthused over the series until he discovered the author's democratic sympathies. America gave her an immense and fervent welcome, until it found that she supported the negro slaves as well as the French republicans. She was everywhere fearless, unselfish and un-snubbable—not a revolutionary, like Ruskin, but a radical, the heir of the young Wordsworth, the young Coleridge, of Shelley and of Byron.

But in 1839, while on a tour of the continent, her health broke down. She returned to England, going for a few weeks to her sister's at Newcastle, and then to lodgings at Tynemouth, where she could be under the care of her brother-in-law. For nearly five years she suffered continual pain, sickness and exhaustion. She was led to believe, or led herself to believe, that her case was incurable, but continued, as well as she could, with her work and her correspondence, though all she saw of the world was a view of the harbour with the bare, blunt moors of Northumberland behind it, and a few farms and a railway which she could spot through a telescope.

Then suddenly she tried mesmerism and, almost like a miracle, she was cured. We need not now consider the circumstances of this cure, nor ask how far it may have been an intense effort of the will, a bursting out of natural vitality. What matters to us is that the invalid of five years was soon taking long walks through wind and rain, and feeling her powers flooding up like a river after a thaw. She did not throw her hat over the chimney, of course. There was no time for that, no time for celebration. She must make up for the lost years; she must work; she must write. She wanted to be away from doctors and sisters and landladies, to run her own life without help or hindrance. She was used to the North now and did not fancy returning to London—for one thing there would be too many interruptions, too many callers and too much dining-out. She decided, therefore, on the Lakes, and in May 1845, at the age of forty-three she came to Ambleside.

"My life," she said, ". . . began with winter. Then followed a season of storm and sunshine, merging into a long gloom. . . . But the spring, summer and autumn of life were yet to come."[1]

[1] Harriet Martineau: *Autobiography* (3 vols., London 1877).

How different was this from the reproachful resignation with which Ruskin retired to Coniston! Here was a middle-aged woman with the enthusiasm and energy of a girl of fifteen. She had neither the eye of an artist nor the sensibility of a poet, yet she could sit in her lodgings at the head of Windermere and enjoy to the full even the sight of the rain. She could plan and build a house and gather about her a family of nieces and servant maids who could bring into her life some of the warmth and affection she had always missed. Without ever knowing that she had done so—she could even fall in love with a young philosopher, and, linking her name with his, could renounce the faith of her first life and declare herself to her neighbours and the world as an agnostic and an enemy of the established religion.

It is not surprising that at first the more respectable neighbours did not call. The postman, however, did, bringing every day pamphlets and tracts and homilies, anonymous letters threatening her with hell, reviling her as an abandoned woman, or begging her, with tears and prayers, to repent. Yet she had also her friends. When she needed turf for the new house at *The Knoll*, on the way to Grasmere, a pile of cut sods mysteriously appeared in the garden during the night. The Arnold family, at Fox How, were her friends, and above all the old poet of Rydal Mount gave her both welcome and guidance.

Harriet Martineau did not really get on well with Wordsworth. She knew him at the most unhappy time of his life, when he was half-blind with grief at the death of his daughter. Moreover, conversation between them was always difficult— she with her ear trumpet and he without his teeth. Difficulties apart, her nature could not adjust itself to his. She was practical about the everyday business of living but indifferent to money. With Wordsworth it was just the other way round. When she moved into her new house he came and planted a stone pine for her, then took both her hands and gave her some advice. She would get many callers he said—at Rydal Mount at least five hundred total strangers turned up every summer— and she must deal with them as he did: tell them that if they wanted a cup of tea they were welcome, but if they wanted anything to eat, they must pay for it. Miss Martineau, however, had not Wordsworth's lofty unconcern about the impression he made, and after having been accosted beside the flower-beds and stared at through the windows, she decided that she must leave Ambleside for a month or two each year during the tourist season.

She began her new life with immense energy. The house was built and furnished. She built also a cowhouse and a pigsty, imported a dairyman from Norfolk, successfully feeding her cows on half the acreage that the local farmers said she would need. She had a pit dug in a little garden behind the Methodist Chapel, a pit like a grave filled with rain water, to which she would come out naked to take her bath in the open air. She would rise early in the morning, in winter long before daylight, and walk seven or eight miles, by Rydal and Grasmere or along the Kirkstone road, returning for breakfast at half-past seven. Even in her old age, the winter before she died, she was up in her room by six o'clock, and sat at the window, drinking her tea, and watching the lights come on in the valley and the stars go out in the sky.

She began, also, to work with a determined, almost violent concentration. Book after book was published, and hundreds and hundreds of articles for *The Daily News* and *Once a Week* —articles on the American Civil War, on the Lancashire Cotton Trade, on India, on royalty, on almost every social and political question of the day. The small retreat at Ambleside became a powerful force in popular radical thought.

Such a woman could never have declined into a passive and sentimental admirer of Lake scenery. She had no hidden longing for the Primitive, for Eden and the Earthly Paradise. A "simple child of nature" was to her not a creature to be admired or envied, but one to be pitied. She wanted to make him less simple. Therefore, she set about the education of the village children, the working-classes and the shopkeepers, giving them a regular course of lectures on English history, the United States, the Crimean War, and sanitation. There was one lecture on the effects of alcohol on the stomach, illustrated with diagrams so vivid that a notorious drunkard had to go outside and be sick. She founded a building society for the workers,

and got cottages in spite of the opposition of the local land-
owners. The young men borrowed books from her library; the
old men had their Christmas party in her kitchen. She liked to
think of *The Knoll* as a beacon, a lantern, shining with the light
of knowledge among the dark and trackless hills.

As for herself, she burned with the bright, mental optimism
of the nineteenth century. Any doubts she may have had, any
shadowy irrational fears, were flicked out of the window or
kicked under the stairs. The light, shining into the attic of her
mind, showed everywhere the bare angular walls, swept,
scrubbed, and cleared of lumber. She would not keep a single
memory that might hold dust. In her garden was a sundial
with a motto of her own choosing: "Come, Light! visit me!"
Wordsworth, she said, "gave it his emphatic approbation."
One would like to think that for once in his life he may have
risen to a little, not-unfriendly irony.

It was not, however, until five years after the death of the
poet that Harriet Martineau published her own *Complete
Guide to the Lakes*—with separate editions for the Windermere
and the Keswick districts. It is, as we might expect, a work
which shows a goodish knowledge of the topography of the
district, and absolutely no knowledge at all of its real character.
She took on the job rather reluctantly, persuaded into it by a
local bookseller, but set about it with her usual gumption. She
hired a wagonette and toured the entire district with six
friends, testing the routes and passes, trying all the inns, and
being agreeably surprised at the cheapness of the latter until
she found that the friend, who was in charge of the arrangements, had been bargaining for reduced terms on the strength
of the coming guide. The book is competent and readable, for
Miss Martineau knew how to give life and point to her argument by anecdote and scraps of autobiography. But after
nearly ten years in the Lakes her view of them was as scrappy,
as superficial, as that of a week-end visitor. As she rode in her
wagonette over Whinlatter or Cold Fell, or up Borrowdale or
along Ullswater, she saw just what the visitor saw, she asked
the same questions as he did, though, unlike him, she remembered the answers. Indeed, much of her book consists simply of
the organization of such answers:

When the turn to the left, which leads up to the chapel, is reached, the stranger must alight and ascend it. He is ascending Rydal Mount; and Wordsworth's house is near the top of the hill,—within the modest gate on the left. By kind permission of the lady now residing there, strangers may obtain entrance to the poet's garden on two days in the week, Tuesday and Friday.

The *Guide* is remarkable, however, not for what Miss Martineau says about the Lakes, but for what she says about the people. It is not to be expected that she understood them, any more than she understood the fells, but she saw clearly the social conditions in which they lived. She was not to be humbugged into thinking that here was a new Arcady, with its people still living miraculously in the Age of Gold. She knew very well that they were living in the nineteenth century, that they belonged to the age of industrialism, and that it was impossible to isolate them from the rest of their time. To do so, to attempt to deny the dalesman his rightful part in the economic development of the country, would bring him to poverty and bankruptcy. Already the old self-supporting statesmen were dying out, and the old home manufacture was dead. Cottages were falling into ruins, fields were untilled, land was un-drained.

The unhealthiness of many settlements is no less a shame than a curse, for the fault is in Man, not in Nature. Nature has fully done her part in providing rock for foundations, the purest air, and the amplest supply of running water; yet the people live—as we are apt to pity the poor of the metropolis for living—in stench, huddled together in cabins, and almost without water. The wilfulness of this makes the fact almost incredible; but the fact is so.

For all this she saw only one remedy: the Lakes must no longer be cut off from the rest of England, living in almost medieval squalor so as not to disturb those immigrants who could afford the comfortable new villas. The Lakes must accept the railways, against which Wordsworth and others had been campaigning; they must seek new markets outside the district; they must open their villages to new trades and their minds to new ideas. No doubt, she exaggerated the good which would come from increased communication with the outer world; no doubt, she over-estimated the understanding and intelligence of the townsman; but at least she realized that to condemn the people of the Lakes to an unnatural, archaic existence in an artificial, preserved countryside was both economically absurd and morally wrong. To subjugate man to the scenery was to de-humanize him, to treat him as no more than a thing. To reduce the world to a mere picture was the primary heresy of the Picturesque; to reduce man to the scale of that picture was its ultimate folly.

CHAPTER TWELVE

TODAY

PERHAPS the most significant point about the Picturesque is the date at which it emerged. For fifteen hundred years the people of England had been an agrarian people, with a society built around hamlet, village and country towns. Throughout the Middle Ages the cities belonged to the country, earning their living from the marketing of country produce. Even in London, life was always next door to rural. The green of the summer rolled up and among the streets like the spring tide, frothing along the parks and gardens, up the gutters and over the walks. Cows were driven along the streets for milking or for slaughter. Every city child grew up with horses and hens, with manure and mud. The great wastes lay right against the walls of the cities; the creeping, misty thickets scrimmaged about the outer suburbs; the black night of the open country stretched up to the first ale-house's light. Everywhere, even in the most sophisticated notches of society, in the Court, in the abbeys, in the universities, in the shops and warehouses—everywhere life swung and lifted and unfronded to the rhythm of the seasons. The smell of the country blew in on the winds, the smell of hay and apples, of dung and old leather. Eggs were still warm from the fowl; venison was what you had hunted across the common three days before. The vitality, the beauty, the bitterness, the dirt, the cruelty, of the countryside were all as much a part of the city as of the village. Man was still a creature of nature and knew himself to be such.

In the country, of course, this was still more obvious. In the feudal villages with their castles and serfs, in the seventeenth-century estates with their great houses and tenants, life was bound tightly to the discipline of the soil, to the curve and conduct of leaf and beast. The land grew and shaped and gave colour to its vegetation. Every variation in subsoil and contour

203

had its own human ecology—the salt, tamed, tough-as-seaweed men of the rocky coasts; the bare, bony, long-sighted men of the hills; the slow, mud-coloured, viscous-speaking men of the heavy Midlands. Man changed his coat with the climate, like the stoats and the mountain hares; he changed his speech with the composition of the soil and adapted his whole life to the shape of the few dozen acres around him and the winds and clouds that blew over.

It is no aim of this book to idealize this unity between man and his environment. It was gained only through immense human suffering. There was disease, hunger, bitter cold. The vast majority of human beings born into this world never lived long enough to know much more of it than a calf sees or smells when first it crutches itself on its splay legs and hobbles after the udders of its mother. But among those that survived there was a dim, and yet, in a way complete, sense of the every-whereness, the all-bringing and all-taking, the lift and thrust of Nature. They lived in Nature as fishes live in the sea.

Moreover, man had not yet lost the sense of an interdependence between himself and his environment which went beyond the mere physical interdependence of bodies and earth. Christianity had suppressed the primitive pagan religions, but the rituals of the old fertility cults survived, and survived not only in the secret conclaves of hidden societies. The ache of adoration which lifted itself towards the Virgin contained much that belonged to the earlier worship of the Earth Mother, the recurring feminine processes of breeding and feeding. The great sacramental structure of the Christian church was itself a new acknowledgment and a new interpretation of the close interdependence of spirit and the natural world. To say that God became man was to say that God became matter; became flesh and bones and blood; became, in fact, a body which itself was made of meat and wheat, of water and soil. So the liturgy and rituals of the Church gathered to themselves echoes and shadows of the old earth worship. Eggs emblemed the Resurrection; holly and mistletoe remembered the Hanged Man even on the tree of the Nativity; sacred wells and streams attached themselves to the saints like lost dogs to a new master. A man caught in a cellar with a barrel of gunpowder put a spark not only to a political scare but to thousands of Beltane Fires which for centuries had lain unlit. For three hundred years already, and perhaps for many more, these fires have gone on burning, on village greens, in suburban gardens, in waste plots of towns and cities, beside railway sidings and in allotments and under the dark cliffs of slagbanks. And while the bonfires kick and crackle and the smoke flaps into the mist, every child shares dimly the understanding that once belonged to the Vikings, and to the witches and warlocks and covens of the secret god.

Yet throughout the Middle Ages, in spite of this unity between man and nature, we get scarcely a mention of landscape. Indeed, the very conception of landscape presumes a detachment, a separation, which people did not then feel. Landscape is not an environment but a background. You must be away from it, outside it, to see it at all—no longer a participant but a spectator; no longer a performer, but a looker-on. The man of the Middle Ages never saw a landscape; he saw only the land. He enjoyed the country as he enjoyed eating and drinking and making love—a spontaneous animal enjoyment in sun and air, in dew and freshness, in light and colour, the greenness, the brightness, the juice and jollity of all things living and growing. Chaucer gives us the full taste and tang of it in the very first lines of the *Prologue*:

> Whan that Aprille with his shoures sote
> The droghte of Marche hath perced to the rote,
> And bathed every veyne in swich licour,
> Of which vertu engendred is the flour . . .

By Elizabethan times there was another note, learned from Virgil and the pastoral poets—the note of a people conscious of their sophistication, of a certain over-intellectualizing which interfered with the spontaneity of their response. It was still, however, a people who were very close to nature; the shepherd's pipe had become a madrigal, the country smock and jerkin had become the doublet and hose, the silks, the gowns, the elaborate pattern and counter-pattern of lining and slash; but the air was still fresh outside the window, the rain was cool and clean on a lifted face.

But with the Industrial Revolution man began to withdraw

from the country. Polite society shut the windows and drew the curtains. A new kind of dirt came into civilization—and hovels, which before had smelt of dung and pigs and human sweat, now smelt of soot, of slag, of oil, of cotton-waste, of the dust of a dead, inorganic, mechanical world. Man was beginning to live in the fug and smother of his own avarice.

It was at this time that landscape was discovered, for man was so broken away and blocked off from the countryside that he could see it with a new detachment. Almost suddenly the Picturesque emerged and developed after the fashion which we have already seen. At first it was largely a matter of æsthetics; then of sensation. Then it merged into the full tide of romanticism. Wordsworth, in particular, made his generation aware of the immense vitality of the country and of the dignity of its way of life. He shifted the interest from the picture to the fact. After him came the field naturalists, the archæologists, the conservers, the preservers, The Friends of the Lake District, the Society for the Preservation of Rural England.

Again, in our own century, and particularly between the two wars, there appeared, in a changed form, something of the animal enjoyment which had belonged to the Middle Ages. It was, perhaps, less natural, less spontaneous, than it had been. It was, perhaps, more self-conscious, more self-assertive. It had something of the inevitable defiance of men who spend their lives checked and repressed in cities. To them, the country was a vast park or playing field. They wanted to run wild like children let out of school. They wanted to swim in the lakes, to climb the hills, to cycle along the roads. They were happy when they were hiking: "... ten, twenty, thirty, forty, FIFTY miles a day." They wanted to do all those things which were absurd and unnecessary in their ordinary life: to be dog-tired without being paid for it, and to be uncomfortable when it could be avoided. The girls would expose a yard of bare red leg to the March wind; the men would cycle all day through the pouring rain, their hair oiled like a duck's back, their bodies wigwamed in an oilskin cape. They would sleep in camps or hostels—sometimes in farms; liking, for the most part, to be in groups or gangs, liking to gather together in the evening to share what they can never have in cities, the comradeship of a community, even though a temporary community, relaxing from a shared effort, a shared experience of wind and weather.

The intellectuals among them were usually more solitary in their pleasures. They turned to rock-climbing, to the exploration of small islands or the systematic pilgrimage to spots where rare plants grew. They were not, for the most part, men who felt any cramp and stuffiness in their daily life, for their jobs were interesting and their studies varied. They were, perhaps, men specially concerned with the organization of society, with the cataloguing and dissemination of knowledge, with the technical processes of industry: civil servants, teachers, laboratory workers, overseers and clerks. To them it must often have seemed that man's life and the natural world were being reduced to a formula—to the memorandum, the curriculum, the blue-print, the chemical equation. Man had nature in his crucible; he always knew the answer to $A + B$. The mystery was going out of the world. Man was so sure of his complete control over physical processes, that he was becoming bored with his own virtuosity. Nature could no longer make a challenge to him, and where there was no challenge there could be no response.

It was all an illusion, of course. Society was beginning to erupt like a volcano, and soon the very atoms of matter would erupt more alarmingly still. But about such things the individual could do nothing. Instead, he could try to seek, at least for a week-end, a more heroic and adventurous relation with the world about him. If nature could make no challenge in his daily life, thanks to wireless, weather forecasts, vitamins, X-ray, electricity, the spectroscope—nevertheless, he could find some small department of experience, some kept corner of nature, where he could set himself a task or a quest in which he would have no habit to guide him or apparatus to help him, but would have to trust to his own wit, his nerve and his muscles.

It will be clear by now, I hope, that these modern cults of nature—the Picturesque, the Romantic, the Athletic—are all symptoms of a diseased society, a consumptive's gasp for fresh air. They have arisen because modern man has locked himself off from the natural life of the land, because he has tried to break away from the life-bringing, life-supporting rhythms of nature, to remove himself from the element that sustains him. Because, in fact, he has become a fish out of water.

The cult of nature in a predominantly urban society is, however, not only a sign of disease; it is also a sign of health—a sign, at least, that man guesses where the remedy can be found. Yet, at present, it is only a very desperate remedy. The sense of man's true place in the natural world cannot be regained merely by week-ending in the Home Counties, by holidays in the Lakes, by cycle runs along Midland lanes, by forsythia in suburban gardens or hyacinth bulbs under the attic bed. I do not intend to disparage these things; my own happiest days have been spent among the Cumberland hills and on the coast, and I am myself a passionate and obstinate grower of bulbs in bowls. But the divorce between man and the land, the mechanization of society, the urbanization of the mind, the unnaturalization of human life, is a problem that cannot be settled merely by the creation of National Parks and Garden Suburbs. All such plans presume that civilization is an urban affair. They all keep up the heresy that the country is a place to be preserved for the sake of the town; that the town is the place for work and life and the country for recreation. All of them overlook or disguise the fact that man himself is a part of nature, a product of soil and water and sun, just as much as are the grass and the trees and the birds. The country is not man's picture gallery, his pleasure garden, his playing field; it is his workshop, his home, his bed and his board. It is the food he eats, the air he breathes, the blood that gives him life, the bones that give him shape. Until this is acknowledged, until man learns once more to adjust his life to the greater life of which he is a part, then all these cults of nature will be mere sops, salves, safety-valves. Nature, indeed, the physical reality in which alone we have our physical being, is in danger of being seen as a mere dream, a half-believed-in vision of Paradise, of the Fortunate Isles, the Garden Enclosed, the lotus, the womb.

It is particularly unfortunate that, in the popular mind, this point of view seems to have the authority of Wordsworth. To most people in the Victorian age, Wordsworth was a moral teacher, colour-washing a few simple platitudes with a Turnerian glow. His "natural piety" became merely the sort of piety which seemed natural to them. To most people today, he is the arch-hiker, the lover of hills and daffodils. It is not, one feels, a reputation that would make a poet popular. Yet a most astonishing thing has happened, as was shown quite clearly during the centenary year in 1950: for Wordsworth has become part of the general furniture of the average modern mind; he has become the stock figure for the poet. It is not that he is read very much, but that one or two of his poems, in particular "I wandered lonely as a cloud", have become the accepted types of what a poem is expected to be. The romantic conception of the poet—the revolutionary, the passionate young man, dying of tuberculosis or getting killed in a battle for freedom—this has been replaced by the figure of an old man at Rydal, listening to the cuckoo and stroking the heads of buttercups.

Nature, to many, is not only the most likely subject for poetry, but practically the only one. Love, war, religion no longer seem quite suited to verse, and almost every school-child, asked to write a poem, will produce lines about snow-drops or sunsets. Not very long ago I saw some verses beginning:

> I love thee, Cumberland,
> The land where I was born;
> And now that I am far away
> My heart is sad, forlorn.

The child who wrote them was about eight, and I doubt if she had ever been away from Cumberland in the whole of her life up to then, yet, in order to write the poem, she found it necessary to imagine an absence she had never known and to pretend to a regret she had never felt. In fact, she was responding to the suggestions made to her at home, at school, at church, by pictures, by calendars, by Christmas cards, by embroidered cushion-covers, by hanging plates embossed with waterwheels and old-world cottages, and by all the fragrant minutes and sniffy seconds in a dozen newspapers and women's magazines—the suggestion that there is something peculiarly poetic in a sentimental nostalgia for the countryside.

*   *   *

P

For a great deal of this Wordsworth is indirectly responsible; but for none of it is he to blame. It is true that in his old
age he became averse to change at Rydal or Windermere, to
the coming of the railways and steamboats. Yet he never at any
time saw the Lakes merely as a glorified pleasure garden, a
human Whipsnade with the inhabitants in their natural surroundings. He saw, instead, a living unity between man and
the land, and if this unity did not include industry, this did
not mean that he regarded the Lakes as an area insulated from
the economy of its time, the Irish Free State of the Industrial
Revolution. It was rather that he drew from his memory of the
statesman an image of life as he wanted it to be. The Lakes
were not an Eden in the wilderness of the world; they were a
working model for that world to study : not a might-have-been
but an ought-to-be.

We have been concerned, in this book, with various ways of
looking at landscape. Wordsworth's way, however, involved
also a way of looking at man. We need not consider here
whether or not he was a pantheist, or whether or not his
beliefs were really consistent with the Christianity he professed
in his later years. But in order to see clearly that his attitude
to Nature involved also an attitude to life, let us take him away
from Loughrigg Terrace and Upper Easedale and place him in
the greater context of Christendom. For though his philosophy
may not be specifically Christian, yet I believe that it can only
be fully understood in the framework of Christian morality.
I realize that by doing so I am in danger of alienating some of
my readers, yet, as my aim here is not to preach Christianity
but merely to clarify Wordsworth, I will ask them to be tolerant. If they like, they may re-interpret, in their own minds, the
specifically Christian terms which I shall use. Thus, when I
speak of a sacramental grace acting through the medium of
a physical body or object (bread, wine, water, a girl, a mountain), they may say to themselves that I really mean that sense
of appropriateness, of rightness, of wholeness, which comes
from a complete harmony or unity between purpose and function, between ends and means, between the mind that acts and
the matter that re-acts, between the imagination that shapes
and the creation that responds. This is not, in fact, what I

really mean, or at least it is not the whole of what I mean, but it is near enough, I hope, to make intelligible what I am trying to say.

Wordsworth, then, belongs to one of the great Ways of Christian teaching, the Sacramental Way, or, in the term popularized by Charles Williams, the Affirmative Way. It is a wonderful and illuminating phrase. It shows the other side of the coin; it turns the clouds inside out; it makes some of the darkest caves and corners of religion shine with a blinding light. Moreover, by relating itself to the Negative Way it creates a structure for itself, and, by negating the negative, it illuminates, in one flash, a new territory and a positive direction. It invents, in the twinkling of an eye, a new Ten Commandments of "Thou shalts" instead of "Thou shalt nots".

The Negative Way came into being first of all as a method of metaphysics, a technique of knowing. God, it said, is far beyond man's understanding. No image drawn from the physical world, no thought conceived in the human brain, can help us in any way to know what God is like. All such images, all such thoughts, can only confuse us, deceive us, can only come between ourselves and God. We can never hope to know what God is, we can only know what He is not; but by eliminating from our minds all that we know He is not, all images, all ideas, all human conceptions, we can arrive, as closely as will ever be possible to us, at what God is.

Gradually that which began as a Way of knowledge ended as a Way of life. Its many branches and sidetracks were explored and charted. Hermits went to live among the rocks of the North African desert; the monastic rules were devised and tested. The inbred puritanism of the Near East, the fanatic fear of the flesh which had revealed itself in the monstrous doctrines of Manichaeism, now found a way to compromise with the new faith which said that it was God, and not a devil, who had created the world. At the same time, the ordinary layman, seeking a track that he could follow, found it in the outer footpaths of the Negative Way. The religious rises at four and fasts for forty days; the bank-clerk gives up the cinema for Lent and goes without sugar in his tea.

The Negative Way, as practised by the monk and the hermit

is based on three main self-denials or rejections of the world; solitude or the rejection of society, celibacy or the rejection of sexual love, and poverty or the rejection of material wealth. Against these, the Affirmative Way, as outlined by Charles Williams, places three modes of acceptance. Against solitude, the acceptance of society in the Way of the City, the sanctified Church-state; against celibacy, the Way of Romantic Love, the acceptance of marriage and the senses; and against poverty, the Way of Nature, the acceptance of the beauty and rightness of the material world. For an image and interpretation of two branches of the Way, the Way of the City and the Way of Love, Charles Williams turned to Dante, finding the first in the poet's vision of Rome, the Holy City, and the second in the figure of Beatrice. For the third he turned to Wordsworth.

Now Wordsworth and Dante have more in common than is at first apparent. Each based his whole life on a vision given to him in childhood, and a vision which was an illumination rather than a revelation. Each saw the beloved object shining with supernatural light, but it remained still a completely natural object—in Dante's case, a very real girl, and in Wordsworth's the mountains and lakes of Cumberland and Lancashire. Moreover the vision of each began with an impulsive giving, a dedication of the self to the beloved. Neither, of course, understood at the time what was happening to him, but the vision was like a sacrament; it did not require intellectual co-operation, but merely that there should be no obstacles to the efficacy of grace, and the greatest of all obstacles is self-consciousness. The true sacrament is a complete acceptance, and complete acceptance is only possible when there is complete submission. Grace has its demands as well as its gifts. There must be self-surrender; there must be effort; there must be discipline and rules.

This meant, for Wordsworth, that man must acknowledge himself to be a creature of nature, bound by the laws of his environment and finding his peace, his purpose, his salvation, in the fulfillment of those laws. Man had to co-operate with nature; to adjust himself to the great biological process, to the seasons, to the climate, to the laws that governed the growth and fertility of grass and tree and beast and bird. Man had to learn the ways of nature, to test all his hopes and ambitions by the standards of nature, to modify his efforts until they were in harmony with the aims of nature. His work, his recreation, his education, his art, his architecture, his industries—these were to be judged and assessed according to their conformity with the practice and precepts of external nature. All man had to do, in fact, was to be natural.

The trouble is that there is no word in the dictionary which is harder to define than "natural". In one sense we may say that it is natural for man to seek the fullest development of all his faculties—his intellect, his imagination, his religious understanding, his power of social organization. In another sense we may say that it is natural for him only to be born, to eat, sleep, copulate and die. And that second state is the one to which nature herself would lead us if we let her have all her own way.

This was something that Wordsworth never fully understood, never allowed himself to understand. He did not realize that the Way of Nature is a challenge as well as a guide. Dante had realized that this was true of the Way of Love. Love leads him into Paradise, but only after he has passed through Purgatory. Moreover, next to himself and his Beatrice, the most celebrated, and the most faithful pair of lovers in *The Divine Comedy* are Paolo and Francesca, who are in Hell. As for the Way of the City, we can all see how power can corrupt the benevolent dictatorship or the divinely-appointed church.

The Way of Nature, indeed, presents two simultaneous problems—how to avoid perverting the true order of nature, and how to maintain and assert our own humanity. Failure in either will bring disaster. Today, of course, it is perversion which is the greatest and most obvious danger. Everywhere we see the fertility being dried out of the soil like water from a de-hydrated egg. Valleys are dammed to generate electricity to work vacuum cleaners and hair-driers; acres of wood are ripped up to give a few thousand extra tons of open-cast coal; pasture is burnt and concreted to make a kennel-yard for bombers; ploughland is gouged and bricked to site factories for tin-cans and imitation cheese and synthetic rubber. Miles of forest are felled to make wood-pulp to make plastic to make a substitute for wood. Blinds are drawn and lights are devised to make a substitute for sun; windows are sealed and the atmosphere is reconditioned to make a substitute for fresh air. Even the animals are infected with a disease of unnatural living. Cows calve without knowing a bull; hens, imprisoned in batteries, secrete eggs in their sleep as an oyster secretes a pearl. And now, at last, the earth itself is no longer safe, no longer solid, no longer dependable. The very flowering of matter, the creative fission by which all energy and life enters the material universe, even this has become our greatest and most terrible danger.

In the face of all this, Wordsworth's teaching is vital and urgent. Yet of itself it is not enough, for the challenge of nature has to be met. Those who would ignore it, who would ask only that nature should be left as she is; those who want the country-side to be untouched, unaltered, are as much in error as the more obvious despoilers. They are exploiting the countryside for their pleasure, for a sentimental escape, just as the industrialists are exploiting it for power. It is not enough to say that Man, if he is to survive, must become once more farmer rather than miner, cultivator rather than exploiter; that he must turn to the organic world rather than the inorganic, to the biological rather than the chemical, to the living world of corn and cows rather than the lifeless world of iron and electricity and nuclear fission. For, if he is to live truly, he must find a balance between the two. He must be farmer *and* miner; he must seek for the fruitfulness of the earth, *and*, in its rightful proportions, for physical power.

That balance, when it is truly found, will surely show itself in a balanced and realistic view of landscape. No more coddling of the countryside; no more rambler-rose calendars pinned above the cocktail cabinet. Man will once more be an integral part of his own environment. He will know the rhythm of the seas, the sun, and the seasons; he will eat, drink and breathe the natural vitality of the earth in food, water and air. And, at the same time, he will modify that environment by the action of his own intellect, living in a continual reciprocity of challenge and response, giving and taking, shaping and being

shaped. Or if he fails, it is unlikely that he will be able to go
on living at all.

There is one other point which must be mentioned. In
tracing the development from the Picturesque to a scientific
attitude I have taken for granted that this meant a change
from fancy to fact, from a subjective invention to a clearer
consciousness of objective reality. In a way, of course, the term
"objective reality" has no real meaning for man. Even if one
does not accept an idealist or Gnostic view, even if one does
not believe that the physical world is an illusion, an emanation
of the spirit—still one must allow that we can be aware of this
world only so far as our senses can interpret and our minds can
understand. Shape and colour, as we know them, are what
happens in our eyes; sound is what happens in our ears; weight,
size, bulk, roughness and smoothness, heat and cold, are what
we conclude from what we have learned by the touch of our
hands. Yet, if we accept the proposition that the world is there
at all—a proposition of which the truth cannot be demonstrated—then, for practical purposes, we are forced to assume
that our senses give us some reasonable idea of what that world
is like. In this way we must admit that the science of the
early nineteenth century took us nearer to objective reality
than did the fantasies of Hutchinson and William Bellers. The
botanist helped us to look more clearly at a daisy; the geologist
helped us to know the character of the rocks; the physicist
explained the forces which impelled and directed the universe
which we could see around us. All of them, in their several
ways, worked to clarify and classify the observations of our
own senses, to illuminate and elucidate the world which we felt
to be solid and certain.

But today the case is different. Science now deals with
aspects of the physical world of which our senses have no knowledge. Plants and animals disappear into a new order of cells
and bacteria. The solid rock disappears into the atom, and the
atom itself dissolves into a mathematical abstraction of elec-
trons and neutrons. We are becoming more and more aware
that our simple conceptions of external nature are completely
inadequate; that a bird, a tree, a mountain, exist not as we

have always thought of them, but as an infinite physical and biological complexity. We are puzzled and perturbed by an intellectual conception of the external world which seems totally unlike what we have been told about it by our eyes, our ears, our hands. By a process of materialism we have abolished matter.

It follows inevitably that the imaginative man has become suspicious of the evidence of his senses. He fears that when he calls to mind the image of, say, a sparrow, he is, in fact, creating merely a convenient formula which suggests a certain scope of experience to his eyes, his ears, and his fingers, while the truth about the sparrow remains completely outside his image. Above all he fears when he looks at a landscape that he may be seeing only himself, or perhaps nothing at all. Because of this, at a time when landscape is now universally appreciated, it is nevertheless disappearing from living art; it is ceasing to provide valid symbols for the creative imagination. The detailed record of landscape is now left to the photographer; the artist, if he turns to it at all, turns to it subjectively.

No doubt, this is a transition stage. One day we shall achieve a new synthesis of the scientific and the imaginative vision. We shall be able to see the atoms swirling round in our own thumbs; we shall no longer shudder when we think of bacteria in our blood. When this happens our view of the external world may be clearer, richer, and of greater significance. Then, perhaps, we may be able to look at the fells of Cumberland with a new understanding, a new confidence. For they rear themselves in the middle of our civilization like an ancient boulder lying in a garden. An archaism, belonging to the world of nature as it was long before man came to look at it; belonging, also, to the world which will survive man. They are a sign both of what man comes from and what he is up against. They may be mapped, footpathed, sign-posted, planted with conifers, gouged with quarries, titivated with tea-shops. They may even, in some gigantic explosion, be blown out of shape. Yet they will remain the same, for they are a fact, a fact we cannot alter and perhaps cannot even understand. They are the past which shaped us and the future in which we shall have no shape. To talk of preserving them is both irrelevant and irreverent. All that matters is how long they will allow us to preserve ourselves.

APPENDIX A

QUERIES

ORIGINALLY composed and printed by Order of the SOCIETY OF ANTIQUARIES, and now addressed to the Gentlemen and Clergy of *North-Britain*, respecting the Antiquities and natural History of their respective Parishes, with a View of exciting them to favor the World with a fuller and more satisfactory Account of their Country, than it is in the Power of a Stranger and transcient Visitant to give.

7. Are there any mineral springs, frequented for the drinking of the waters; what are they; at what seasons of the year reckoned best, and what distempers are they frequented for?

8. Are there any periodical springs, which rise and fall, ebb and flow, at what seasons, give the best account you can?

9. Are there any mills on the rivers, to what uses are they employed?

10. Are there any and what mines; what are they; to whom do they belong; what do they produce?

11. Have you any marble, moorstone, or other stone of any sort, how is it got out, and how worked?

12. What sorts of manure or amendment do they chiefly use for their land, and what is the price of it on the spot?

13. What are the chief produce of the lands, wheat, rye, oats, barley, peas, beans, or what?

14. What sorts of fish do the rivers produce, what quantities, and what prices on the spot, and in what seasons are they best?

*14. What quadrupeds and birds are there in your parish? What migratory birds, and at what time do they appear and disappear?

15. Are there any remarkable caves, or grottoes, natural or artificial? give the best description and account thereof you can.

16. Are there any and what quantities of saffron, woad, teazels, or other vegetables of that sort, growing in the parish, and the prices they sell for on the spot?

17. Is the parish remarkable for breeding any cattle of remarkable qualities, size or value, and what?

18. Are there any chalk-pits, sand or gravel-pits, or other openings in the parish, and what?

19. On digging wells or other openings, what strata's of soil do they meet with, and how thick is each?

20. How low do the springs lye, and what sort of water do you meet with in the several parts of the parish?

21. Is there any marl, fuller's earth, potter's earth, or loam, or any other remarkable soils, as ochre, &c?

22. Are there any bitumen, naptha, or other substances of this nature found in the earth?

23. Does the parish produce any quantities of timber, of what sort, and what are the prices on the spot, *per* load or ton? Are there any very large trees, and their size?

24. Are any quantities of sheep raised or fed in the parish, and on what do they chiefly feed?

25. Are the people of the country remarkable for strength, size, complexion, or any bodily or natural qualities?

26. What are the diversions chiefly used by the gentry, as well as the country people, on particular occasions?

27. What is the nature of the air; is it moist or dry, healthy or subject to agues and fevers, and at what times of the year is it reckoned most so? and, if you can, account for the causes.

28. Are there any petrifying springs or waters that incrust bodies, what are they?

29. Any hot waters or wells for bathing, and for what distempers frequented?

30. Are there any figured stones, such as echinitae, belemnitae, &c. Any having the impression of plants or fishes on them, or any fossil marine bodies, such as shells, corals &c, or any petrified parts of animals; where are they found, and what are they?

31. Is there any part of the parish subject to inundations or land floods, give the best account, if any things of that nature have happened, and when?

32. Hath there been any remarkable mischief done by thunder and lightning, storms or whirlwinds, when and what?

33. Are there any remarkable echoes, where and what are they?

34. Have any remarkable phaenomena been observed in the air, and what?[1]

[1] Printed as an appendix to Pennant's *Tour in Scotland in 1769.* (1771).

APPENDIX B

EXTRACTS FROM *ODE TO THE SUN* BY RICHARD CUMBERLAND, PUBLISHED IN 1776.

Soul of the world, refulgent Sun,
Oh take not from my ravisht sight
Those golden beams of living light,
Nor, 'ere thy daily course be run,
    Precipitate the night.
Lo, where the ruffian clouds arise,
Usurp the abdicated skies,
And seize the aetherial throne;
    Sullen sad the scene appears,
Huge Helvellyn streams with tears!
Hark, 'tis giant Skiddaw's groan,
I hear terrific Lowdore roar;
The Sabbath of thy reign is o'er,
    The anarchy's begun;
Father of light, return; break forth, refulgent sun! . . .

Trembling now with giddy tread,
Press the moss on Gowdar's head;
But lo, where sits the bird of Jove,
Couch'd in his eyrie far above;
Oh, lend thine eye, thy pinion lend,
Higher, yet higher let me still ascend:
    'Tis done; my forehead smites the skies,
To the last summit of the cliff I rise;
    I touch the sacred ground,
    Where step of man was never found;
I see all nature's rude domain around. . . .

Press not so fast upon my aching sight
Gigantic shapes, nor rear your heads so high,
    As if ye meant to war against the sky,
Sons of old Chaos and Primaeval Night. . . .

    Now downward as I bend my eye,
    What is that atom I espy,
    That speck in nature's plan?
    Great Heaven! is that a man?
And hath that little wretch its cares,
Its freaks, its follies, and its airs;
And do I hear the insect say,
"My Lakes, my mountains, my domain?"
O weak, contemptible, and vain!
    The tenant of a day.
    Say to old Skiddaw, "Change thy place."
    Heave Helvellyn from his base,
    Or bid impetuous Derwent stand
At the proud waving of a master's hand.

    Now with silent step, and slow,
    Descend, but first forbear to blow,
    Ye felon winds let discord cease,
And nature seal an elemental peace:
    Hush, not a whisper here,
    Beware, for Echo on the watch
    Sits with erect and listening ear.
    The secrets of the scene to catch.
    Then swelling as she rolls around
    The hoarse reverberated sound,
    With loud repeated shocks
    She beats the loose impending rocks,
    Tears down the fragments big with death,
And hurls it thundering on the wretch beneath. . . .

APPENDIX C

COPY OF ADVERTISEMENT BILL FOR CROSTHWAITE'S MUSEUM.

"Keswick, August, 25 1792.

PETER CROSTHWAITE

Formerly Naval Commander in India, Surveyor and Seller of the Maps of the Lakes, MASTER of the Celebrated MUSEUM, (of eleven years standing), at the Quadrant, Telescope, and Weathercock, A little below the Middle of Keswick,

RETURNS his most grateful Thanks to the *Nobility, Gentry,* and *Others* for crowning his labours with Success. His house is the loftiest in *Keswick,* and has the Advantage of most delightful Prospects quite round the Vale.

In 1784, *Sir Ashton Lever,* and several other able Virtuosos, declared his Museum the most capital one *North* of *Trent.* Since which time it is improved as Three to One. ———— It consists of many Hundred Natural and Artificial Curiosities, from every Quarter of the World; the *Fossils,* Spontaneous *Plants,* and *Antiquities* of *Cumberland; Coins, Medals, Arms, Quadrupeds, Birds, Insects, Shells, Landscapes, Pictures, Grottos,* and his much admired *Organ;* together with many Models and useful Inventions of his own; and if it were not for the low Cunning, and mischievous Falsehoods continually circulated against him by an ungrateful JUNTO of Impostors in the Place, it is thought few of the Gentry would pass him; but, being covetous to an Extreme, and much hurt by Envy, they take all Advantages of misleading the Gentry to this Day; and all this after he has laid out several Hundred Pounds in the Museum, and spent near Thirteen Years of his time in collecting Curiosities, making and repairing Roads, Surveying the Lakes, &c &c, all which has been done for the better Entertainment of the Gentry, and an honest Livelihood for his Family.

Admittance to LADIES and GENTLEMEN, *One Shilling* each; COUNTRY PEOPLE, *Sixpence* each.
Open from 7 A.M. till 10 P.M.

He has sold many thousand Maps of the Lakes, and shews undeniable Certificates as to their Accuracy and masterly Engraving. They are now sold at his MUSEUM, at *Nine Shillings* per set, (single Maps at *Eighteen Pence each*) he having made an additional Survey, and added every Thing which could be thought necessary or useful to the Tourist.

He also sells Mr *Farrington's* Twenty *Landscapes* of the *Lakes*; *Mr Donald's Map of Cumberland*; his *Map* of the *Environs* of *Keswick; West's* and *Shaw's* GUIDES; *Gray's* Landscape Glasses; *Claude Lorrain's* Do.; Pocket Compasses, Music, Spar, &c, and hopes to merit the future Favour of the Nobility, Gentry, and Others: having added several capital Curiosities since last November."

PICTURESQUE BIBLIOGRAPHY

Only books bearing directly on the Picturesque have been included. Biographical books and works of criticism are mostly omitted, and there has been no attempt to list all the many guides and handbooks, often anonymous and mostly mediocre, published after 1810. The books are arranged approximately in the order in which they are relevant to the text.

William Camden. *Britannia*. First edition in Latin, 1586. Translated newly into English by Philémon Holland, 1610.

Sir Daniel Fleming. *Description of the County of Cumberland*, 1671. Ed. by R. S. Ferguson, Kendal, 1889.
Description of the County of Westmorland, 1671. Ed. by Sir G. F. Duckett, Kendal, 1882.

Thomas Robinson. *The Anatomy of the Earth*, 1694. (Facsimile, Kendal, 1905).
Essay Towards a Natural History of Westmorland and Cumberland, 1709.

Ralph Thoresby (1677–1724). *Diary*, Ed. by the Rev. J. Hunter, London, 1830.

Celia Fiennes. *The Journeys of*, Ed. by Christopher Morris, Cresset Press, 1949.

Daniel Defoe. *A Tour through the Whole Island of Great Britain*, 1724–7.

Thomas Cox. "Cumberland and Westmorland" in *Magna Britannia*, 1720–31.

J. E. Weeks. *A Poetical Prospect of Workington and Whitehaven*, 1752.

John Brown. *Description of the Lake and Vale of Keswick*, Newcastle, 1767.

John Dalton. *Descriptive Poem Addressed to Two Young Ladies at their Return from Viewing the Mines near Whitehaven*, 1755.

Thomas Pennant. *Tour in Scotland in 1769*, (1771).
Tour in Scotland and Voyage to the Hebrides in 1772, (1774–6).
Tour from Downing to Alston Moor, 1801.

Arthur Young. *A Six Month's Tour through the North of England.* 4 vols, London 1770.

Thomas Gray. *Journal in the Lakes,* (In a letter to Dr Wharton, Oct. 1769, published in the Memoir of his life by Mr Mason.)

William Mason. *The Poems of Mr Gray,* to which are prefixed Memoirs of his life and Writings. York, 1775.

Hartley Coleridge. "Life of William Mason", in *Biographia Borealis,* or, *Lives of Distinguished Northerners,* 1833.

William Gilpin. *Observations on the River Wye in 1770,* 1782.

Observations Relative Chiefly to Picturesque Beauty made in the Year 1772, in several parts of England, particularly the Mountains and Lakes of Cumberland and Westmorland, 2 vols, 1786.

Three Essays on Picturesque Beauty, 1792.

Memoirs of the Gilpin Family of Scaleby Castle together with an Account of the Author by himself. Ed. by W. Jackson, for the Cumb. & West. Archaelogocial Soc., 1879.

The Life of Bernard Gilpin, 1752.

T. D. Fosbroke. *The Wye Tour or Gilpin on the Wye,* 1818. Revised edition, 1822.

―――. *A Memoir of the late Rev. William Gilpin, M.A.* By an Admirer of his Character and Works, 1851.

Richard Warner. "Biographical Sketch of the late Rev Wm Gilpin" (Included in the second vol. of Warner's *Miscellanies*), 1819.

[W. Combe]. *The Tour of Dr Syntax in Search of the Picturesque.* Pubd. anonymously; illustrated by Rowlandson. 1812.

William Hutchinson. *An Excursion to the Lakes in Westmorland and Cumberland in 1773 and 1774,* London, 1776.

History of the County of Cumberland and some Places Adjacent, 2 vols, Carlisle, 1794.

Thomas West. *The Antiquities of Furness,* 1774. New edition with additions by William Close, 1805.

[Thomas West]. *A Guide to the Lakes* by the author of *The Antiquities of Furness,* 1778. Second edition, revised by William Cockin, with an appendix, 1780.

Joseph Nicholson and Richard Burn. *History of Cumberland and Westmorland,* 2 vols, 1777.

T. Newte. *Tour in England in 1785,* 1798.

James Clarke (Land Surveyor). *A Survey of the Lakes,* 1787.

Joseph Budworth (Later Palmer). *A Fortnight's Ramble to the Lakes,* First edition by "A Rambler", 1792. Second edition by

Q

"A Rambler", 1795. Third edition by "Jos. Budworth", 1810. *Windermere*, a poem. London, 1798.

Anon. *The Life of John Hatfield* commonly called The Keswick Impostor. Carlisle, 1846.

————. *The Echoes of the Lakes and Mountains* (containing the Life of John Hatfield) by an "Antiquarian, Guide, Philosopher and Friend". London, No date.

Anon. *James [sic] Hatfield and the Beauty of Buttermere*, Illustrated by Robert Cruikshank, 3 vols, 1841.

Henry Mayhew *1851* or *The Adventures of Mr & Mrs Sandboys*, with drawings by George Cruikshank.

W. C[ockin]. *Occasional Attempts in Verse*, Printed only for the Writer's Particular Acquaintance, Kendal, 1776.

William Cockin *The Rural Sabbath*, a poem, London, 1805 (Written about 1792).

A[dam] Walker. *Remarks made on a Tour from London to the Lakes*, London, 1792.

Andrew Pringle. *General View of the Agriculture of the County of Westmorland*, 1794.

J. Bailey and G. Culley. *General View of the Agriculture of Cumberland*, 1797.

Charlotte Smith. *Ethelinda* or *The Recluse of the Lake*, 1789.

Anne Radcliffe. *A journey made in the Summer of 1794 through Holland and the Western Frontier of Germany, with a Return down the Rhine, to which are added Observations During a Tour of the Lakes in Westmorland and Cumberland*, London. 1795.

Anon [James Plumtre]. *The Lakers*, A Comic Opera in Three Acts. London, 1797.

G. Thompson. *Sentimental Tour from Penrith to London*, 1798.

Sarah Aust (The Hon. Mrs Murray) *A Companion and Useful Guide to the Beauties of Scotland and the Lakes*, 1799. (Third edition, 1810, under the name of Hon. Mrs Murray Aust.)

J. Grant. "Journal of a Three Weeks' Tour in 1797 through Derbyshire to the Lakes." Mavor's *British Tourist*, (Vol IV) 1800.

Henry Kett. "A Tour in the Lakes of Cumberland and Westmorland in August 1798." Mavor's *British Tourist*, (Vol V) 1800.

John Housman. *A Topographical Description of Cumberland, Westmorland, Lancashire, and a part of the West Riding of Yorkshire*, Carlisle, 1800.

A Descriptive Tour and Guide to the Lakes, Caves and other Natural Curiosities in Cumberland etc., 1802. (This consists of a reprint of part of the previous volume.)

Richard Warner. *A Tour through the Northern Counties of England and the Borders of Scotland*, London, 1802.

Anon. *Sketch of a Tour from Lancaster round the Principal Lakes in Lancashire, Cumberland, and Westmorland*, 1803.

Anon. *Observations chiefly Lithographical made in a Five Weeks' Tour to the Principle Lakes of Westmorland and Cumberland*, London, 1804.

James Denholm. *A Tour to the Principal Scotch and English Lakes*, Glasgow, 1804.

J. Mawman *An Excursion to the Highlands of Scotland and the English Lakes*, 1805.

[Benjamin Travers] *A Descriptive Tour to the Lakes of Cumberland and Westmorland, in the autumn of 1804*, 1806.

Thomas Sanderson. *A Companion to the Lakes in Lancashire, Westmorland, and Cumberland*, 1807.

Don Manuel Alvarez Espriella [Robert Southey] *Letters from England*, 3 vols, London, 1807. One vol. Ed. Jack Simmons, The Cresset Press, 1952.

Robert Southey. *Sir Thomas More* or *Colloquies on the Progress and Prospects of Society*, John Murray, London, 1829.

S. T. Coleridge. *Diary of a Tour to the Lake District Oct.–Nov. 1799.*
Tour—August 1802, in the form of a Letter Journal. (The text of both these tours is printed in *Wordsworth & Coleridge*, ed. by Earl Leslie Griggs, Princeton & Oxford, 1939. The text of the 1802 tour is printed in *Inquiring Spirit*, ed. by Kathleen Coburn, Routledge, 1951. The quotations in this book are from the latter.)

John Wilson ("Christopher North") *Letters from the Lakes*, Ambleside, 1889. (First printed in Blackwood's Mag. 1819.)
Recreations of Christopher North, Edinburgh, 3 vols, 1842.

Thomas De Quincey. *Recollections of the Lake Poets.*
Autobiography.
Confessions of an English Opium Eater, etc, etc.
The Collected Writings, ed. by David Masson, Edinburgh, 1889–90.

Elizabeth Smith. *Fragments in Prose and Verse, with some account of her life and character*, by H. M. Bowdler. 1808. Second edition, London, 1811.

Charles Farish. *The Minstrels of Winandermere, A Poem*. London, printed for the author, c. 1811.

Joseph Wilkinson. *Select Views in Cumberland, Westmoreland and Lancashire*, 1810.

William Wordsworth. *A Description of the Scenery of the Lakes*, 1822, 1823.
A Guide through the District of the Lakes in the North of England, with A Description of the Scenery etc., For the Use of Tourists and Residents, Kendal & London, 1835.

J. Hudson (Edit.) *A Complete Guide to the Lakes, comprising Minute Directions for the Tourist with Mr Wordsworth's Description of the Scenery of the Country, &c.*, Kendal, 1842, 43, 53, 59, 64.

J. H[udson]. *Handbook to the English Lakes, with an Introduction by the late William Wordsworth*, Kendal.

Dorothy Wordsworth. *Journals of Dorothy Wordsworth*, ed. by E. de Selincourt. Two vols, Macmillan, 1941.

Anon. "Letter of a Wanderer to the Lakes in Cumberland and Westmorland," *Monthly Magazine*, vol 31.

John Robinson D. D. *A Guide to the Lakes*, London, 1819.

William Green. *The Tourist's New Guide*, Two vols, Kendal, 1819.

Jonathon Otley. *The English Lakes*, 1823.

Thomas Wilkinson. *Tours to the British Mountains*, London, 1824.

John Briggs. *Letters from the Lakes etc*, Kirkby Lonsdale, 1825.

Ed Baines, Jun. *Companion to the Lakes*, 1829.

M. A. Leigh. *Guide to the Lakes*, 1832.

J. Allison. *Tourist's Guide to the Lakes*, 1834.

George Tattersall. *The Lakes of England*, 1836.

William Ford. *Scenery in the Lake District*, 1840.

Black's *Picturesque Guide to the English Lakes*, 1841.

Sylvan. *Pictorial Handbook*, 1847.

Mrs William Hey. *Recollections of the Lakes and other poems* by the author of *The Moral of the Flowers* and *The Spirit of the Woods*, 1841.

Edwin Waugh. *Rambles in the Lake Country*, including *Over Sands to the Lakes*, Manchester, 1882.

"A Laker". *Mrs Ann White's Tour to the Lakes of Westmorland and Cumberland*, Keswick, 1867.

John Ruskin. *Iteriad*: or *Three Weeks among the Lakes* (Included in *Poems*, George Allen, 1903).

The Storm Cloud of the Nineteenth Century (From *The Queen of the Air*)

Yewdale and her Streamlets (From *Deucalion*).

Harriet Martineau. *Complete Guide to the Lakes*, London and Windermere, 1855. (Portions of the Guide published separately for Windermere and Keswick).

Autobiography, Three vols, London, 1877.

SOME PRINTS AND ILLUSTRATED
BOOKS OF THE PERIOD

S. and N. Buck. *Castles, Abbeys and Priories of Cumberland,* 1739, reprinted 1837.

William Bellers. Etchings after paintings by W. B., 1753.
Eight Views of Lakes in Cumberland, Pub. by John Boydell, 1774.

Thomas Smith (of Derby). *Four Views of the Lakes in Cumberland,* Pub. by John Boydell, 1767.

William Burgess. Aquatints engraved by F. Jukes, 1792.

John Smith. *Twenty Views of the Lakes,* 1791–5
Scrapbook Containing Views of the Lakes, 1798.

P. Holland (Engraved by C. Rosenberg). *Select Views of the Lakes in Cumberland and Westmorland,* 1792.

LaPorte. Drawings engraved by B. Comte.

William Green. *Sixty Views of the English Lakes,* 1814.
Seventy-eight Studies from Nature, 1809.

Joseph Wilkinson. *Select Views in Cumberland, Westmorland, and Lancashire,* 1810.

Joseph Farington *The Lakes in Cumberland, Westmorland, and Lancashire,* Forty-three engravings described by T. H. Horne. 1816.
Twenty-eight Views in Cumberland, (1815–16).

T. H. Fielding. *A Picturesque Tour of the English Lakes, Illustrated with 48 Coloured Views drawn by T. H. Fielding and J. Walton, During a Two Years' Residence among the Lakes,* London, Ackermann, 1821.
Cumberland, Westmorland, and Lancashire, Illustrated in a series of 44 engravings exhibiting the Scenery of the Lakes, Antiquities and other Picturesque Objects. London, 1822.

William Westall. *Views of the Lake and of the Vale of Keswick,* 1820.
See also engravings contributed to *The Life and Correspondence of Robert Southey,* ed. by his son, Charles Cuthbert Southey, 1850.

Rose and Allom *Westmorland, Cumberland, Durham and Northumberland Illustrated,* from original drawings by Thomas Allom, with descriptions by T. Rose. Three vols, London, 1832.

J. B. Pyne. *The English Lake District,* portfolios, 1853.

INDEX

233